Selected Correspondence of Bernard Shaw

Bernard Shaw and His Publishers

Bernard Shaw and His Publishers

Edited by Michel W. Pharand

UNIVERSITY OF TORONTO PRESS
Toronto Buffalo London

Bernard Shaw Letters
© 2009 the Trustees of the British Museum,
The Governors and Guardians of the National Gallery of Ireland,
and Royal Academy of Dramatic Art
Introductory and editorial matter © 2009 Michel W. Pharand

Published by University of Toronto Press Incorporated
Toronto Buffalo London
www.utppublishing.com
Printed in Canada
ISBN 978-0-8020-8961-8

   Printed on acid-free paper

Library and Archives Canada Cataloguing in Publication

Shaw, Bernard, 1856–1950
   Selected correspondence of Bernard Shaw.

   Includes bibliographical references and index.
   Contents: [V. 1] – Bernard Shaw, theatrics / edited by Dan H. Laurence – [v. 2] –
Bernard Shaw and H.G. Wells / edited by J. Percy Smith – [v. 3] – Bernard Shaw and
Gabriel Pascal / edited by Bernard F. Dukore [v. 4] Bernard Shaw and Barry Jackson /
edited by L.W. Conolly – [v. 5] Bernard Shaw and the Webbs / edited by Alex C.
Michalos and Deborah C. Poff – [v. 6] Bernard Shaw and Nancy Astor / edited by J.P.
Wearing – [v. 7] Bernard Shaw and his publishers / edited by Michel W. Pharand

   ISBN 0-8020-3000-9 (v. 1). – ISBN 0-8020-3001-7 (v. 2). –
   ISBN 0-8020-3002-5 (v. 3) : bound). – ISBN 978-0-8020-3572-1 (v. 4). –
   ISBN 0-8020-4123-X (v. 5 : bound). – ISBN 978-0-8020-3752-7 (v. 6). –
   ISBN 978-0-8020-8961-8 (v.7)

   1. Shaw, Bernard, 1856–1950 – Correspondence.   2. Dramatists, Irish 20th century –
Correspondence.   I. Title.

   PR5366.A4 1995   822'.912   C959-301518-rev

This book has been published with the help of a grant from the Canadian Federation
for the Humanities and Social Sciences, through the Aid to Scholarly Publications
Programme, using funds provided by the Social Sciences and Humanities Research
Council of Canada.

University of Toronto Press acknowledges the financial assistance to its publishing
program of the Canada Council for the Arts and the Ontario Arts Council.

University of Toronto Press acknowledges the financial support for its publishing
activities of the Government of Canada through the Book Publishing Industry
Development Program (BPIDP).

for Ginger, who makes everything possible

and

for our daughter Angéline, who makes everything beautiful

Contents

General Editor's Note ix

Introduction xi

Editor's Note xxxi

Abbreviations xxxvii

LETTERS 1

Table of Correspondents 223

References 229

Index 233

General Editor's Note

This volume is the seventh in the series entitled *Selected Correspondence of Bernard Shaw*. The first two volumes – *Bernard Shaw and H.G. Wells*, edited by J. Percy Smith, and *Theatrics*, edited by Dan H. Laurence – appeared in 1995. The third – *Bernard Shaw and Gabriel Pascal*, edited by Bernard Dukore – was published in 1996, and the fourth and fifth volumes – *Bernard Shaw and Barry Jackson*, edited by L.W. Conolly, and *Bernard Shaw and the Webbs*, edited by Alex C. Michalos and Deborah C. Poff – appeared in 2002. The sixth volume – *Bernard Shaw and Nancy Astor*, edited by J.P. Wearing – was published in 2005.

The volumes in this series are of two kinds. Percy Smith's inaugural volume represents an example of the first kind: correspondence between Shaw and another individual of distinction in his or her own right. Bernard Dukore's, J.P Wearing's, and my own editions are further examples of this kind. *Bernard Shaw and the Webbs* is a minor variation on this model in that it deals with Shaw's relationship with *two* distinguished individuals.

This approach replicates other editions of Shaw correspondence published prior to this series: Christopher St John's *Ellen Terry and Bernard Shaw: A Correspondence* (1931), or Alan Dent's *Bernard Shaw and Mrs. Patrick Campbell: Their Correspondence* (1952), among others. The advantage of this approach, of course, is that it gives the reader two (or more) voices rather than one, with all the stimulation that can arise from complementary or adversarial views on issues, events, or people. Such an approach also allows for insights into the nature of close personal and professional relationships, with all the emotional and intellectual drama that usually accompanied such Shavian associations. While matching the epistolary Shaw in full flow is a tough challenge, people such as Wells, Pascal, Jackson, the Webbs, and Nancy Astor – hardened professionals all – were not easily intimidated by Shaw's sharp wit, searing logic, or intellectual aggression. Thus the sparks sometimes fly, from which light as well as heat is generated.

This attempt to capture Shaw's *dialogue* with friends and colleagues differs, of course, from collections solely of Shaw's letters to individuals, be they single individuals as in C.B. Purdom's *Bernard Shaw's Letters to Granville Barker* (1957) or Samuel Weiss's *Bernard Shaw's Letters to Siegfried Trebitsch* (1986), or hundreds of individuals as in Dan H. Laurence's monumental edition, *Bernard Shaw: Collected Letters* (4 volumes, 1965–88). And both of these approaches differ again from the second kind of volume in this series, Shaw's letters to a variety of individuals *on a particular subject*. Thus, Dan Laurence's *Theatrics* provides the opportunity to explore Shaw's ideas on theatre and theatricality, and this new volume in the series, *Bernard Shaw and His Publishers*, deals comprehensively with Shaw's views on publishers and publishing.

And so through a variety of approaches the magnificent edifice of Shaw's correspondence is gradually constructed, drawing, in this series, largely on previously unpublished letters, and, in many instances, opening up new insights into Shaw's life and achievements, as well as the life and achievements of his correspondents. Nearly half of the letters in this volume, for example, are here published for the first time, offering, as Professor Pharand puts it in his introduction, 'a unique insight into a relatively little-known facet of Shaw's long career, one that was vital to his renown as an author.' Shaw's often contrary dealings with publishers – who, he said, 'combine commercial rascality with artistic touchiness and pettishness, without being either good business men or fine judges of literature' – are here splendidly documented, as is his meticulous attention to the details of copyright protection, publishers' contracts ('booby traps'), and printing styles. Shaw couldn't do without publishers, of course, including American publishers ('shocking duffers'), but throughout his dealings with the twenty-five covered in this edition he unwaveringly followed his own injunction: 'It is up to the author to take care of himself.'

Introduction

Publishing Is a Gamble

'I always tell young authors who consult me,' Bernard Shaw wrote to publisher Stanley Unwin in 1929, 'that publishing is a gamble in which the publisher, who must make one best-seller pay for several duds, must take every advantage he can obtain, and that it is up to the author to take care of himself' (Letter 124). Fifty years earlier, however, few publishers would gamble on Shaw's novels, written one per year with workmanlike regularity: *Immaturity* in 1879, *The Irrational Knot* in 1880, *Love Among the Artists* in 1881, *Cashel Byron's Profession* in 1882, and *An Unsocial Socialist* in 1883. 'Your demand for "something more substantial" takes my breath away,' Shaw told Macmillan & Co. in 1885 when they rejected *An Unsocial Socialist* (Letter 5). But eventually all of Shaw's novels, with the exception of *Immaturity*, were serialized, and two of them were published – *Cashel Byron* sold out its printing – and even pirated. The letters in this volume to Swan Sonnenschein (who published *An Unsocial Socialist* in 1887) evidence Shaw's early struggles with copyright issues and his efforts to make the most of his literary property. From the onset of what became a very long publishing career, Shaw took care of himself – and of his money.

Realizing that novels were not his forte, Shaw turned his energies to political activism – he joined the Fabian Society in 1884 – and journalism: book reviews in *The Pall Mall Gazette* (1885–8), art criticism in *The World* (1886–9), and music criticism in *The Star* (1888–89) and in *The World* (1890–4). In early 1892 he told publisher T. Fisher Unwin that 'the Fabian business and my own hand-to-mouth journalistic jobbing leave

me without a moment for literary work' (Letter 20). Yet that October
Shaw completed his first play (begun in 1884), *Widowers' Houses*. When it
was published the following year and sold poorly, Shaw kept writing, but
without publication in mind. 'I object to publishers,' he complained to
bookseller Frederick H. Evans in 1895; 'the one service they have done
me is to teach me to do without them. They combine commercial rascality with artistic touchiness and pettishness, without being either good
business men or fine judges of literature. All that is necessary to the production of a book is an author and a bookseller, without any intermediary parasite' (Letter 24).

   As evidenced by the letters in this volume, if some publishers were not
good businessmen, neither could Shaw do without them. His close ties
with publishing house presidents, vice-presidents, directors, partners,
managers, and agents, as well as with his printers R. & R. Clark, were crucial to his literary and economic success. Although Shaw dealt primarily
with five publishers – Grant Richards, Constable, and (much later) Penguin in England, and Brentano's and Dodd, Mead in the United States –
his works appeared under more than thirty imprints. For over half a century, Shaw tried to control the fate of his books from proofs to bookshop,
and to have the last word on prices, advertising, copyright, and royalties
– as well as typeface, type size, margins, paper, binding, and colour.[1]
Nothing was taken for granted, especially not a publisher's competence.

   Given his myriad obligations and pursuits – 'journalistic jobbing,' play-
writing, lecturing, directing, travelling, and writing countless letters –
Shaw's management of the technicalities and legalities involved in publishing his works is astonishing. Seldom pleased with what his publishers
did (or rather did *not* do) to sell his books, Shaw intervened to rewrite a
contract or outline a more effective advertising strategy, took precau-
tions to ensure airtight agreements, and often tried to shame publishers
into parting with profits he thought rightfully his. When it came to his
books, Shaw was no gambler.

   In fact, at the outset he was not convinced that his plays were worth
publishing. Sales of *Widowers' Houses* had been disappointing: Henry &
Co. printed fewer than five hundred copies, and according to Shaw 'the
sale, which was only effected by great perseverance & determination on
the part of the purchasers, was 150 copies!'[2] About *Arms and the Man*
(performed in 1894), Shaw asked T. Fisher Unwin in early 1896: 'Do you

think there is really any chance of its being worth my while or yours to publish the play?' (Letter 27). Shaw's doubts were well founded: despite exceptions such as Ibsen in English translation (see Letter 36), there were few incentives to publish plays, at least not for profit. Playtexts were bought mostly as inexpensive keepsakes of performances, while acting editions were riddled with technical jargon. Moreover, printed drama was overshadowed by triple-decker novels which, although expensive, reached a vast public via circulating libraries and dominated the market until 1894, when the one-volume, six-shilling novel became the standard format.[3]

There were also serious legal impediments to publishing plays. Katherine E. Kelly explains that prior to the 1911 Copyright Act, 'the weakness of nineteenth-century copyright protection for dramatic scripts and the absence of a significant reading public for drama made it virtually impossible for most playwrights to earn a sustained income from their published works.' England and the United States had 'mutually discouraging laws governing dramatic copyright.' English publication of a playscript meant forfeiting the British playwright's American rights, while Americans publishing in their country lost British copyright protection. What is more, 'British law treated US stage performance as "publication"; therefore, when a British play was pirated in a US city in advance of performance in Britain, the author forfeited his or her British copyright protection.' Shaw himself 'coined the term "stagerighting" to describe what became his and others' common practice of staging at least one (typically hasty and low-budget) British production of a play to secure its copyright.' Stagerighting was essential, as it prohibited the first American performance of a British play that would nullify its copyright protection in Britain.[4]

'If I could secure both copyrights & stagerights intact here and in America,' Shaw told T. Fisher Unwin in 1895, 'I should be strongly tempted to try a volume of dramas' (Letter 26). The following year, thanks to an upstart young would-be publisher, Shaw succumbed to temptation.

Grant Richards

A twenty-year-old Grant Richards (1872–1948) had seen *Widowers' Houses* at the Royalty Theatre in December 1892. Four years later he was ap-

proaching writers to help him launch the publishing house that would
open on 1 January 1897.[5] One evening in November 1896, Richards followed Shaw home after a theatrical first night and tried to solicit his work.
Shaw was not convinced: 'As far as I have been able to ascertain ... the
public does not read plays, or at least did not a very few years ago. Have
you any reason to suppose that it has changed its habits?' (Letter 31).

The Shavian solution, of course, was to give the public new habits: reading volumes of plays disguised, so to speak, as novels. At three plays per
volume, minus the usual technical terms but with descriptive stage directions and (later) long, polemic prefaces, Shaw's books would be thick,
portable, and inexpensive. Readers would get their money's worth. But
Shaw's initial ideas about packaging his novelized dramas were peculiar.
He had a catchy title for his two-volume 'Plays: Pleasant and Unpleasant,'
but he wanted the unpleasant plays 'printed on light brown paper (Egyptian mummy color) in an ugly style of printing, and the pleasant ones on
white paper (machine handmade) in the best Kelmscott style.' Such a
'piebald volume,' he assured Richards, would 'make a sensation' (Letter
32). Fortunately, no such volume materialized.

Soon a third party joined the Shaw-Richards partnership. At the suggestion of fellow Fabians Sidney and Beatrice Webb, Shaw selected Edinburgh printers R. & R. Clark – who paid 'fair wages' – and continued to
work with them until his death. At their 1946 centenary, Shaw said they
had been 'as natural a part of my workshop as the pen in my hand.'[6] So
had William Maxwell (1873–1957), the firm's secretary (1914–20), director (1920–6), and then managing director: 'our business relations devel-
oped into a cordial personal relationship which has been of inestimable
value to me as an author.'[7] Included in this volume are seven letters to
Clark and Maxwell out of the few hundred that survived the Second
World War.[8]

Almost immediately the Shaw-Richards-Clark ménage was grappling
with Shaw's idiosyncratic printing requirements, which included eliminating apostrophes from contracted words, emphasizing words using
spaced letters rather than italics (used for stage directions), and banish-
ing what Shaw (and his mentor William Morris) called 'rivers of white,'
which coursed through the page when an extra space was added between sentences. Nine months after Richards had accosted him, Shaw
was 'an exhausted wretch who, after a crushing season, has slaved these

four weeks for four hours a day at your confounded enterprise' (Letter 37). Finally, in April 1898, a watershed date in Shaw's publication history, the first collection of his dramas, *Plays: Pleasant and Unpleasant*, was published in two volumes, appearing simultaneously in the United States with Herbert S. Stone & Co. of Chicago.

Although Richards went on to publish *The Perfect Wagnerite* (1898), *Three Plays for Puritans* (1901), a new edition of *Cashel Byron's Profession* (1901), and the first separate impression of *Mrs Warren's Profession* (1902), his business practices were slipshod, at times reckless. Not only did he borrow heavily and incur tremendous debts, he did not effectively advertise Shaw's plays. Eager to publish *Man and Superman* (completed in June 1902), Shaw began to look elsewhere. 'I may publish [the play] myself on commission & do my own advertising,' he informed Richards in late 1902 (Letter 58). After a few rejections – John Murray opined that the object of the play was 'to assail marriage and other social & religious institutions' (Letter 65) – Shaw contacted Archibald Constable & Co., and an agreement 'of a few lines scribbled by Shaw on a sheet of letter paper' lasted the remaining forty-seven years of his life.[9] Constable published *Man and Superman* in August 1903.

Meanwhile, Richards's business was unravelling. 'I must get out of your hands in any case,' Shaw told him on 6 January 1905. 'I have given up the royalty system definitely: it does not pay me nor suit me ... Henceforth I manufacture for myself & publish on commission' (Letter 81). Three months later Richards went bankrupt. His brief Shavian role was crucial: he had placed Shaw's plays in the hands of the novel-reading public.

Constable; Brentano's; Dodd, Mead; and Penguin

As a result of what Shaw called Richards's 'poetic inaptitude for business' (Letter 82), sales were meagre and Shaw duly abandoned the conventional royalty system, which he had considered doing as early as 1881 (Letter 2). In effect, Shaw became his own publisher, dealing directly with printers R. & R. Clark and paying for his own composition, machining, paper, and binding. Beginning with *Man and Superman* in 1903 until Shaw's death in 1950, Constable served as his distributing agents, Shaw selling them plays on a commission basis.

Constable (1903–50)

Senior partner Otto Kyllmann (1860–1959) handled Shaw's affairs at Constable & Co. But like Richards, he sometimes mishandled them. Whereas Richards was prodigal with his earnings, 'Kyllmann was a penny-pincher who put off paying accounts as long as possible.'[10] Shaw cajoled and badgered him for money: 'When are you going to send me my money?' (Letter 92); 'Where's my money? How do you expect a poor author to live?' (Letter 99); 'I am stoney broke' (Letter 169). When he did earn money, Shaw grumbled that most of it went to taxes: 'damn it, you are on velvet compared to me. Out of your ten thousand [from *Everybody's Political What's What?* (1944)] £8619-16-11 has already gone to the Treasury' (Letter 172).

But the Shaw-Constable liaison weathered its upheavals. It even withstood Shaw's failure to support Constable during the 1907 *Times* Book Club debacle over the 'net book agreement' (see Letters 87 and 88),[11] when Shaw went so far as to take five hundred copies of *John Bull's Other Island and Major Barbara* (already printed) and substitute the Constable name on the title page with 'This Edition is issued by the Author for *The Times* Book Club.'[12] In any event, Shaw's Constable books were profitable: as Shaw told Kyllmann in early 1920, 'Clark has just sent me in a bill for £682, which I have no means of paying. For God's sake stop selling my books, or I shall be ruined' (Letter 104).

Brentano's (1904–32)

When American publishers Herbert S. Stone sold out to Fox, Duffield & Co. in 1906, they relinquished the plates of all their Shaw books: *Plays: Pleasant and Unpleasant* (1898), *The Perfect Wagnerite* (1898), *Love Among the Artists* (1900), *Cashel Byron's Profession* (1901), and *Three Plays for Puritans* (1901). Dan H. Laurence relates how 'Shaw threatened legal action on the grounds that he had licensed publication rights to Stone for five years only, and that the licences had expired. Fox, Duffield eventually surrendered the plates to Brentano's, the "pirates" of several of Shaw's works, who, in comic opera fashion, underwent sudden conversion, being selected by Shaw to be his authorised publisher in America.'[13] In 1908 the firm's president, Simon Brentano (1860–1915), told Shaw that

'Stone & Co. and Duffield & Co. should have made a more liberal offer so as to have left you at least with larger money compensation.'[14]

While working with Constable on a commission basis, Shaw retained the royalty system with Brentano's. On 30 May 1904 he informed literary agent J.B. Pinker that he had 'closed with an offer from Brentano of 25% for five years' (see Letter 77).[15] By late 1912, however, Shaw was complaining of poor sales and threatening 'to take the manufacture of the books into my own hands, and ... ask you to do no more than to sell them for me on commission' (Letter 93). Matters had not improved six years later, when Shaw's net earnings for 1918 'and for all America [were] $1895, subject to British and American income tax at war rates' (Letter 102). The problem was that Brentano's, according to Shaw, were selling his books at 'ridiculous prices' (Letter 147).

The firm was hit hard by the Depression and by March 1930 was in serious financial straits. Despite reassurances from Simon Brentano's son Lowell (1895–1950), now vice-president (see Letter 129), bankruptcy proved inevitable. 'I held on as long as I could with any sort of prudence,' Shaw told him on 6 January 1933 (Letter 142). Ten days later, Brentano's plates and copyrights were surrendered to Dodd, Mead & Co.; Brentano's were declared bankrupt in March. Shaw had told Otto Kyllmann in 1922, 'You cannot reverse the order of Nature, which is, that great authors should bankrupt their publishers, not that publishers should bankrupt great authors' (Letter 114).

Dodd, Mead (1933–50)

Dodd, Mead arrived on the scene long after Shaw was world-famous but had wanted to publish his works as early as 1905 (see Letter 86). Their first Shaw publication was *The Adventures of the Black Girl in Her Search for God* (1933), for which Shaw sent vice-president Howard C. Lewis (1890–1952) an agreement in December 1932. Lewis and the firm's president, Frank C. Dodd (1875–1968), first met Shaw in New York on 11 April 1933 and took him on a whirlwind drive through Manhattan (see Letter 143). In September Shaw sent them a detailed overview of his publishing guidelines and principles (Letter 147).

Dodd, Mead's relationship with Shaw differed from Brentano's in that they acted more or less as Shaw's agents, retaining half the royalties from previously published Shaw works. They also issued reprint editions of the plays using the plates of the Ayot St Lawrence edition (1930–2) published by William H. Wise, also of New York (see Letters 126 and 129), as well as one-volume collections: *Nine Plays* (1935), *Six Plays* (1941), and *Seven Plays* (1951). By 1940, only seven years after his first Dodd, Mead publication, Shaw was growing frustrated that they were not widening his circulation by following its $2.50 editions with cheaper ones. 'You have refused to take any such risks, very wisely; but for your refusal you demand 50% of my royalties. The proportion bereaves me of breath' (Letter 166). Frank C. Dodd replied on 9 July, 'Indeed, we would never voluntarily relinquish our proud position as the accredited publishers of Bernard Shaw in America!' (Letter 167). And despite Shaw's ultimatums and objections, they never did.

Penguin (1937–)

Shaw's impatience with Dodd, Mead may have stemmed from the fact that his circulation had begun to widen through Penguin Books. In 1935, when paperbacks were low-quality books of ephemeral fiction and romances, often with lurid covers, publisher Allen Lane (1902–70) proposed a series of sixpenny reprints of respectable contemporary works. The idea was greeted by most as radical, but Shaw saw it as an opportunity to reach the masses.

The first Shaw book to be Penguined was *The Intelligent Woman's Guide to Socialism, Capitalism, Sovietism and Fascism* (1937), an enlarged edition of Constable's *The Intelligent Woman's Guide to Socialism and Capitalism* (1928). Ironically, Lane, who objected to what he called 'bosoms and bottoms' covers,[16] had chosen a book whose original dust jacket (designed by Eric Kennington) depicted 'a nude female Intelligencer looking down a well.'[17] The illustration on the cover of Shaw's two sixpenny paperbacks, which inaugurated the Pelican series, was a mere pelican.

Then came *Back to Methuselah* (1939), the screen version of *Pygmalion* (1941), and in 1946 the 'Shaw Million': ten titles at 100,000 copies each to celebrate Shaw's ninetieth birthday. 'A bombshell!' Shaw exclaimed (Letter 174). The edition sold out in six weeks. Penguin had become – and would remain – Shaw's major UK publisher.

Familiar Green Volumes

Shaw's progress from would-be novelist to his apotheosis by Penguin was not without incident. Shaw may have discarded the idea of a 'piebald volume,' but he was adamant that all his idiosyncratic (often eccentric) printing requirements be followed to the letter. He outlined some of them in 'Notes on the Clarendon Press Rules for Compositors and Readers' (1902), including this memorable one about discarding apostrophes: 'I have written aint, dont, havnt, shant, shouldnt and wont for twenty years with perfect impunity, using the apostrophe only where its omission would suggest another word: for example, hell for he'll. There is not the faintest reason for persisting in the ugly and silly trick of peppering pages with these uncouth bacilli.' As for spelling, 'I always use the American termination *or* for *our* ... Such abominable Frenchifications as programme, cigarette, etc, are quite revolting to me. Telegram, quartet, etc., deprive them of all excuse.'[18]

Shaw owed many of his ideas about book production to fellow Socialist William Morris (1834–96), poet, designer, and founder of the Kelmscott Press (1891–8). Shaw adopted 'Morris margins' (wide below and at the outside, narrow above and at the inside) and Morris's preference for the blackest ink, fine paper, and evenly spaced words. The last was particularly important for Shaw because extra spacing within a word replaced italics.[19] Shaw was especially keen to eliminate 'mutton quads,' the extra blank space at the beginning of paragraphs or following a full stop that created unsightly 'white rivers' meandering through the black print. 'Oh those proofs, those proofs!' wrote an exasperated Shaw to Ellen Terry on 5 January 1898 as he struggled with *Plays: Pleasant and Unpleasant*. 'Imagine going though a play again & again, scanning the commas, & sticking in words to make the printing look decent – to get the rivers of white out of it!' (CL 2, 8). He emphasized to book designer William Dana Orcutt in 1903 that '*White* is the enemy of the printer. *Black*, rich, fat, even, black, without grey patches, are, or should be, his pride' (Letter 74).

Shaw's insistence upon these typographical elements, including Caslon Old Face type (used by Morris) and a distinctive light grey-green or olive brown binding with pale greenish dust jackets, made his books immediately recognizable. Their title pages were striking, with letters in

24-point Caslon and short, uncentred lines, and words broken in odd
places, such as 'Unple-asant' (see figure 2, p. xlii). 'I had much rather
see even syllables divided than a line spaced so widely as to make a whit-
ish bar across the black of the letterpress,' affirmed Shaw. 'The compositor should be taught that the evenness of the color of his letterpress is
far more important than the philological pedantries of word division.'[20]
Thanks to his distinctive typography, Shaw created 'a visual signature for
his works' and introduced 'a performative print style into play publishing that called attention to the singularity of his plays by the material appearance of type, paper, and white space on the printed page.'[21]

But this print style did not please everyone. In an issue of *The Fleuron:
A Journal of Typography* (1925), publisher and bibliophile Holbrook Jackson (1874–1948) related how Morris's *The Roots of the Mountains* (1892)
had inspired Shaw's solid, black page with uneven margins printed in
unleaded Caslon Old Face, and praised the 'superb rectangular efficien-
cy' of Shaw's printed page.[22] Eminent scholar-printer Bernard H. Newdigate (1869–1944), one of England's best-respected typographers and
book designers, responded to Jackson in *The London Mercury* (August
1925) with '"G.B.S." and the Typography of his Books.' He pointed out
that 'the chief fault in [Shaw's] books is the smallness of the type in
which they are printed,' and that 'those of us whose sight is growing dim
would find them [his plays] pleasanter if they were printed in pica [12
point] Caslon instead of long primer [10 point].'[23] Shaw himself replied
to Newdigate in the September issue: 'If Mr. Newdigate will reset in pica
Caslon one of my familiar green volumes, ... the size of the resultant volume will astonish him ... If my lines were an eighth of an inch apart,
there would be no complaints. Yet what tries the eyes in reading is not
the black on the page (the letters) but the white (the leads). Morris's
principle of having as much black and as little white as possible was good
for sore eyes as well as pleasing to sound ones.'[24]

Newdigate picked up Shaw's challenge in the October issue by obtaining a stereo-plate from Clark of a page from Richards's *The Philanderer*
(1898), resetting it in pica Caslon, and juxtaposing it with the Richards
original. The result, he calculated, 'would add about 42 pages to the
book, ... The "resultant volume" astonishes not by its great size, but by its
comparative smallness,' and might easily be made portable by the use of
less bulky paper. He also noted that 'The spacing in the reset page is

much closer than in the original. That, of course, is merely following Morris's own practice, which Mr. Shaw interprets as "having as much black and as little white as possible."[25]

The controversy continued in the November issue, with typographer and printer Gerard T. Meynell attacking Newdigate: 'Large type, with or without spacing, does not necessarily mean legibility,' he argued, enclosing his own version of the *Philanderer* excerpt set in Imprint type, long primer leaded.[26] Immediately below it was a letter from William Maxwell of R. & R. Clark which, understandably, also took issue with Newdigate. The increase in pages from the use of pica, he wrote, was not 42 pages but 68; and if *The Doctor's Dilemma* of 512 pages were set on Newdigate's page, 'it becomes 644 pages, *i.e.*, a 26 per cent. increase in extent, and I don't think Mr. Newdigate can risk the suggestion that such a book ought to be in two volumes, as Mr. Shaw's public fully appreciates his policy of giving good value for price charged.'[27]

Newdigate had the last word in the December issue, sarcastically congratulating Meynell on 'his excellent eyesight if ... he is able to read the Caslon long primer of Mr. Shaw's page as easily as the Caslon pica of mine,' and chiding Maxwell for being 'unkind to Mr. Shaw's readers in printing his plays in a type which, by Mr. Shaw's own admission, many of them find too small to read with comfort.'[28]

As these lively exchanges demonstrate, Shaw's playtexts remained controversial, their 'performative print style' flouting established printing conventions and arousing passions among scholars and bibliophiles long after Richards first published Shaw's plays in 1898. Many letters in this volume record Shaw's tenacious struggle to have both printers and publishers respect the integrity of his playtexts.

Man and Businessman

'It's art when you are writing a play but business when you are selling it,' Shaw once quipped.[29] This is a fitting motto for Shaw's dealings with all his publishers, whose business sense he usually found wanting. For Shaw, 'business' was synonymous with profits and protection, and the latter meant primarily copyright protection: 'An author who gives a manager or publisher any rights in his work except those immediately and specifically required for its publication or performance is for business purposes an imbecile,' he wrote in 1931.[30] Protection also meant preventing his plays from being anthologized or turned into school texts. Shaw tersely, rebuffed requests to reprint his work for such purposes. Replying at the bottom of a 23 April 1938 letter by John R. Crossland, 'Editor and Educational Manager' at William Collins Sons & Co. (Glasgow), asking permission to include a passage from the preface to *Saint Joan* and a few lines from *The Dark Lady of the Sonnets* in a secondary school anthology, Shaw wrote: 'No: the advantage to the book would be negligible, and the damage to me incalculable. Publishers should refuse to abet efforts to make English Literature a school subject. People who have suffered from them in their schooldays never buy or read books afterwards. The very names of the authors make them sick. G. Bernard Shaw 27/4/38' (see also Letter 120).[31]

Shaw was well aware of the uncertain nature of the publishing business: as he told Stanley Unwin in 1929, 'publishing is a gamble.' He reiterated the idea in a 22 November 1932 letter to G.H. Thring, secretary of the Society of Authors, which Thring published as the preface to his book *The Marketing of Literary Property* (1933): 'All publishers whose business is concerned with contemporary copyright literature are gambling on the inscrutable caprices of public taste.'[32] Shaw was fond of the analogy and used it again in 'Sixty Years in Business as an Author' (1945): publishing 'is not ordinary trade: it is gambling. The publisher bets the cost of manufacturing, advertizing and circulating a book, plus the overhead of his establishment, against every book he publishes exactly as a turf bookmaker bets against every horse in the race. The author, with his own book, is an owner backing his favorite at the best odds he can get from the competing publishers.'[33] What made things worse, as he told Daniel Macmillan, chairman of Macmillan & Co., in 1943, is that 'the publisher often knows everything about publishing practice and nothing about its economic theory, whilst the author as a rule knows nothing about either, and is constitutionally unfit to conduct his own business' (Letter 170).

Shaw, however, never doubted his own fitness to conduct his business affairs. Long experience made him something of an expert on authors' rights, copyright law, and especially contractual agreements. In early 1921, when actress Mrs Patrick Campbell began writing her autobiography, *My Life and Some Letters* (1922), Shaw warned her, 'Let nothing in-

duce you to accept a publisher's contract without expert advice: *all*
publishers' contracts are booby traps.'[34] Shaw duly scrutinized and
emended any legal document binding author and publisher, whether
his or someone else's. His changes to his contract with Penguin Books
for the two-volume *Intelligent Woman's Guide* made headlines. In 'Shaw
"First Edition" at 6d. a Copy,' the *News Chronicle* for 21 May 1937 reported, 'There was a Shavian exchange over the signing of the contract
which contained the customary clause that the author should guarantee
that the work did not contain any libellous, defamatory, obscene or improper material. G.B.S. crossed this clause out, wrote in its place, "any
hidden libels," and added a footnote: "These clauses are publishers' de-
lusions. A publisher cannot evade his responsibility for every word of the
author's. He might as well murder his mother-in-law and produce in defence a contract in which the author agreed to hold him blameless for all
murders committed by him."'[35]

So refined was Shaw's business acumen that authors sought his advice.
He made numerous annotations to the draft agreement between
Jonathan Cape and T.E. Lawrence[36] for the publication of *Revolt in the
Desert* (1926), and defaced the one between Duckworth & Co. and poet
W.H. Davies by drawing lines through most of the clauses, writing beside
the one protecting Duckworth from being sued for libel: 'This is all non-
sense. The publishers cannot contract out of their responsibility to the
law. They must protect themselves by reading the MS.'[37]

Or take the case of Cyril Clemens (1902–99), Mark Twain's third cousin twice removed. In 1939 Shaw began rewriting Clemens's agreements
and proffering advice on registering copyright, how much royalty to demand, and how big an advance to request. Clemens kept sending Shaw
documents until, in 1942, Shaw warned him: 'Make these terms and stick
to them. Dont argue or listen to arguments. If the book is not worth your
terms it is not worth publishing on any terms. Now you know all about it;
so dont send me any more agreements. If you do I will burn them.'[38] Five
years later, he sent Clemens a personalized 'stereotyped' postcard of the
1911 Copyright Act – Shaw called it an author's 'Magna Charta'[39] – that
spared him the trouble of writing separate replies to requests from publishers wishing to reprint excerpts from his works, or from groups wishing to perform his plays:[40]

THE COPYRIGHT ACT, 1911.

Clause 2   Copyright in a work shall be deemed to be infringed by any person who without the consent of the owner of the copyright does anything the sole right to do which is by this Act conferred on the owner of the copyright.

PROVIDED that the following Acts shall not constitute an infringement of copyright.

(i) Any fair dealing with any work for the purpose of private study, research, criticism, review, or newspaper summary.

(iv) The publication in a collection, mainly composed of non-copyright matter, bona fide intended for the use of schools ... Provided that not more than two of such passages from works by the same author are published by the same publisher within five years.

(v) The publication in a newspaper of a report of a lecture delivered in public.

Private domestic and school class performances of plays are also privileged; but if numerous spectators are invited to witness them in large buildings they may damage the Author. Admission without payment is not a valid defence in such legal action as may ensue.

In view of the above, Mr. Bernard Shaw begs writers, publishers, and managers not to ask him for unnecessary authorizations.

AYOT SAINT LAWRENCE,
WELWYN, HERTS.

Shaw finally lost patience with the bothersome Clemens the following year (1948): 'Now as to the agreement you have sent me and have signed ... Your signature to such a document shews that you are mentally incapable of managing your business as an author.'[41]

The Last Word

As exacting as he was with legal documents, Shaw was even more so with his books. 'Shaw stood guard over his works like a hen over her chicks,' recalled Blanche Patch, his secretary for thirty years. 'Nobody dared disturb a comma.'[42] Shaw's need to have the last word about how his books were printed and marketed resulted in a steady stream – often a torrent – of correspondence between Shaw and his publishers and printers. Delays caused by his travels, an always-heavy workload, wartime conditions, and, in the case of his American publishers, distance, led to misunderstandings and further letters. Undaunted, Shaw advised, corrected, and rewrote. Specimen typeset was scrutinized and amended; errors and typos were rectified, sometimes one per postcard; section by section, proofs went back and forth from Clark's in Edinburgh to Shaw's London flat at Whitehall Court or his country home at Ayot St Lawrence.

If publishing was a gamble, all the more reason to leave nothing to chance. Even Shaw's signature and date (1944) below the now-famous Yousuf Karsh photograph published in *Everybody's Political What's What?* were arrived at only after twenty attempts,[43] an example of Shaw's relentless perfectionism. Everything was important: typeface and margins, royalties and copyright, payments large and small: 'Checks for $1,500 and a stamp value of 35c. arrive on the same morning and are acknowledged with equal courtesy.'[44]

But Shaw did not always have the last word. In 1896, when the Roycroft Printing Shop of East Aurora, New York, issued an unauthorized edition of his essay 'On Going to Church' (see figure 1, p. xli), Shaw was livid. Publisher Elbert Hubbard and his 'Roycroft idiots' (see Letter 74) had taken unconscionable liberties with Shaw's text to accommodate their pseudo-Morris ornamentations. Although his letter excoriating Hubbard has not been located, some of Shaw's critiques found their way into 'The Author's View: A Criticism of Modern Book Printing' (1902), which was reprinted in 1915 as 'Bernard Shaw on Modern Typography' (see figure 3, p. xliii).

Even Shaw's legitimate publishers sometimes faltered. In 'The Typographical Shaw: GBS and the Revival of Printing' (1960), Joseph R. Dunlap rightly observes that in *Plays: Pleasant and Unpleasant*, despite 'Shaw's efforts for close spacing, you will find larger gaps between the sentences than between the words,' a practice that continued 'until the *Collected Works* and *Standard Edition* were issued between the wars.'[45]

Indeed, Constable's limited edition of *The Works of Bernard Shaw: Collected Edition* in 33 volumes (1930–8) and the less expensive *The Works of Bernard Shaw: Standard Edition* in 37 volumes (1931–51) proved challenging – and frustrating – undertakings. For the *Collected Edition*, William

Maxwell convinced (in fact tricked) Shaw into giving up the Caslon handset type he had used since 1898: 'I told him it [the edition] would not be set by hand. I argued long and then took a risk. I told him I would show him a hand-set and a machine-set page side by side and let him choose. When the pages were ready I took them to him and did not, of course, indicate which was which. Shaw got out his magnifying glass and various other gadgets, and retired to another room to examine the pages. Eventually he decided in favour of the one that happened to be machine-set.'[46] (For Shaw's reaction, see Letter 104.) When Otto Kyllmann asked if the type for the *Collected Edition* should be distributed and the texts reset for the *Standard Edition*, Shaw replied (on 9 July 1930): 'Yes: we are bound to destroy the type. I shall view the operation with malignant pleasure, as I have conceived an extraordinary hatred to this particular edition, blast it!'[47]

A year or so later, when Maxwell presented Shaw with specimens for the *Standard Edition* in various typefaces (Caslon, Baskerville, Scotch Roman, Old Style, and Fournier), Shaw told him: 'I like them all but I'll stick to Caslon until I die: and after I am dead you can do what you like.'[48] Alas for Shaw, not only was Fournier adopted, but the font size changed to a slightly larger type, with more white space ('leading') between the lines. Maxwell even convinced him 'to scrap the long-used Venetian blind green binding cloth in favour of a non-fading Venetian red sailcloth fabric' (CL 4, 129).

Dunlap reports how Shaw's American publishers – Shaw thought *all* US publishers 'shocking duffers' (Letter 73) – also took liberties with his texts. 'Brentano first used Caslon but about 1913 switched to Scotch-Roman which is a transitional type between the old style and the so-called modern faces, not approved by Morris ... Furthermore, both Stone and Brentano were inclined to use capitals without lower case on title pages, and their word spacing in the text was often un-Shavian. They were also prone to substitute parentheses for square brackets as boundaries for the stage directions. All this may have contributed to Shaw's astringent views on America ... Since the early '30s Shaw's plays have appeared in Caslon, Scotch-Roman, and Fournier under the Dodd, Mead imprint.'[49] Shaw expressed his 'astringent views' – what he called in Letter 143 'unpopular but necessary things' – in his 11 April 1933 New York lecture 'The Future of Political Science in America,' published under that title by Dodd, Mead and as *The Political Madhouse in America and Nearer Home* by Constable.

This collection of 187 letters between Shaw and twenty-five publishers, ninety of them previously unpublished, offers a unique insight into a relatively little-known facet of Shaw's long career, one that was vital to his renown as an author. These letters reveal how Shaw, in attempting to convince his publishers of the prescience of his views while simultaneously denouncing their business myopia, took very seriously his injunction that 'it is up to the author to take care of himself.' And if he did not always have the last word, Shaw took care of himself efficiently enough to become one of the best-selling authors of the twentieth century.[50]

Notes

1 See Michel W. Pharand, 'A Selected Bibliography of Writings by Bernard Shaw on Publishing, Printing, and Related Topics,' *SHAW: The Annual of Bernard Shaw Studies* 27 (2007): 80–4.

2 Shaw to John Lane, 16 April 1894, in Dan H. Laurence, ed., *Bernard Shaw: Collected Letters 1874–1897* (New York: Dodd, Mead, 1965), 424. In his *Bernard Shaw: A Bibliography*, 2 vol. (Oxford: Clarendon Press, 1983), vol. 1: 23, Dan H. Laurence notes that 156 copies had been sold by April 1894 and six more over the next fifteen months, for a total of 162. Katherine E. Kelly places the figure at 'two or three hundred copies' in her excellent overview, 'Imprinting the Stage: Shaw and the Publishing Trade, 1883–1903,' in *The Cambridge Companion to George Bernard Shaw*, ed. Christopher Innes (Cambridge: Cambridge University Press, 1998), 36.

3 For an informative survey of the era's evolving book-market conditions, see Stefan Collini, 'Boomster and the Quack,' a review of *Writers, Readers and Reputations: Literary Life in Britain 1870–1918*, *London Review of Books* (2 November 2006): 11–14.

4 Kelly, 'Imprinting the Stage,' 25, 36–7.

5 Richards was the first publisher of G.K. Chesterton and John Masefield. As 'Grant Richards Ltd' he issued the first edition of James Joyce's *The Dubliners* (1914).

6 Quoted in James Shand, 'Author and Printer: G.B.S. and R. & R. C[lark].: 1898–1948' (1948), in *Books and Printing: A Treasury for Typophiles*, rev. ed., ed. Paul A. Bennett (Cleveland: The World Publishing Co., 1951), 387.

7 Ibid., 399.

8 Dan H. Laurence notes that many of Shaw's letters 'were in the office files commandeered for war scrap; there was no time to hunt them out and

preserve them' (*Collected Letters 1874–1897* [New York: Dodd, Mead, 1965], xii).

9 Dan H. Laurence, ed., *Bernard Shaw: Collected Letters 1898–1910* (New York: Dodd, Mead, 1972), 335.

10 Jonathan Rose and Patricia J. Anderson, eds, *Dictionary of Literary Biography: British Literary Publishing Houses, 1881–1965*, vol. 112 (Detroit: Gale Research Co., 1991), 67.

11 In a letter to *The Times* of 17 November 1906, 'Publishers and the Public,' Shaw writes: 'But, in the name of common sense, let us have no more moral attitudes and attempts to persuade the public that the publishers are a body of high-minded patrons of literature, organizing the book supply *en grands seigneurs* for the benefit of authors, whilst *The Times* represents a gang of vulgar tradesmen employing Yankee methods for the hideous and unheard-of purpose of making money.' Ronald Ford, ed., *The Letters of Bernard Shaw to The Times* (Dublin: Irish Academic Press, 2007), 73.

12 See Dan H. Laurence, ed., *Bernard Shaw: Collected Leters 1874–1897* (New York: Dodd, Mead, 1965), 78.

13 Ibid., 1: 9–10.

14 Simon Brentano to Shaw, 10 April 1908 (TLU (c): Guelph [see Abbreviations List, p. xxxvii]). On 26 May 1909 Brentano's sent Shaw a cheque, 'on the monthly account from Messrs. Stone & Co.,' for '£24–19–2, representing in our money $121.98,' promising 'additional remittance' (TLS: HRC).

15 According to Dan H. Laurence, Brentano's paid Shaw a royalty of 25% on all volumes except the following: .066 $^2/_3$% on *Imprisonment*; 15% on *Cashel Byron's Profession, The Irrational Knot, The Perfect Wagnerite, An Unsocial Socialist*, and individual plays in paper wrappers; and 20% on *Three Plays for Puritans, Plays: Pleasant and Unpleasant*, and *The Quintessence of Ibsenism*. 'Information obtained from a copy of a letter to Brentano, April 1928, in the Mugar Library, Boston U' (TNU: Guelph).

16 Quoted in Rose and Anderson, eds, *Dictionary of Literary Biography*, vol. 12, 253.

17 Shand, 'Author and Printer,' 394.

18 Shaw, 'Notes on the Clarendon Press Rules for Compositors and Readers,' *The Author* 12 (1 April 1902): 171–2.

19 Even spacing was also a corrective to the practice by nineteenth-century compositors of permitting 'excessively wide spacing between words, particularly after full stops and other marks of punctuation, to minimize their typesetting efforts and maximize their fees' (Kelly, 45).

20 Bernard Shaw, 'Notes on the Clarendon Press Rules for Compositors and Readers,' *The Author* 12 (1 April 1902): 172.

21 Kelly, 'Imprinting the Stage,' 45, 42.

22 Holbrook Jackson, 'Robert Bridges, George Moore, Bernard Shaw and Printing,' *The Fleuron: A Journal of Typography* 4 (1925): 52.

23 B.H. Newdigate, '"G.B.S." and the Typography of His Books,' *London Mercury* 12 (August 1925): 420.

24 Shaw, 'The Typography of G.B.S.,' *London Mercury* 23 (September 1925): 524.

25 B.H. Newdigate, 'Book-Production Notes,' *London·Mercury* 12 (October 1925): 645–6.

26 Gerard T. Meynell, 'Newdigate *v.* Shaw,' *London Mercury* 13 (November 1925): 72.

27 William Maxwell, 'To the Editor of *The London Mercury*,' *London Mercury* 13 (November 1925): 72–3.

28 B.H. Newdigate, 'Meynell *versus* Shaw and Others,' *London Mercury* 13 (December 1925): 189.

29 Quoted in George Middleton, 'Shaw's Royal Royalties: Dramatist Knew Values of Literary Property Rights – and Protected Them to the Hilt,' *Variety*, 9 January 1957: 31.

30 Shaw, 'Mr. Bernard Shaw on "imbeciles" who are "afraid to say no,"' *The Author* 41 (Spring 1931): 88. See Letter 166 for similar comments.

31 John R. Crossland to Shaw, 23 April 1938 (Colgate).

32 Shaw, 'A Letter to the Author from Bernard Shaw,' in G. Herbert Thring, *The Marketing of Literary Property: Books and Serial Rights* (London: Constable, 1933), xi–xxiii, repr. in *Bernard Shaw: The Complete Prefaces, Volume 3: 1930–1950*, ed. Dan H. Laurence and Daniel J. Leary (London: Allen Lane, Penguin, 1997), 135.

33 Shaw, 'Sixty Years in Business as an Author,' *The Author* 55 (Summer 1945): 57.

34 Shaw to Mrs Patrick Campbell, 20 January 1921, in Dan H. Laurence, ed., *Bernard Shaw: Collected Letters 1911–1925* (New York: Viking, 1985), 708.

35 Quoted in Steve Hare, ed., *Penguin Portrait: Allen Lane and the Penguin Editors 1935–1970* (Harmondsworth, UK: Penguin, 1995), 57–8.

36 Reproduced in Rose and Anderson, 56–7.

37 Undated photocopy (Guelph). Shaw wrote the preface to W.H. Davies's *The Autobiography of a Super-Tramp* (London: A.C. Fifield, 1908).

38 Shaw to Cyril Clemens, 2 February 1942 (TLS: UNC).

39 'A Letter to the Author,' 139. The 1911 Copyright Act had its detractors. In
'G. Bernard Shaw as the Champion of Capitalism: An Open Letter on the
New Copyright Bill' (*Everyman*, 7 February 1913), Belgian Charles Saroléa
(1870–1953), head of Romance Languages at the University of Edinburgh,
inveighed against the 1911 act (effective 1 July 1912) that extended copyright
to fifty years after an author's death. Bemoaning the unavailability for
another half-century of 'hundreds of masterpieces of world literature,'
Saroléa expressed 'bewilderment' that 'the Superman of Socialism' had
given the act his approval and accused him of being pledged 'to the materi-
alistic conception of human society' (521–2).

40 Shaw sent the card to Clemens on 20 August 1947 (UNC). See Laurence, *Bernard Shaw: A Bibliography*, vol. 2: 848–9, for a description and variants.

41 Shaw to Cyril Clemens, 31 December 1948 (TLS: UNC).

42 Blanche Patch, *Thirty Years with G.B.S.* (London: Victor Gollancz, 1951), 48.

43 Undated autograph note (NLS). Shaw lamented that his signatures were 'all
decrepit. I have to write slowly, like a child.'

44 Quoted in Middleton, 'Shaw's Royal Royalties.'

45 *Bulletin of the New York Public Library* 64 (1960): 534–47, reprinted in *The Shavian* 2.3 (February 1961), 10.

46 William Maxwell, 'Printing for Bernard Shaw,' *The Listener*, 10 September
1949: 797.

47 Dan H. Laurence, ed., *Bernard Shaw: Collected Letters 1926–1950* (New York:
Viking, 1988), 193.

48 Quoted in Shand, 'Author and Printer,' 391.

49 Dunlap, 'The Typographical Shaw,' 14; his ellipses.

50 Some of the material in this introduction appeared in Michel W. Pharand,
'Getting Published: Grant Richards and the Shaw Book,' *SHAW: The Annual
of Bernard Shaw Studies* 27 (2007): 69–80.

Editor's Note

When Dodd, Mead & Co. wrote to Shaw in 1949 suggesting the publication of his collected letters, the nonagenarian replied that there were 'billions of them; and I am adding to them every day' (Letter 183). The 133 letters to 24 publishers in Dan H. Laurence's four-volume edition of Shaw's *Collected Letters* is only a fraction of Shaw's correspondence with them. He sent them hundreds of letters, postcards, and telegrams and received countless documents in return: letters, memos, proofs, invoices, receipts, accounts of sales, bills for printing and binding, royalty statements, copyright agreements, and income tax records. In addition, judging from allusions made by Shaw and his publishers to correspondence sent or received, numerous letters have gone astray.

This edition contains 187 pieces of correspondence, of which 165 are from Shaw. A total of 90 letters are published here for the first time, of which 72 are by Shaw. Short extracts from other unpublished letters are found in the headnotes and notes. Archival and published sources for each letter are given in brackets at the start of a letter, with full information in the Abbreviations section.

The primary source for previously published correspondence is Laurence's *Collected Letters*. Note that letters listed therein as located in the Mary and Donald F. Hyde Collection, Four Oaks Library, are now marked 'BL'; following the death in 2003 of Mary Hyde, Lady Eccles, her papers were transferred from her home at Four Oaks Farm (Somerville, New Jersey) to the British Library. Letters listed by Laurence as located in the British Museum are now also marked 'BL.' Minor discrepancies between a letter published in *Collected Letters* and the original have been silently corrected in favour of the latter (as in Letter 166).

Shaw's idiosyncratic spelling ('shew' for show, 'Shakespear'), elimination of apostrophes in contractions ('dont' for don't), and ampersands have been retained, except in the case of previously published documents (when originals were missing or unavailable) that standardize spelling. A few obvious typographical errors have been silently corrected to keep the use of '[*sic*]' to a minimum. As is to be expected when the topic is business, many of Shaw's letters deal with technicalities that, when reiterated from one letter to the next, become tedious. These, as well as peripheral or irrelevant passages, have been omitted and replaced with ellipses (which, unless otherwise noted, are mine).

The letters are numbered consecutively and printed chronologically, with headnotes providing a letter's context and notes following the letter clarifying references and allusions, with the subject of each annotation in boldface type. Where relevant, annotations include some of Shaw's many utterances on publishers and the publishing trade that appeared in print during his lifetime. As Shaw's American publishers were often prolix, only key excerpts from their very long letters are quoted in headnotes.

As with previous volumes in this series, Shaw's addresses and dates have been standardized. Letters lacking an address (either because Shaw did not provide one or because, if the letter is a copy, it was omitted) are designated 'no address.' Where an address is conjectural but can be inferred from the context, it appears in brackets. The recipient or author is identified in boldface type at the head of each letter.

Many letters in this volume deal with financial matters, from printing costs and book prices to royalties and taxes. Readers outside the UK (and younger ones *in* the UK) may appreciate the following information. Before 1971, when decimalization divided the pound into 100 pence, British currency consisted of three basic units: pounds (£), shillings (s), and pence (d). Shilling notations sometimes appear as '/–' (thus six shillings is 6/–) and references to shillings and pence are sometimes abbreviated (thus two shillings and sixpence is 'two and six'). Simply put:

1 pound = 4 crowns = 10 florins = 20 shillings = 240 pence = 960 farthings
1 shilling = 12 pence

2 shillings = 1 florin
2 shillings 6 pence = half a crown
10 shillings 6 pence = half a guinea
21 shillings = 1 guinea

Acknowledgments

I am grateful above all for the unwavering friendship, Shavian expertise, and keen editorial eye of Leonard Conolly, who offered me this project many years ago one evening by the fireside of his elegant home in Peterborough, Ontario. (He beguiled me into it.) The University of Toronto Press has been most supportive, and the patience of editor Jill McConkey has, I hope, been rewarded. My heartfelt thanks to her, Richard Ratzlaff, Barb Porter, and everyone at UTP who helped refine my work. My very special thanks to UTP copy-editor John St James, whose scrupulous reading and astute suggestions did away with numerous errors and omissions. I am also most grateful for the invaluable corrections and suggestions made by the two readers of the Canadian Federation for the Humanities and Social Sciences, Aid to Scholarly Publications Program.

    Bernard Shaw and His Publishers has had a nomadic history. I began it while teaching at the University of Ottawa and am indebted to Keith Wilson, former Chair of the English Department, for helping me obtain a travel grant to visit two Shaw archives. I continued my research while a Visiting Research Scholar at the University of South Carolina, under the generous sponsorship of Matthew J. Bruccoli. I then moved to Japan, where I obtained travel grants to visit other Shaw collections thanks to two English Department Chairs: Masashi Sasaki of Hokkaido Bunkyo University and Shigenobu Saito of Kobe University. This book has now made its circuitous way back to Canada, as have I. It has been a long journey.

    It is a great pleasure to convey my appreciation to those who facilitated my work. Don B. Wilmeth, eminent American theatre historian, alerted me to Brown University's extensive Dodd, Mead archive. *A Bernard Shaw Chronology*, by Shaw biographer A.M. Gibbs, rendered effortless the challenge of accurately tracking Shaw's whereabouts. Gabriel Austin, former secretary to the late Lady Eccles, generously provided me with a checklist of her Shaw collection. The doyen of Shaw studies, the late Dan H. Laurence, kindly gave me full access to the extensive vertical files in his Shaw collection at the University of Guelph Library. In addition, the head-notes to his outstanding edition of Shaw's *Collected Letters*, and the wealth of details in his indispensable *Bernard Shaw: A Bibliography*, have been crucial resources: this book owes its existence to his scrupulous research. On a personal note, in May 2001, prior to a road trip to visit a Shaw archive, Dan sent me a cheque, 'to do me the courtesy of thanking, after all these years, the collectors and scholars' who had been generous to him in the past. 'You, in your turn, will recognize that you repay debts, not to the last generation, but to the present and future ones. So pass the generosity on, when you can, to the scholars and researchers of the future.' Rest assured, Dan, I shall indeed.

Grateful acknowledgment is made to the following institutions for permission to publish correspondence from their collections, and to the archivists and librarians who answered my queries, sent me information and photocopies, and otherwise assisted me in accomplishing the daunting task of examining and duplicating masses of documents:

Brown University: Mark N. Brown, former Curator of the Manuscripts Division, Timothy Engels, Senior Library Associate Specialist, Rosemary L. Cullen, Senior Scholarly Resources Librarian, and Stephen L. Thompson, Gateway Services Librarian, The John Hay Library. Bucknell University: Doris Dysinger, Curator of Special Collections / University Archives, Ellen Clarke Bertrand Library. Colgate University: Carl Peterson, Head of Special Collections and University Archivist, Everett Needham Case Library. Cornell University: Eleanor Brown, Curator of Media and Digital Collections, Ann L. Ferguson, former Curator of Rare Books and Burgunder Curator for George Bernard Shaw, and present Rare Books and Burgunder Curator Katherine Reagan, all at the Carl A. Kroch Library. Georgetown University: Scott S. Taylor, Manuscripts Processor, and Nicholas B. Scheetz, Manuscript Librarian, Special Collections Research Center, Joseph Mark Lauinger Library. Harry Ransom Humanities Research Center, The University of Texas at Austin: Patrice S. Fox, Library Assistant II, and Richard Workman, Research Librarian. Houghton Library: Heather G. Cole, Assistant Curator, and Leslie A. Morris, Curator, Modern Books and Manuscripts, Houghton Library of the Harvard College Library. National Library of Scotland: Sally Harrower, Curator of Manuscripts, and Sheila Mackenzie, Senior Curator, Manuscripts Division. Princeton University Library: Meg Sherry Rich, Reference Librarian/Archivist, and AnnaLee Pauls, Special Collections Assistant III, Rare Books and Special Collections. University of Guelph: Lorne Bruce, Head of Archival and Special Collections, University of Guelph Library. University of North Carolina at Chapel Hill: Elizabeth Chenault, Geneva R. Holliday, Laura Brown, Matthew Turi, and Curator of Rare Books Charles McNamara, Wilson Library. Washington University: John Hodge, Curator, and Sarah Patton, Special Collections Assistant, Modern Literature Collection / Manuscripts, John M. Olin Library. Yale University Library: Mellissa Hughes and Stephen C. Jones, Head of Public Services, The Beinecke Rare Book and Manuscript Library.

I would also like to thank Jeremy Crow, Head of Literary Estates at The Society of Authors, for his ongoing support. Shaw's letters in this edition are published by permission of The Society of Authors, acting for the Estate of Bernard Shaw. All efforts have been made to obtain information on copyright holders of letters to Shaw included in this volume. For their kind permission to publish such letters, grateful acknowledgment is extended to Constable & Robinson Ltd and Rights Director Eryl Humphrey Jones for a letter from Otto Kyllmann of Constable & Co dated 24 July 1929, and to The Orion Publishing Group Ltd and Rights Assistant Paul Stark for a letter from A.J. Hoppé of J.M. Dent and Sons Ltd dated 7 February 1940.

Without the encouragement of family members, friends, and colleagues, who listened patiently to my progress reports over the years, this book would have foundered. I heartily thank my father, Donat Pharand, the first published author I ever knew, for introducing me early on to the intricacies of manuscript revision by allowing me to proofread his books on international law: you continue to inspire my work. My sincere thanks also to his companion Sylvia Herrera, a fellow bibliophile and voracious reader, for her faith in all I undertake. My sister Gisèle, her partner Tom Schneider, their son Peter, my brother Bernard, and my ninety-five-year-old aunt Florence have always been my steadfast advocates: for your love and support, merci beaucoup. One could not ask for more gracious hosts than my parents-in-law, Gayle and Larry Lutgen, whose South Carolina home and cozy seaside condo are always havens of repose. To Rodelle and Stanley Weintraub, for over two decades of unflagging friendship and mentorship, I express my deepest appreciation and es-

teem. My colleagues at Hokkaido Bunkyo University – in particular
Stephen Toskar, a poet and true friend – were congenial to a fault. So
were the members of the Bernard Shaw Society of Japan – in particular
Hisashi Morikawa – with whom it was a privilege to share my research at
their conferences. My thanks to Christopher S. Schreiner, fellow Penn
State graduate and long-time friend, for his invaluable counsel (and for
introducing me to the woman I married). Special thanks are due to Barbara Conolly for allowing me to hone my editorial skills at Broadview
Press. My thanks to Ellen Hawman for her indexing assistance. I am especially grateful to Mel Wiebe, Director of The Disraeli Project at
Queen's University, Kingston, for unwittingly providing the needed im-
petus that helped me complete this book.

My wife Ginger and our children Logan and Rees, who followed me
from North America to the other side of the globe and back again,
showed more forbearance than I deserved while I brought my work to a
close in Kobe, Japan. Ginger's contribution to this book, and to my life,
is inestimable.

Abbreviations

Type of correspondence

ACCS	Autograph 'compliments' card signed
ADS	Autograph draft signed
ADU	Autograph draft unsigned
ALCS	Autograph letter-card signed
ALS	Autograph letter signed
ALU	Autograph letter unsigned
ANS	Autograph note signed
ANU	Autograph note unsigned
APCS	Autograph postcard signed
APCU	Autograph postcard unsigned
(c)	Carbon copy
(e)	Extract or truncated text previously published
FP	Facsimile publication
PP	Previous publication
SHDS	Shorthand draft or copy signed
SHDU	Shorthand draft or copy unsigned
TDU	Typed draft unsigned
TEL	Telegram or cable
TLS	Typed letter signed
TLT	Typed letter typed signature
TLU	Typed letter unsigned
TNS	Typed note signed
TPCS	Typed postcard signed

TR   Transcription: original unlocated
(tr)   Typed transcription or copy

Sources of the correspondence

Archival Sources

Albert   Sidney P. Albert Bernard Shaw Collection, John Hay
              Library, Brown University
BL   British Library
BLPES   Shaw Business Papers, British Library of Political and
              Economic Science, Archives Division, London School
              of Economics and Political Science
Brown   Dodd, Mead & Co. Records Pertaining to George Ber-
              nard Shaw, Brown University Library
Bucknell   Special Collections / University Archives, The Ellen
              Clarke Bertrand Library, Bucknell University
Colgate   Richard S. Weiner Collection of George Bernard Shaw,
              Special Collections, Case Library, Colgate University
Cornell   Bernard F. Burgunder Collection, Division of Rare and
              Manuscript Collections, Carl A. Kroch Library, Cornell
              University
Dartmouth   Baker Library, Dartmouth College
Delaware   Bernard Shaw Collection, Special Collections Depart-
              ment, University of Delaware Library, University of Del-
              aware
Georgetown   The Max Reinhardt Papers, Special Collections
              Research Center, Georgetown University Library,
              Washington, DC
Guelph   Archival and Special Collections, University of Guelph
              Library
Harvard   Houghton Library, Harvard University
HRC   Harry Ransom Humanities Research Center, The Uni-
              versity of Texas at Austin
NLS   Manuscripts Division, National Library of Scotland
NYPL   New York Public Library
Oregon   University of Oregon Library

Princeton	Princeton University Library
UNC	Southern Historical Collection, Wilson Library, University of North Carolina at Chapel Hill
Virginia	Tracy W. McGregor Library, University of Virginia
WU	Modern Literature Collection / Manuscripts, John M. Olin Library, Washington University
Yale	Beinecke Rare Book and Manuscript Library, Yale University

Printed Sources

Note: Full publication information for printed sources can be found in the References.

Author	Grant Richards, *Author Hunting*
Bowes	Bowes and Bowes, *Catalogue 523*
CL 1	Dan H. Laurence, ed., *Bernard Shaw: Collected Letters 1874–1897*
CL 2	Dan H. Laurence, ed., *Bernard Shaw: Collected Letters 1898–1910*
CL 3	Dan H. Laurence, ed., *Bernard Shaw: Collected Letters 1911–1925*
CL 4	Dan H. Laurence, ed., *Bernard Shaw: Collected Letters 1926–1950*
CP 1–7	Dan H. Laurence, ed., *Bernard Shaw: Collected Plays with their Prefaces*, 7 vols.
Diaries 1	Stanley Weintraub, ed., *Bernard Shaw: The Diaries 1885–1897*, vol. 1
Diaries 2	Stanley Weintraub, ed., *Bernard Shaw: The Diaries 1885–1897*, vol. 2
Ervine	St John Ervine, *Bernard Shaw: His Life, Work and Friends*
Exhibit	Dan H. Laurence, *Shaw: An Exhibit*
Gibbs	A.M. Gibbs, *A Bernard Shaw Chronology*
Hare	Steve Hare, *Penguin Portrait: Allen Lane and the Penguin Editors 1935–1970*
Henderson	Archibald Henderson, *Bernard Shaw: Playboy and Prophet*
King	Raphael King, *Catalogue 5*

Laurence 1	Dan H. Laurence, *Bernard Shaw: A Bibliography*, vol. 1
Laurence 2	Dan H. Laurence, *Bernard Shaw: A Bibliography*, vol. 2
Memories	Grant Richards, *Memories of a Misspent Youth*
Morgan	Charles Morgan, *The House of Macmillan*
Mumby	F.A. Mumby and Frances H.S. Stallybrass, *From Swan Sonnenschein to George Allen & Unwin Ltd.*
Nowell-Smith	Simon Nowell-Smith, *Letters to Macmillan*
Orcutt	William Dana Orcutt, *Celebrities Off Parade*
Patch	Blanche Patch, *Thirty Years with G.B.S.*
Publishing	Sir Stanley Unwin, *The Truth About Publishing*
Rhys	Ernest Rhys, *Letters from Limbo*
SHAW 27	*SHAW: The Annual of Bernard Shaw Studies*, vol. 27
Unwin	Sir Stanley Unwin, *The Truth About a Publisher*
Weintraub	Stanley Weintraub, ed., *Bernard Shaw's Nondramatic Literary Criticism*

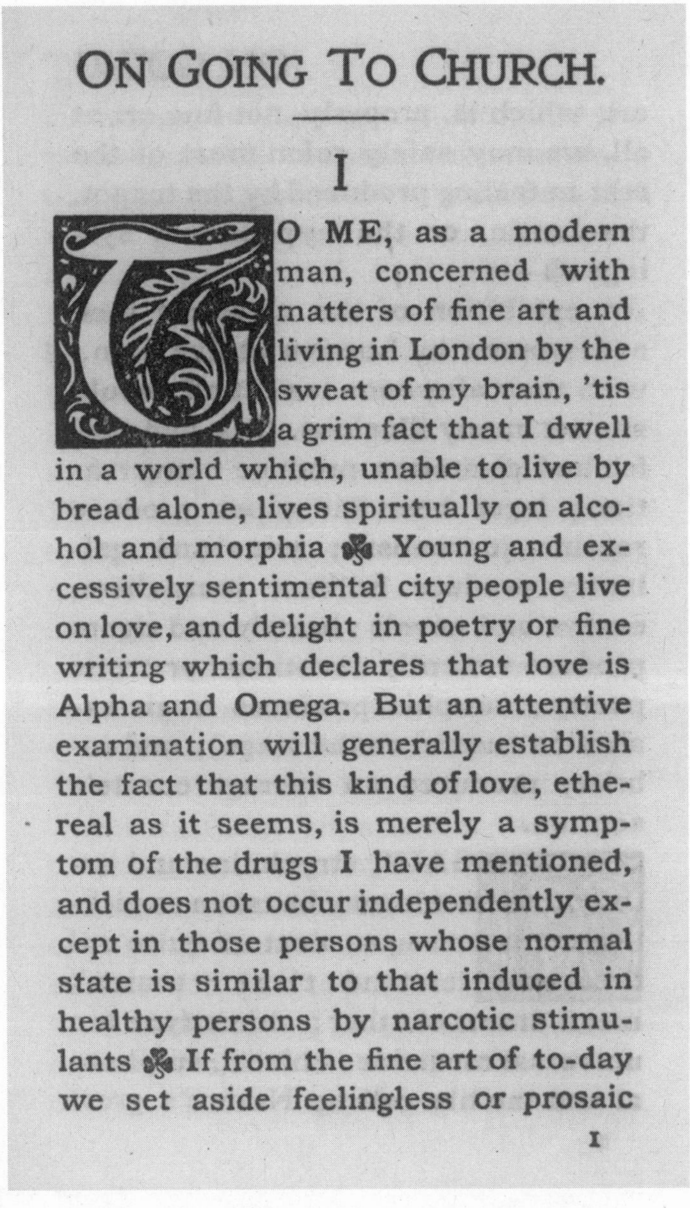

ON GOING TO CHURCH.

I

TO ME, as a modern man, concerned with matters of fine art and living in London by the sweat of my brain, 'tis a grim fact that I dwell in a world which, unable to live by bread alone, lives spiritually on alcohol and morphia ❧ Young and excessively sentimental city people live on love, and delight in poetry or fine writing which declares that love is Alpha and Omega. But an attentive examination will generally establish the fact that this kind of love, ethereal as it seems, is merely a symptom of the drugs I have mentioned, and does not occur independently except in those persons whose normal state is similar to that induced in healthy persons by narcotic stimulants ❧ If from the fine art of to-day we set aside feelingless or prosaic

1

Figure 1. *On Going to Church.* East Aurora, NY: Roycroft Printing Shop, 1896. Photo courtesy of Brown University

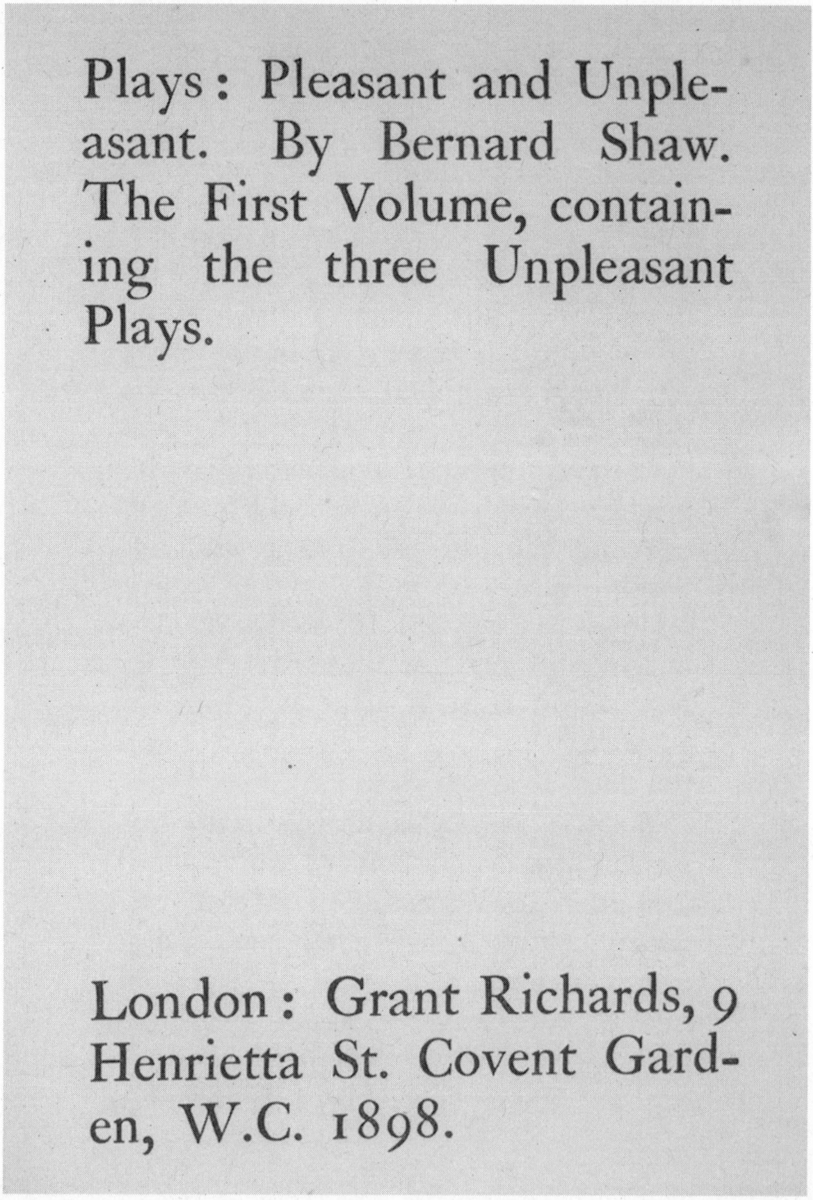

Plays : Pleasant and Unpleasant. By Bernard Shaw. The First Volume, containing the three Unpleasant Plays.

London : Grant Richards, 9 Henrietta St. Covent Garden, W.C. 1898.

Figure 2. *Plays: Pleasant and Unpleasant,* volume 1. London: Grant Richards, 1898. Photo courtesy of Brown University

BERNARD SHAW

ON

MODERN TYPOGRAPHY

REPRINTED FROM
THE CAXTON MAGAZINE
LONDON

HORACE CARR
AT THE PRINTING PRESS
CLEVELAND
1915

Figure 3. *Bernard Shaw on Modern Typography.* Cleveland: Horace Carr at The Printing Press, 1915. Photo courtesy of Brown University

Figure 4. *Saint Joan: A Chronicle Play in Six Scenes and an Epilogue.* London: Constable and Company Ltd, 1924. Limited edition with illustrations by Charles Ricketts. Photo courtesy of Brown University

Letters

1 / To Macmillan & Co. 13 Victoria Grove SW

1st February 1880

[ADU: BL; CL 1]

Shaw's first novel, Immaturity, *had been rejected by Hurst & Blackett on 25 November 1879 (Shaw's acknowledgment included a request for the MS to be forwarded to Kegan Paul & Co.) and by Richard Bentley & Son on 8 January 1880; 'You cannot possibly regret the unfavourable result more than I do,' Shaw wrote to them on the 15th (CL 1, 26). Macmillan's 31 January reader's report called* Immaturity *'the work of a humourist and a realist, crossed, however, by veins of merely literary discussion. There is a piquant oddity about the situations now and then: and the characters are certainly not drawn after the conventional patterns of fiction. It is dry and ironic in flavour ... It is undoubtedly clever, but most readers would find it dry, unattractive, and too devoid of any sort of emotion. And then it is very long' (Morgan, 119). Macmillan rejected the novel on 3 February after receiving the following letter.*

Gentlemen

My MS has arrived safely with a very kind letter from you, and a critical description of my book which could not, I believe, be more accurate.

The flatness of the novel was so involved by its design, that in writing it, I did not propose to myself to save it from appearing dull to a reader who should seek for excitement in it. This design was, to write a novel scrupulously true to nature, with no incident in it to which everyday experience might not afford a parallel, and yet which should constantly provoke in [a] reader full of the emotional ethics of the conventional novel, a sense of oddity and unexpectedness. In short, not to be ironic, but to deal with those ordinary experiences which are a constant irony on sentimentalism, at which the whole work is mainly directed. The machinery employed is an arrangement of two heros & 2 heroines, strongly contrasted and shuffling about, changing partners, and playing on one another throughout. Thus, one of my alternative titles to 'Immaturity,' was 'A Quadrille'; but I rejected it for the same reason that led me to excise every word that betrayed the least consciousness on my part of my own design. I also cut out pages of analysis of character, because I think the dramatic method of *exhibiting* character the true one, and that analysis has been carried so far in the furthest point to which novel writing has been brought, that future advances will discard it rather than develop it.

The result is a panorama without a descriptive lecture. Now, if, in order to stamp the book as a meditation on life, I insert a lecture, I violate my own crotchets as to art workmanship. On the other hand, if I heighten the interest by unusual and exciting incidents, I abandon my design and spoil my moral. I am too raw a workman to fulfil the conditions and avoid the difficulties at the same time, and therefore anxious as I am to get introduced to the public so as to be more at my ease with them next time, I confess that I am utterly at a loss when I attempt to plan such a recasting of the book as you suggest. I would give up the idea of publishing it altogether, but that there are portions of it (small ones, unfortunately) which I have not the heart to consign to oblivion without making some sort of plea for, particularly since your critic has relieved me of some of my worst doubts concerning them. Would it be possible to publish the book as a series of magazine papers, or in some form from which the ordinary reader would not look for his accustomed stimulants?

I hope to avail myself of your invitation to call in the course of the week, so I need not add anything more at present. I suppose you are sufficiently used to the communicativeness of young authors on the subject of their own works to excuse the length at which I have already troubled you.

I am, gentlemen,
yours faithfully,
[G.B. Shaw]

Shaw's sister Lucinda Frances ('Lucy') (1853–1920) and mother Lucinda Elizabeth Gurly ('Bessie') (1830–1913) left Dublin on 17 June 1873 and settled in London at **13 Victoria Grove**. Shaw joined them on 1 April 1876. On 23 December 1880 they moved to 37 Fitzroy Street (walking distance to Shaw's frequent haunt, the British Museum). A **quadrille** is an intricate 18th-century French dance performed by four couples. Daniel (1813–57) and brother Alexander (1818–96) **Macmillan** co-founded their publishing house in 1843. For Shaw's reminiscences of his early novel-writing days, see Letter 170.

2 / To Remington & Co.   37 Fitzroy Street W
                                              26th November 1881

[SHDU: BL; CL 1]

Even though Joseph M. Langford of W. Blackwood & Sons rejected Immaturity *on 28 September 1880, in thanking Macmillan on 4 January 1881 for their attention to* The Irrational Knot *(which they rejected), Shaw asked that the MS be forwarded to Langford. Shaw was unaware that Macmillan's reader had described it as 'a novel of the most disagreeable kind,' whose 'characters have a curious flavour and "sapidity" about them.' The whole idea of the book 'is odd, perverse and crude ... There is too much adultery and the like matters' (Morgan, 120). Shaw wrote to Bentley & Son on 14 July following their rejection of the MS – 'I fear the book has graver faults, of which you have spared me a recital' (CL 1, 39) – and on the same day sent it to Smith, Elder & Co. Below Shaw replies to an offer by Remington & Co. to publish* Immaturity *in three volumes at a cost of £95, to be sold at one and a half guineas. To Remington's 30 November reply that advertising would exceed £25, Shaw replied the same day that the 'offer' was that Shaw should pay £100 and receive ¾, concluding with 'I am merely trying who will make the best bargain with me' (CL 1, 44).*

Gentlemen

I have received your proposal to publish my novel 'Immaturity,' and, as far as I can judge at present, it is less advantageous than an offer made me by another firm for the same book. At what rate would you account to me for the copies sold? Do you still estimate the advertising at £25? I should like to have an exact basis for calculation, because, as I do not possess £95 (or, indeed, 95/–) I must endeavour to borrow the money on the security of the novel – not a very tempting speculation for a man of business.

I may say at once, however, that your proposal is not an encouraging one. I am told that £95 will practically secure you against loss. If that is so, what consideration do you offer for the share of ⅓ which you require? If I am to be capitalist as well as artist, might I not as well publish on commission and retain my copyright entire? Again, it is not likely that there will be any occasion to print 1000 copies at 1½ guineas, and I presume your right to a third will be established not only in the first issue, but in the copyright, and would extend to colonial editions, railway editions, &c, should such be called for.

If the book has really inspired you with any confidence in its success, I should be very glad to sell you the copyright [for] what you may choose to offer for it, or to take a small royalty in lieu of finding £95 and having ⅔. It will be neither easy nor pleasant to borrow money in the face of the obvious remark that if the book was worth anything, some publisher would have taken it up. Let me add that if it will not pay, I had rather it remained in MS.

> I am, gentlemen,
> yours faithfully
> [G.B. Shaw]

When applied to writing, **sapidity** means 'not vapid or uninteresting' (*Concise Oxford Dictionary*). The other **firm** was Newman & Co. Shaw would **publish on commission** beginning in 1903 with *Man and Superman*. To **retain copyright** remained a crucial publication criterion throughout Shaw's career. **Railway** and **colonial editions** were inexpensive, the latter 'intended for circulation only in India and the British Colonies.' *Cashel Byron's Profession* was published in 1901 in 'Grant Richards's Colonial Library' (see Laurence 1, illustration facing p. 9).

3 / To Richard Bentley & Son

c/o W.J. Gurley, Esq.
Leyton, Essex
18th February 1882

[SHDS: BL; CL 1]

Shaw had completed his third novel, Love Among the Artists, *in December 1881. Bentley informed him that the novel was 'not of a sufficiently encouraging nature to enable us to make overtures to you for its publication. The work is written with a smart and apparently practised pen, but the whole story would seem to be lacking in point of interest for the general reader' (CL 1, 48).*

Gentlemen

I am much obliged to you for the attention you have given to my novel 'Love among the Artists,' and trust that the result will not discourage you from conferring a similar favour on me on a future occasion [if] I ask you to do so. I am not without a hope that the point of my work, obscure though it seems to be, will yet strike your reader, who (if you will excuse my saying so) either underrates the capacity of 'the general reader,' or applies the term to a class of persons who – like himself – read little else but the newspapers, and whom therefore a novelist is not concerned to please.

Kindly return the MS to 37 Fitzroy St., W, at your convenience.

> I am, gentlemen,
> yours faithfully
> G.B. Shaw

After what he called 'a light attack of scarlet fever,' Shaw convalesced at the home of his maternal uncle, **Walter John Gurly** (not Gurley), who placed him under 'a species of quarantine' (quoted in Gibbs, 45). During this period, Shaw completed the first draft of *Love Among the Artists* and revised *The Irrational Knot.*

4 / To Richard Bentley & Son

36 Osnaburgh Street NW
31st May 1883

[ADU: BL; CL 1]

Shaw completed his fourth novel, Cashel Byron's Profession, *in early February 1883. It was subsequently serialized between April 1885 and March 1886 (without payment) in the Socialist monthly* To-Day. *Macmillan's reader, perhaps repelled by pugilism itself or by the idea of a retired boxer as successful politician, said its author had 'some promise of writing in him if he did not disgust us by his subject' (Morgan, 126). Bentley returned the MS after several months' delay, explaining that it had been read twice, the last time in March. It was rejected later in the year after a third reading.*

Dear Sirs

I have received 'Cashel Byron' safely, and beg to thank you for the attention you have given it. I read it twice (and wrote it twice) myself, but certainly would not have done so except under the strong compulsion of authorship, and your repetition of the experiment seems to me either a remarkable proof of your conscientiousness in judging the novel, or a flattering tribute to its interest. But why did you not send it back to me last March? Is it possible that, with your great experience, you did not know that if you looked you would never leap – that when you could no longer defer your decision, you would act on the principle, 'When you are in doubt, don't.' I do not ask you this with any idea of troubling you for a reply, but merely as a defence to a certain strain in your letter which seems to reproach me with having inconsiderately pressed you for an answer.

You are quite right as to the horrible blackguardism of the book, but pray remember that I have tried science and the finer arts as subjects in vain, and that the lower I go, the better I seem to please.

Should you ever contemplate a reprint of the works of the late Pierce Egan, I will be happy, in the capacity of editor, to place at your disposal the historical research which I have wasted on 'Cashel Byron.'

Forgive me for thus trifling with your valuable time, and believe me,

dear Sirs,

yours faithfully

[G.B. Shaw]

Shaw, Lucy, and their mother had moved to **36 Osnaburgh Street** in April 1882. In the British Museum, Shaw had consulted the boxing articles of English sports writer **Pierce Egan** (1772–1849), collected as *Boxiana* (five volumes, 1813–28), as background for *Cashel Byron.*

5 / To Macmillan & Co.

36 Osnaburgh Street NW

14th January 1885

[CL 1; PP: Morgan]

Shaw completed his fifth novel, An Unsocial Socialist, *on 1 November 1883 and revisions on the 15th. He had written to Kegan Paul, Trench & Co. inquiring about sending them the MS, rewriting on the 18th that they 'were less likely to be repelled by the appearance of a few economic considerations in a novel than firms who deal chiefly in popular fiction' (CL 1, 78). Following its serialization in To-Day (again gratis) from March to December 1884, Shaw sent the MS to Chatto & Windus on 26 December 1884 and in early 1885 to Macmillan, whose rejection was accompanied by an offer to 'look at anything else [the author] might write of a more substantial kind' (CL 1, 111).*

Gentlemen

Many thanks for reading An Unsocial Socialist. Your demand for 'something more substantial' takes my breath away. Your reader, I fear, thought the book not serious – perhaps because it was not dull. If so, he was an Englishman. I have only met one reviewer and one oral critic who really took the book in. They were both Scotchmen. You must admit that when one deals with two large questions in a novel, and throws in an epitome of modern German socialism as set forth by Marx as a makeweight, it is rather startling to be met with an implied accusation of triviality.

yours faithfully

George Bernard Shaw

The **one reviewer** was journalist John Mackinnon Robertson (1856–1933). The **one oral critic** was Shaw's friend William Archer (1856–1924), dramatic critic for *The World* 1884–

1905. In 1884 he had suggested to Shaw that they collaborate on a play entitled *Rhinegold* (Archer supplied the plot); years later Shaw reworked it (without Archer) into his first play, *Widowers' Houses*, completed in late 1892 and published in 1893.

6 / To Macmillan & Co. 36 Osnaburgh Street NW
22nd January 1885

[SHDS: BL; CL 1]

Replying to the preceding letter on the 22nd, Macmillan enclosed their reader's report, apologizing for 'the epithet "unsubstantial" which was perhaps not quite fortunate though we could not think of any other that would better express our meaning. What we really doubt is whether the book would find enough readers' (Morgan, 129). The report summed up the book as 'theories with a whimsical and deliberately extravagant story, served up with pungent literary sauce. The result is a dish, which I fancy only the few would relish' (CL 1, 114).

Gentlemen

Many thanks for your letter. I forgive your critic, although the book is perfectly serious – which is precisely why people take it as a joke. Its impossibilities are the commonplace occurrences of life. All my readers, as far as I know them, like the book; but they tell me that although they relish it they dont think the general public would. Which is the more discouraging, as this tendency of each man to consider himself unique is one of the main themes of the novel. Surely out of thirty millions of copyright persons (so to speak) there must be a few thousand who would keep me in bread and cheese for the sake of my story-telling, if you would only let me get at them.

However, I hope to attack you again with something more or less tremendous, if I can afford to write.

I am very sensible of your kindness in sending me your reader's opinion, and am,

yours faithfully
George Bernard Shaw

Shaw's **attack** occurred only in June 1903, when he offered them *Man and Superman* (Letter 67), which Macmillan rejected in July (Letter 70).

7 / To Swan Sonnenschein & Co.   36 Osnaburgh Street NW
25th February 1885

[SHDS: BL; CL 1]

Swan Sonnenschein & Co., founded in 1878 by William Swan Sonnenschein (1855–1931), published a monthly journal, Time, *to which Shaw twice contributed. In 1911 the firm merged with George Allen & Co. On 16 February Shaw offered them* An Unsocial Socialist *with a view to 'reprinting in cheap form' (CL 1, 116). They agreed on the 23rd to do so (first at six shillings, then in a cheaper edition) at their expense, with Shaw to receive a royalty of 5 % on the first thousand, 10 % on further sales, to which he agreed. However, upon examining the contract, Shaw discovered that he would have to assign his copyright to the publishers indefinitely. This he refused to do, offering instead to 'lease' the rights for five years, subject to renewal. 'This limitation of licence,' writes Dan Laurence, 'was a principle from which Shaw throughout his life never departed' (CL 1, 117).*

Gentlemen

I can by no means persuade myself to let the copyright of 'An Unsocial Socialist' pass away from me for ever. If the book be not dead this time five years I shall most probably have either changed my mind about it entirely, or be ready to do some further work upon it, if not to carry out my original design of a larger book of which it is only the first volume. I am willing that you shall have the exclusive right to publish the book for five years on the conditions named. But the copyright must remain my property, and the book come under my control again to alter, withdraw, or do what I please with. I doubt if it has five years' life in it in its present state.

Kindly explain to me anything unreasonable in this proposition of mine. As it is my commercial instinct that you should come to associate my name with profitable enterprises, I am anxious that the book should prove remunerative to you. It is my artistic instincts upon which I am disposed to take a stand. I wish to guard my right to commit suicide, as it were – to make alterations in the book that might destroy its popularity. That is not very likely, but it is quite possible that (after the five years) I might wish to effect a change which you might consider fatal and which I might regard as a necessary improvement. You will foresee that I might also, if my fame had greatly increased, propose a new arrangement at a competition price. Doubtless I should; but the efforts I should consequently make to increase my reputation would be all to the advantage of your patent while it lasted. We would also exploit it as vigorously as possible during that period, so that there would most probably be nothing left of it except a shilling edition for which no other publisher would give me any better terms. These are the only economic aspects of the case which occur to me. Your greater experience will apprise you of the others, most likely. I am open to conviction, except as to the copyright.

I am, gentlemen,

yours faithfully

George Bernard Shaw

8 / To Swan Sonnenschein & Co.　　　36 Osnaburgh Street NW

1st March 1885

[SHDS: BL; CL 1]

Shaw discusses the possible consequences of letting Swan Sonnenschein keep the stereo-plates of An Unsocial Socialist.

Gentlemen

If by the copyright you only mean the stereo-plates, I am quite willing that they shall remain your property for all time. But at the expiration of the five years they would only serve you in this manner. Let us suppose that the five years have elapsed, and that another publisher, learning that I am receiving ten per cent on the nominal price of the book, offers me twenty. I go to you and say 'You must give me 20% or I will take the book out of your hands.' You, having the stereo-plates, will be better able to comply than your competitor, who would have to case new plates, get the book on his list anew, and so forth.

As you say, it is a pity in your view, to limit the publisher's interest; but your interest is already, by the terms of form of agreement, limited by mine, as mine is by that of the community. My proposition does not limit your interest even to five years; for I can never extort more than the market value of the book. More than that, if its circulation be very languid five years hence, you can reduce the royalty, just as, on the opposite supposition, I can raise it. Only in the event of the book proving profitable to you is there the slightest chance of any firm bidding against you for it.

Your greatest risk is that the book may fail at first, but that some subsequent literary achievement of mine may suddenly raise its value just too late for you to profit by it. You might partially insure against this by publishing all my subsequent achievements, so as to make on the success what you would lose on the failure.

As to a joint property in the stereos, I have no right to any such joint property as I am not prepared to contribute towards their cost. Neither would such joint property be of the least use to me.

Can we not agree for a definite number of editions and copies, with an outside limit which I must permit, but which you need not produce unless there is a demand, the whole transaction to cease after five years?

I am, gentlemen,
yours faithfully
[George Bernard Shaw]

Stereo-plates (or stereotypes) or **stereos** are metal printing plates cast from a matrix molded from a raised printing surface, such as type. Shaw would later use electroplates (see Letter 75). Only 244 **copies** of the novel were bound in cloth at publication in February 1887; see Laurence 1, 10–12, for the book's complex bibliographical history.

9 / To Swan Sonnenschein & Co.

36 Osnaburgh Street NW
16th March 1885

[CL 1; PP: Bowes]

In the following letter 'Shaw correctly predicted falling printing costs, rising values of monopoly copyrights, the bankrupting of compositors, the lowering of profits for the selling and publishing of works with competitive value, and a new preference for publishing on commission' (Kelly, 'Imprinting the Stage,' 27).

Gentlemen

I want more than 10% for the fifteen years lease of 'An Unsocial Socialist.' As offers go, and as trade stands at present, I am aware that the offer is a reasonable one. If I thought that the relations of authors, publishers, and booksellers would not alter for fifteen years, I should accept it. But I believe that within that time machinery will so diminish the cost of printing that the value of copyrights which are genuine monopolies will be greatly increased. At the same time the compositors will be ruined; and the profits of bookselling and publishing matter which is subject to competition will be so reduced that only the very large capitals will be able to stand it. Speculation in ordinary copyrights will not be worth attempting; and even the old fashioned publishers will begin to find that publishing on commission is the safest and the most lucrative. Monopoly copyrights, supplying a public demand which cannot be met by hack writers, will rise in value; and if an International Copyright Treaty be concluded (and fifteen years may take us past even that) authors of reputation and the commonest knowledge of business will deal directly with publishers in America. These considerations, and others which spring out of them, make one think fifteen years a long time. Further, I am no longer in any danger of finding no opening. I have already provided for the publication of the novel which is about to appear as a serial in To-Day; and one of my juvenile works has been secured on rather better terms than I ever dreamt of getting for it by another magazine. As it is prodigiously long, it will keep me alive modestly for some time to come. On the whole I had rather wait a year or so than close with you for ten per cent.

I am, Gentlemen
yours faithfully
George Bernard Shaw

Compositors set up type for printing. An **International Copyright Treaty** was signed the following year (1886) in Switzerland: the Berne Convention for the Protection of Literary and Artistic Works. *Cashel Byron's Profession* appeared in four issues of *To-Day* from April 1885 to December 1886. The **juvenile work** was *The Irrational Knot* and the **magazine** was *Our Corner*, where it was serialized between April 1885 and February 1887; it was published only in 1905 (by Constable and Brentano's).

10 / To Swan Sonnenschein & Co.   36 Osnaburgh Street NW
30th March 1885

[SHDS: BL; CL 1]

When Swan Sonnenschein suggested a seven years' lease at 10 % royalty, Shaw (on 24 March) accepted the offer 'on condition that you are not to sublet your assign' and 'that you do not limit me in the matter of proof corrections to £5 ... lest I have the printer charging me for having given me a great deal of trouble [specifically on punctuation] on the pretext that it is I that have troubled him.' As for foreign copyrights, 'I think I may ask for 33 % of the proceeds without undue

rapacity' (CL 1, 128). Shaw received the agreement (with a £10 limit on correc-
tions) with assurances that they would not pay the printer for any changes to
Shaw's punctuation. Shaw returned it with numerous alterations and additions,
including the following strictures on copyright:

... For 3rdly I have altered 'shall be the property of' to 'is hereby assigned
by the author to.' Although a copyright is personal property, I believe we
have no power to declare by a deed that it is the property of anyone in
particular. I have undoubtedly the power to assign my copyright; and the
law will thereupon secure to you the benefit of it. The clause as it stands
in print is not a covenant: it is an act of legislation ... I have added the
9thly to protect myself against a defect (from the author's point of view)
in the law, whereby a publisher can virtually destroy an author's copyright by printing, whilst the agreement is in force, copies enough to
stock the market after the expiry of the term ...

11 / To William Swan Sonnenschein 29 Fitzroy Square W
2nd May 1887

[SHDS: BL; CL 1]

Shaw signed and returned the agreement on 6 April 1885: 'I hope your venture
will be a profitable one,' he concluded, 'apart from my share in the returns. If I
could only make your fortune, your competitors would hasten to make mine' (CL
1, 130). Meanwhile, Cashel Byron's Profession *was published in March 1886 by*
the Modern Press, whose proprietor, Henry Hyde Champion (1859–1928), had a
taste for pugilism. Although Shaw had hoped An Unsocial Socialist *would 'reach*
the reviewers while the impression made by "Cashel Byron" is fresh, and before
they are swamped with Xmas literature' (CL 1, 159), it was published only in
February 1887. Having failed to convince Swan Sonnenschein's editors to repub-
lish Cashel Byron, *Shaw tried to sell the idea to the publisher himself (to no*
avail).

Dear Sonnenschein

There is a novel of mine, 'Cashel Byron's Profession,' which, after many
queer adventures, got out last year in the most beastly shilling form,
printed from stereos taken from a monthly mag with a page of impossi-

ble size. It got well reviewed; but Champion, the publisher, was unable to take advantage of this, as he was not in a position to push the book with the trade. It was too ugly, and too long; and only 500-odd copies went off. I quite expected this; but the book served my turn as an advertisement; and I left it with Champion until he had got all there was to be got out of his edition of it. Now, however, I have ascertained that the sale has practically ceased; and he says he will not feel aggrieved if I take it out of his hands. I have no time to bother about it just at present; but it occurs to me that you might be able to do something with it. It is not nearly so good as An Unsocial Socialist; but it is generally considered better, is a faster seller, and has been gorgeously reviewed. There are two sets of plates of it in existence: Champion's stereos, which are utterly damnable; and those made for a very neat reprint in Harper's 'Handy Volume Series.' These are presentable, but small; and the few errors of punctuation and attempts at bowdlerizing (such as 'd——' or simply '——' for damn, and the like) have been made by the American printers without the least regard to my feelings. Duplicates of these plates can be obtained; but I had rather have the book set up afresh and issued at a higher price. What do you think? ...

yours

G. Bernard Shaw

Shaw, Lucy, and their mother had moved to an apartment at **29 Fitzroy Square** on 21 March 1887. The **500-odd copies** do not correspond to Shaw's recollection (in his preface to the 1901 edition) of 1000 copies, nor to his 23 December 1885 diary entry of 2500 copies (see Laurence 1, 4). Harper & Brothers (founded 1833) published *Cashel Byron* in its **Handy Series** in December 1886 (see Letter 48). The effect of the **bowdlerizing**, Shaw had complained to publisher James R. Osgood (Harper's London representative) on 7 February, was to suggest 'something much worse. The moral injury to me from the language I have used over these unprovoked assaults on my literary offspring far outweighs that saved to the American nation by the omission of my hero's harmless expletives' (CL 1, 162).

12 / To William Swan Sonnenschein　　　　29 Fitzroy Square W
28th November 1887

[SHDS: BL; CL 1]

The 'postscript' to An Unsocial Socialist *that Shaw discusses below became an 'Appendix' entitled 'Letter to the Author from Mr Sidney Trefusis' (the novel's protagonist); see Letter 13. (Near the close of his 2300-word letter, Trefusis writes: 'In conclusion, allow me to express my regret that you can find no better employment for your talent than the writing of novels.')*

Dear Sonnenschein

I agreed long ago to the issue of 'An US' at a shilling; and I have no doubt that a certain number of workmen and socialists will buy it at that price if it's brought under their notice. If a really new edition is made by the addition of a postscript which I should like to write, several people who have the book already would buy a new copy at a shilling. But nothing worth talking about will ever come out of my books unless they are advertised. 'Cashel Byron' is *the* popular book; but nobody can get C.B. If it were issued uniform with An US, and one book advertised in the other, if nowhere else, they might help to sell each other. I would even consent to let out the I. Knot, which hit the secularist taste remarkably, in order to make something like a series. But I am ashamed of the whole boodle of them, and am not eager to take any more trouble about them unless someone takes them up in earnest. Guarantee me £20 a month on condition of my writing 6 novels in 6 years; and I will begin to believe that you mean business – though you will probably drop a couple of thousand over it.

Let me know whether the new chapter of A U.S. is feasible. I should much prefer to add it to a cheap edition, though I dont think it is likely to go well except [if] it is put on C. Byron's back.

It is 4 years since I gave up fiction; and I am in two minds whether I will ever return to it. Pecuniarily, at least, the failure has been too heavy.

yours
G. Bernard Shaw

13 / To William Swan Sonnenschein 29 Fitzroy Square W
31st December 1887

[SHDS: BL; CL 1; PP: Bowes]

Sonnenschein wrote to Shaw on 30 December, 'I fear U.S. has not done much good this half year ... I certainly don't regret the small sum of money we probably have in U.S. still; and shall not do so unless you choose to drop your pen, or die, or do something else foolish' (Mumby, 24). An Unsocial Socialist had sold poorly; the remaining sheets (more than half the edition of 1000 copies) were rebound in a two-shilling 'cheap edition' with the new appendix (sent by Shaw to Sonnenschein on 29 December).

Dear Sonnenschein

Hi! Stop! Murder! Thieves! Fire! What are you dreaming about? If Trefusis's letter is put *before* the story I swear I will set fire to Paternoster Square. It would be utterly unintelligible to anyone who had not learnt all about the book. It would discount the story, destroy the illusion, and drive me mad. Give it to a reader, and observe his lively interest, his tears, his cheers, his irrepressible laughter. No: it must come at the end; but as the last page of the novel is a left hand one, everyone will see the appendix on the right hand one. Ugh! you have made my blood run cold ...

As to the cover for 'An U.S.,' I have no practicable ideas. Your books are generally happily turned out; and my notions as to catching covers are not bright. I greatly prefer yellow to pink; but there is a red that used to be called Mahdi red that would look startlingly socialistic. We used to print Fabian tickets in it; and it was a great success. But I question the policy of suggesting a sensational dynamite story when the book is so much the reverse. As to an illustration, Trefusis shooting the statue's head off is the only incident that lends itself. If I can think of anything, I will let you know.

yrs
G. Bernard Shaw

Swan Sonnenschein's offices were in **Paternoster Square**, a centre of the London publishing trade (until the Second World War Blitz). The **cover** of *An Unsocial Socialist* was orange. In 1884 Shaw joined the **Fabian** Society, which was dedicated to gradual social change through progressive legislation and mass education; their watchword was 'the inevitability of gradualism.' In chapter 15 of *An Unsociable Socialist* Trefusis shoots the **head off** one of the many life-size plaster statues (already similarly defaced) in the niches surrounding his study.

14 / To William Swan Sonnenschein 29 Fitzroy Square W
4th January 1888
[SHDS: BL; CL 1]

The 'whatdoyoucallit' that Shaw is objecting to below is the ornate William Swan Sonnenschein device on the title page: a rectangle containing a shield (flanked by two unicorns on their hind legs) bearing the large initials WSS hanging from an apple tree laden with fruit. It appeared on the cover of An Unsocial Socialist *in the bottom right corner.*

... I strenuously object, however – and here I call Lowrey to my aid – to the enlargement of your whatdoyoucallit on the cover. I invite you to study the original, with its really crisp decorative foliage in black and white at the top, and its game and skittish unicorns, who have tucked in their tails for a joke. Look at the dejected unicorns, with their trotters hanging like stuffed things, and their tails between their legs. Look at the foolish formal foliage (oh, forgive me, I am alliterating like G——e M——e) and the shield spoilt in shape and proportion. Such a cover would justify a revolution. The backing is much better. But you really must get a new design for the front ...

Francis **Lowrey** was Sonnenschein's partner. Sonnenschein published *Confessions of a Young Man* by 'naturalist' novelist **George Moore** (1852–1933) in 1888.

15 / To T. Fisher Unwin

29 Fitzroy Square W
4th September 1888

[ALS: Colgate; CL 1; FP: American Art Association, Catalogue of sale, 18 December 1928]

*Thomas Fisher Unwin (1848–1935) had founded the publishing house bearing his name in 1882. Shaw knew him socially, as early as 4 March 1886 (*Diaries *I, 150). Shaw had written to him on 20 March 1888 asking him to take up* Cashel Byron's Profession, *but 'Unwin replied that the proposal was too speculative' (Weintraub in* Diaries *I, 359).*

Dear Unwin

I see that you are issuing a series of novels. Perhaps the enclosed [*Cashel Byron*] might interest you. The author referred to, whose regard for you is only equaled by his own great personal merit, has been approached on the subject by Cassells. (I mention this to impress you with a sense of the demand he is in, and of the importance of your at once seizing the golden opportunity). Cassells have not made up their mercenary minds with becoming eagerness; and the author is growing uneasy as he feels a sense stealing on him that the book is not at bottom right, or it would not have been so well received by a detestable individualistic press. He wants it out before he comes to the point of feeling bound to suppress the volume altogether. He is growing middle-aged, and feels that the works of his early youth (the book was written in 1882) hardly become the dignity of his graver years.

He is a man of moderate views, and never expects more than a simple royalty of 25% on four times the nominal price of his books. And even this he does not always get.

Think over it in the course of the coming season. No immediate communication expected.

Yrs
G. Bernard Shaw

Publishers **Cassell** & Co. were founded in 1848 by John Cassell (1817–65). 'Wrote to Cassell's proposing that they should publish *Fabian Essays*' (10 April 1889, *Diaries* 1, 488). Cassell never published Shaw's work.

16 / To T. Fisher Unwin

29 Fitzroy Square W
19th November 1888

[ALS: Colgate; CL 1; PP: Ervine]

Dear Unwin

No thank you: no more novels for me. Five failures are enough to satisfy my appetite for enterprise in fiction. I have no intention of lowering myself to the level of Bruce's spider. The success of future attempts must be guaranteed beforehand by a cheque for £500 for seven years copyright. Otherwise the attempts will not be made.

Seriously, I have no longer either time or inclination for tomfooling over novels. And your repudiation of 'Cashel Byron' is a positive relief to me; for I hate the book from my soul.

I have just run a really pretty novel through 'Our Corner,' which you ought to read if you ever come across the volumes of that moribund magazine; but it would be of no use to you professionally. 'Love among the Artists' is the name. When you are tired of saleable novels, and want to read something really dainty, you will find it the very thing for you.

G.B.S.

According to legend, Scottish king Robert the **Bruce** (1274–1329), while hiding in a cave after numerous defeats, was so inspired by a **spider**'s unrelenting attempts (and eventual success) at spinning its web that he led his army to victory. *Love Among the Artists* was being serialized in *Our Corner* from November 1887 to December 1888.

17 / To G. Bernard Shaw

[no address]

21st February 1889

[ALS (tr): Guelph]

The Walter Scott Publishing Co. Ltd (1882–1931), founded by Sir Walter Scott (1826–1910) – no relation to his famous namesake – published a revised, one-shilling edition of Cashel Byron's Profession *(the topic of Letters 17 and 18) in April or May 1889, a 'cheap' edition of* Fabian Essays in Socialism *(1889) in 1890, and* The Quintessence of Ibsenism *in 1891. Shaw offered Scott* An Unsocial Socialist *on 20 July 1891 (Diaries 1, 740). Shaw replied to the following on the 22nd (Diaries 1, 471) and got his way.*

Dear Sir

In instructing my printers to rigidly follow your instruction, which I understand they have done accordingly, I overlooked the fact that you had not instructed that the usual decorative sign of abbreviation in 'didn't,' 'can't,' 'don't' etc should be inserted! Now I object entirely to such typographical aberrations and monstrosities as 'didnt' 'dont' etc., signs which no doubt have enormous significance for the individual who conceived them, but which are simply an aggravation and a puzzle to the ordinary person who tries to decipher them. I beg to inform you, then, that I shall instruct my printer to print the usual contractions in the usual way.

yours faithfully,

For Walter Scott

D. Gordon, Manager per. D.

Although managing editor **David Gordon** had little education, he contributed significantly to Scott's publishing success; Will Dircks (see Letter 19) called him 'a Napoleon of business' (quoted in Rose, *Dictionary of Literary Biography*, vol. 12: 286).

18 / To G. Bernard Shaw   [no address]
                                          25th February 1889
[ALS (tr): Guelph]

Dear Sir

All right; have it your own evil way. To be strictly logical I think you should 'agglutinate' the whole page; a series of continuously unbroken lines would probably look much better typographically than the present series of lines conventionally divided into words. I hope however that the 'youves' and the 'youds' don't abound too pitilessly in *Cashel Byron*.

yours faithfully,
For Walter Scott
D. Gordon, Mgr. per. D.

To **agglutinate** is to form words by combining other words.

19 / To Will H. Dircks   29 Fitzroy Square W
                                          3rd September 1890
[CL 1; PP: Rhys]

Will H. Dircks was editor and reader at Walter Scott, which had just published a cheap edition of Fabian Essays in Socialism, *edited by Shaw (who also contributed two essays). He had written to Shaw on 9 December 1889 asking him to 'name a price less fabulously imaginative' for* Cashel Byron *reprint rights (Diaries 1, 457). Shaw expounded at length on the issue of a cloth edition of the* Essays, *discussed below, to stockbroker Edward R. Pease (1857–1955), secretary (1890–1913) of* The Fabian Society, *on 22 and 25 September (see CL 1, 263–65). 'Dirckes' is Shaw's misspelling.*

Dear Dirckes (it is you, isn't it?)

Tell the London house finally to go to blazes. If people want a copy of the Essays in cloth, tell them to send Pease four and sixpence, and they shall have one by return of post. The body of political economists understand perfectly that you cannot, in the face of competition of speculative binders with no royalty to pay, afford to pay them any royalty whatsoever; and they now see that they should have listened to the voice of Shaw, who maintained that it was impossible to get a royalty of twopence on the shilling edition from you by standing out for it. THE EXTRA HALFPENNY WHICH YOU NOW OFFER IS NOT A ROYALTY ON THE TWO SHILLING EDITION AT ALL, BUT THE IDENTICAL HALFPENNY WHICH YOU SHOULD HAVE GIVEN US ON THE PAPER COPIES. However, we magnanimously make you a present of this, bearing no malice, and desiring your speedy enrichment. But when you propose a perfectly new arrangement as if it were a mere incident of the old one – when furthermore, it is an arrangement which we dont desire and never contemplated – when it is expressly devised to kill the edition which we reserved our right to run for ourselves, then you get to the end of the Fabian patience, and we refuse with objurgations. If you want to run a library edition of the Essays, make us a proposal to that effect. We might not object to allowing you to print a half crown edition on large paper, provided you gave us sixpence a copy or so. Dash it all, do you take the Fabian for a sheepfold?

Personally, I have lost all faith in you because I believe the artistic sense to be the true basis of moral rectitude; and a more horrible offence against Art than what you have put above Crane's design on the cover of the Essays, has never been perpetrated even in Newcastle. I reject your handbill with disdain, with rage, with contumelious epithets. You must reset the authors' names in the same type as 'PRICE ONE SHILLING'; and the words 'Essays by' must on no account be in a different type. To aim at having as many different founts as possible on the same sheet is worthy of a jobbing printer at work on a bookmaker's handbill; but that you, who turn out your Camelot title pages so well, should condescend to such barbarism simply destroys my faith in human nature. And why put Simpkin & Marshall in? Better put 'all booksellers.' If one of the bills falls into the hands of the trade (which is not what they are wanted for) a reference to your London house will shew them whither they must go. Of the hellish ugliness of the block of letterpress headed 'What the Press says' I cannot trust myself to write, lest I should be betrayed into intemperance of language; but I would suggest that the whole should be reset so as to make room for the extracts which I have marked in the enclosed sheet of press notices, from the Methodist Times (which might take the place of the Church Reformer), the Scots Observer, the Pall Mall Gazette, and the Academy. The italic type used in the notices from the Daily News and Scottish Leader appear to me unspeakably revolting.

Some time ago, you mentioned something about changing the cover of 'Cashel Byron,' and introducing a design of some pugilistic kind. This is to give you formal notice that if you do anything of the sort without first submitting the cover to me, I will have your heart's blood.

yours respectfully

G. Bernard Shaw

An **objurgation** is a harsh rebuke. Shaw was absent when the Fabian executive accepted Dircks's proposal for a two-shilling cloth edition, rather than Shaw's **half crown** (2 shillings 6 pence) proposal; Shaw told Pease: 'Ass that I was to trust my copyright to a council of pigeons!' (CL 1, 265). Shaw had supervised the *Fabian Essays* cover design by socialist painter and illustrator Walter **Crane** (1845–1915). **Contumelious**: rudely contemptuous, insolent. Scott's **Camelot** series (renamed the Scott Library in 1892) was edited by Ernest Rhys, who left in 1906 to work for J.M. Dent (see Letter 162). **Simpkin, Marshall**, Hamilton, Kent & Co. was a wholesale book distributor and publishing house that frequently distributed works on a commission basis. In **letterpress** (or 'relief') printing, ink is applied to raised portions of a metal plate that is then pressed onto paper. Shaw had published (or would publish) articles in *Methodist Times*, *Church Reformer*, *Scots Observer*, *The Pall Mall Gazette*, *The Academy*, *Daily News*, and *Scottish Leader*. In 1901 Herbert S. Stone & Co. published the first authorized American edition of *Cashel Byron's Profession* with a **cover** bearing the drawing of a **pugilist**.

20 / To T. Fisher Unwin

29 Fitzroy Square W

4th March 1891

[TLS: Colgate; CL 1]

Herbert S. Stone of Chicago would publish an unauthorized edition of Love Among the Artists *in 1900, but an English edition appeared only in 1914 with Constable & Co. At the outset of what would become a very long publishing career, we find Shaw being adamant about having his books printed by what he calls in the following letter a 'Union' or 'fair' house. Only a few weeks earlier (on 18 February), the House of Commons had passed the first Fair Wages Resolution (revised in 1909 and 1946). In 1903 Shaw warned Methuen & Co. that 'any contract that I make must contain a "fair wages" clause' (Letter 61).*

My dear Fisher Unwin

Your letter of the 16th January has just come to hand, so to speak. My funeral, and the expiration of my copyrights, will come long before I find time to attend to my own business ...

I have nothing to suggest as far as my own work is concerned. I have no time to prepare it: the Fabian business and my own hand-to-mouth journalistic jobbing leave me without a moment for literary work. It is really all your fault. I have no time to go fooling around offering MSS to the eminent firms who regretted that Cashel Byron was not a sufficiently interesting work to warrant them in producing it. I want to republish 'Love among the Artists' from Our Corner, as it is good enough not to disgrace me, and my reputation is now sufficient to make its publication a safe if not a brilliant operation. But I cannot stop to make up the money to get it printed myself; and you most unjustifiably refuse to do your duty except on condition of putting the work into the hands of a firm whose proceedings are emphatically condemned by the organization of the trade to which the workers they employ belong. If you employ a Union house for my books, it will probably secretly sublet the contract (for a commission) to a non-union house; so that Chilworth can rejoice all the same over the baffling of Drummond. Hang it, if these people were friends of yours I could understand your backing them; but brothers! – brothers are natural enemies by the law of nature. I do not mind discussing the question with the Chilworth exploiters; but Drummond, or some other expert representative of the Union must be a party to the conference.

I also want to reprint the cream of Corno di Bassettò from the Star, and to issue Shaw's Tales from Ibsen, uniform with Lamb's Tales from Shakespere; but here too I am deterred by your family, except as to Ibsen, which Scott (who is 'a fair house') wants.

I had hoped to see you at Pennell's on Thursday; but I find I shall have to go to Rosmersholm instead.

G.B.S.

Love among the Artists was serialized in *Our Corner* in 1887–8. When Fisher Unwin's brother Edward (1840–1933), chairman of the Unwin Brothers printing **firm** at **Chilworth**, refused to permit Charles J. **Drummond** (secretary of the London Society of Compositors) to attend a conference in 1889 to discuss fair wages, Shaw withdrew *Fabian Essays in Socialism* (which Unwin was to print). Shaw published music criticism under the pseudonym **Corno di Bassetto** in *The Star* 1888–9 and *The World* 1890–4. The idea fizzled (see Letter 21) and the book materialized only in 1937 (see Letter 154). Norwegian playwright Henrik **Ibsen** (1828–1906) was the subject of *The Quintessence of Ibsenism* (1891). American artist Joseph **Pennell** (1857–1926) wrote art criticism for *The Star*. Shaw was in the first-night audience when Ibsen's *Rosmersholm* (1886), starring Florence Farr, was produced on 23 February.

21 / To T. Fisher Unwin   29 Fitzroy Square W
                                                              22nd April 1891

[ALS: Colgate; CL 1]

*On 19 March Shaw had written Unwin that he had looked over some of the Corno
di Bassetto columns: 'Such sickening, vulgar, slovenly slosh never blasted my sight
before. I cannot believe that there is enough good stuff sunk in this mud to be worth
diving for.' He also reported that Scott's 'formal proposal' for* The Quintessence of
Ibsenism *was forthcoming, and that if Unwin was 'sweet on it,' he should send
Shaw 'a cheque for £5,000, with an agreement securing me a 66⅔% royalty, not
to commence until the sixteenth copy' (CL 1, 286). Scott issued the* Quintessence
in September 1891 at two shillings and sixpence.

Dear Fisher Unwin

I am at present able to do nothing but gasp after the effort to finish the
Ibsen book. All correspondence went by the board during the last three
weeks of the struggle. Hence my neglect to answer your letter.

First, as to the Bassetto papers, I found that a sensible charwoman, seeing a great heap of old Stars lying about, had disposed of them as waste
paper. It is true that enough is left to fake up a Pseudonym volume; but
I hardly feel equal to the job just at present. A festoon of dusty old columns hangs over the gaspipe above me as I write; but the dog is not disposed to return to his vomit immediately after the Ibsen feast. Besides,
most of it is wretched stuff: in the few strips I have looked over there are
not two paragraphs that I would reprint. On the whole, as Walkley wants
to make a book of his Spectator articles, and I have promised not to spoil
his market, I think we had better leave di Bassetto to rot peacefully in his
grave.

The Ibsen MS is not a very large affair. In the type and style of Archer's
translations as published by Scott, it would make a book of only about
120 pages. However, I think you had better let it alone, as it seems to me
that since any sensation it may make will help to sell the translations, in
which Scott has much more capital invested than you have in The Lady
from the Sea, it must be better worth Scott's while than yours to publish
for me. The MS is a present in his hands to enable him to estimate the
cost of manufacture &c. We have come to no agreement as yet; but I have
no doubt we shall soon do so. I am in a certain degree bound to Scott,

provided he offers me no worse terms than anyone else; partly because he has behaved handsomely to Ibsen in the Hedda Gabler difficulty, and partly because he published Cashel Byron, of which immortal work I regret to say he has sold, up to the 31st March last, only 3193 copies. Obviously he can afford to offer anything that you can afford to offer, and even more, because of the reaction on the translations, and also because, having been disappointed in the novel, he has the faith & the interest in me which a publisher always feels in an author who has bled him. (The shilling edition of the Essays – 20,000 of them all sold at one volley – must have recouped him a bit, by the bye).

Someday I shall probably make up a volume of my musical articles in The World – that is, if I ever again find time to go back on old work. I am really too dead beat to entertain anything seriously at present ...

Instead of returning 'Love Among the Artists' to me, will you send it to Mrs Emery, 123 Dalling Road, Ravenscourt Park W. She awaits it with an expectancy which the first few pages will rapidly cool.

G.B.S.

Shaw dedicated *Man and Superman* to Arthur Bingham **Walkley** (1855–1926), dramatic critic (under the pseudonym '**Spectator**') of *The Star* (1888–1900) and of *The Times* (1900–26). Unwin published Walkley's *Playhouse Impressions* (1892), which Shaw reviewed in *The Star* on 9 January 1892. *The Lady from the Sea* (1888) is by Ibsen. The **Hedda Gabler difficulty** refers to the publication by W.H. Baker & Co. in 1891 of a translation of *Hedda Gabler* (1890) by critic Sir Edmund Gosse (1849–1928), which Ibsen had authorized but which conflicted with commitments to Scott by William Archer (translator of numerous Ibsen plays). **Mrs** Edward **Emery** is Florence Farr (1860–1917), one of Shaw's love interests; she created the roles of Blanche Sartorius in *Widowers' Houses* in 1892 and of Louka in *Arms and the Man* in 1894.

22 / To John Lane   29 Fitzroy Square W
                                                      22nd November 1892

[ALS: CL 1; PP: King (e)]

London publisher John Lane (1854–1925) was also co-founder, with Elkin Mathews (1851–1921), of the Bodley Head publishing company in 1887.

Were you serious about publishing that play of mine? I am not sure that it would be a very gorgeous investment; but I suppose a limited edition at a high price would be bought by a certain number of idiots who would not buy anything of mine for a penny or a shilling. However, you can judge for yourself: my chief object in writing to you is to remind you that if the play is to be printed, it will need all the send-off it will get from the criticism and discussion of the performance; and as this is to take place (if it does not fall through) on the 9th Dec., we must literally rush into print. A simple and not too expensive way of making an *édition de luxe* of it will be to illustrate with photographs of the cast in costume. The leading lady is a very goodlooking woman, I might remark. It ought to be quite a quarto – not too large, but just large enough.

Your suggestion came into my mind this afternoon for the first time with full force. To confess the truth, the chief attraction to me is the opportunity of presenting a copy to each of the actors, who are all playing for nothing. So dont set too much store by my favorable view of the chance of a sale.

yours faithfully,

G. Bernard Shaw

Widowers' Houses (**that play**) was produced by the Independent Theatre on **9th** and 13 **Dec**ember 1892 (two performances only) at the Royalty Theatre, London, with **leading lady** Florence Farr as Blanche. Shaw sent Henry & Co. the play on 19 January 1893 and a publication agreement on 13 February (*Diaries* 2, 896, 906). They replied on the 14th that they did 'not think such an elaborate agreement necessary, especially as we do not expect the sale to be sufficient to recoup us for our outlay' (quoted in *Diaries* 2, 907). *Widowers' Houses* was published in May (not 'Feb. 93,' as Shaw states in Letter 34); only 162 copies were sold over the next three years (Laurence 1, 23). 'When Henry & Co. honorably retired in due course,' recalled Shaw in 1929, 'they very magnanimously presented me with the unsold and unbound remainder of the edition' (CL 4, 147).

23 / To Grant Richards   29 Fitzroy Square W
                                              13th November 1893

[ALCS: HRC; CL 1; PP: *Memories*]

At this time, Grant Richards (1872–1948) was secretary and assistant editor to William T. Stead (1849–1912) on the Review of Reviews *(founded 1890); Stead had been editor of* The Pall Mall Gazette *1883–90. Shaw wrote to Richards on 8 December: 'My objection to the Stereoscopic work had no reference at all to the ferocity of the expression; ... I protested against it solely because it was a botched, stippled, falsified, vulgarized abomination as a work of art' (CL 1, 410).*

28

Dear Sir

As usual, the Stereoscopic people have taken a decent photograph and then deliberately ruined it by rubbing every line and mark out of the face, which looks like a piece of dirty drawing paper. Please, in the interests of reasonable art and common sense, do not have it reproduced. There are three alternatives. 1. Don't portray me at all, which I should prefer to any encouragement of this abominable retouching business, which I have always denounced as an art critic. 2. Use the excellent woodcut you published in the R of Rs last January (I think) and which was done for the Ill. London News. 3. Reproduce the enclosed untouched photo, which you can see at least represents a human face with the traces of a human life on it instead of the slab of wet dough which the Stereoscopic people have felt bound to produce. It has never been reproduced before & even a half successful print of it would be better than an entirely successful print of the other.

yrs very truly
G. Bernard Shaw

The **Illustrated London News** began publication in 1842.

24 / To Frederick H. Evans The Argoed, Monmouth
14th August 1895

[ALS: Dartmouth; CL 1]

From 31 July to 21 September, Shaw vacationed at 'The Argoed,' the holiday home of fellow Fabians Sidney (1859–1947) and Beatrice (1858–1943) Webb, in the Wye Valley in South Wales. Frederick H. Evans (1852–1943), who would retire from bookselling to become a full-time photographer in 1898, had approached Shaw with the idea (later abandoned) of editing and publishing his musical criticisms written for The World.

... I want you to consider the question of publishing very seriously. I object to publishers: the one service they have done me is to teach me to do without them. They combine commercial rascality with artistic touchiness and pettishness, without being either good business men or fine judges of literature. All that is necessary for the production of a book is

an author and a bookseller, without any intermediary parasite. The reviewers and editors will look at my name, not at the publisher's. Therefore I propose that you and I, as honest and necessary persons, I the
author and you the bookseller, do follow the wise & lucrative example of
Allen and Ruskin, and, with the help of Providence (technically known
as Simpkin & Marshall) carry this thing through ourselves. I have, out of
the spoils of 'Arms & The Man,' just about enough money lying in the
bank to pay for the manufacture of a book; and I had much rather go to
work in this way than deal with a publisher unless he were to offer me a
sum of money that would ensure him an exemplary loss unless he did his
very utmost by the book ...

yrs sincerely

G. Bernard Shaw

Influential art critic John **Ruskin** (1819–1900) underwrote the costs of printing his *Fors
Clavigera* in 1871, setting up his pupil and assistant George **Allen** (1837–1907) as his agent
and publisher. From this partnership emerged George Allen and Sons (1871) and eventually George Allen & Unwin Ltd (1914). *Arms and the Man*, Shaw's first appearance in the
commercial theatre, ran for seventy-six performances at London's Avenue Theatre beginning on 21 April 1894. It was also the first Shaw play to be seen in the United States (on 17
September 1894).

25 / To T. Fisher Unwin The Argoed, Monmouth
9th September 1895

[ALS: Delaware; CL 1]

*Shaw had asked John Lane on 16 April 1894, 'Has your experience of Lady Win-
demere's Fan &c. led you to suppose that publishing plays is worth while?' (CL 1,
423). (Lane had published Oscar Wilde's play in 1893.) Shaw now queries
Unwin on the same issue.*

Dear Fisher Unwin

... It is very good of you to declare your readiness to become my publisher; but believe me, you deceive yourself. If I sent you anything, you would
open it with joyful anticipation, finish reading it with dismay and utter
disappointment, and only proceed with it to spare my feelings. I should
feel the meanest of mortals if, after nearly sixteen years experience of the
effect I produce on publishers (my first book was finished in 1879) I were

to take advantage of your personal nature to involve you in a very doubtful speculation. Just as your letter arrived, I was engaged in a negotiation with an enthusiastic Shawite bookseller who has actually compiled a volume from my musical criticisms (knowing that I would never take the trouble myself) and wanted me to get it published in the ordinary course. But I will get the book manufactured at my own cost & risk & hand it to him to sell. If it pays its way, well & good: if not, nobody is the worse except myself.

By the way, is there any public as yet which reads plays? When you sent me the Echegaray volumes I wrote them up in the Saturday & urged them on the notice of Richard Mansfield, the actor. I see now that he declares his intention of opening the Garrick (New York) next season with 'The Son of Don Juan.' Do those Cameos sell? I noticed that Heinemann, after trying a 6/– Mrs Tanqueray, relapsed into the old 1/6 for Mrs Ebbsmith; and I know that these cheap Pineros only sell to amateur clubs. But if I thought that people were picking up the French trick of reading dramatic works, I should be strongly tempted to publish my plays instead of bothering to get them performed.

Yours sincerely
G. Bernard Shaw

Shaw wrote *Immaturity* in **1879**. The **Shawite bookseller** was Frederick H. Evans. American actor-manager **Richard Mansfield**'s (1854–1907) most successful production was *The Devil's Disciple* in 1897. Shaw reviewed Spanish dramatist José **Echegaray**'s (1833–1916) *Mariana* and *The Son of Don Juan* (published by Unwin in his **Cameo** Series of translations) in the *Saturday Review* on 27 April 1895. William **Heinemann** (1863–1920) founded his publishing firm in 1890. Mrs Patrick Campbell (1865–1940), who would create Liza Doolittle in the English-language premiere of *Pygmalion* in 1914, starred in the premieres of *The Second Mrs Tanqueray* (1893) and *The Notorious Mrs Ebbsmith* (1895), by the extremely popular Sir Arthur Wing **Pinero** (1855–1934).

26 / To T. Fisher Unwin29 Fitzroy Square W
6th December 1895

[APCS: Delaware; CL 1]

Shaw 'coined the term "stagerighting" to describe what became his and others' common practice of staging at least one (typically hasty and low-budget) British production of a play to secure its copyright' (Kelly, 37). Stagerighting was crucial for Shaw and other British playwrights because it prohibited the first American

*performance of a British play that would nullify its copyright protection in Brit-
ain. (See also Letter 27.)*

Dear Fisher Unwin

It's no use – I am kept so busy over fresh work that I cannot take time to
prepare the old for publication. It will end in a posthumous edition of
my collected writings.

As to plays, I cannot make out the law as to stage rights. The point is,
do I forfeit my American stageright if publication precedes performance? If I could secure both copyrights & stagerights intact here and in
America I should be strongly tempted to try a volume of dramas.

yrs sincerely
G. Bernard Shaw

P.S.   By the way, I hope you did not suffer by the fire. As to the Brothers,
serve 'em right!

The Chilworth printing works of the Unwin **Brothers** had been totally destroyed by fire on
23–4 November.

27 / To T. Fisher Unwin

29 Fitzroy Square W
11th February 1896

[ALS: Delaware; CL 1]

*After receiving Shaw's 6 December 1895 letter, Unwin appealed to American liter-
ary agent Paul R. Reynolds (1864–1944) for advice. Reynolds then contacted
New York publisher George Haven Putnam (1844–1930), of G.P. Putnam's
Sons. Unwin sent Shaw a copy of Putnam's 23 December 1895 reply, which reads
in part: 'The copyrighting of a drama in book form under existing copyright
arrangements secures the full control of the copyright of the printed text, and
includes the right to prohibit the dramatization of the material by any unauthorised parties. While, therefore, the stage right does not secure copyright, a copyright
has been held to give a substantial control over stage rights in the identical material, or in any material which is substantially identical with that copyrighted'
(TLS [tr]: UNC). The following comment by Shaw appears at the bottom of the
letter: 'This does not apply to the case of a printed drama, I believe. Once a play is
published, a stage representation can be given without violation of copyright by
simply using copies of the printed play at rehearsal & for study. But if the author*

publishes a novel ('Lord Fauntleroy,' for instance) the adaptation of it for the stage involves copying portions of the dialogue & thus infringes on the copyright, leaving the question of stage right unraised. Consequently the protection which a novel enjoys against dramatization & representation does not extend to a play. G.B.S.' (ANS [tr]: UNC).

Dear Fisher Unwin

I return Putnam's letter, which rather confirms my notion that nobody does exactly know how the law stands. I have made a note explaining the confusion into which Putnam apparently fell for a moment between the protection of a novel from dramatisation through its *copy*right, and the case of a play which can be performed from the printed copies without illegal copying. I am still very doubtful as to the case of a play published in either England and America before performance. For instance, all Ibsen's stage rights are voided here except those which Heinemann so ingeniously secured by his performances of the last two or three plays in Norwegian at the Haymarket Theatre before they were translated.

The only play of mine which has been performed in England and America is 'Arms & The Man.' It would not make much of a book; but with a preface by the brilliant author, and a reprint of my article in the New Review (on the military questions raised) by way of appendix, it would make a respectable Cameo.

Do you think there is really any chance of its being worth my while or yours to publish the play? You will remember that Heinemann, after trying Pinero's 'Mrs Tanqueray' at 6/–, came down again to eighteenpence for paper covers and half a crown for cloth, mostly for sale to amateur clubs. He sticks to Ibsen at five shillings a play. What do you think? What do you propose?

yours sincerely
G. Bernard Shaw

*Little **Lord Fauntleroy*** (1886) had set a precedent in copyright law in 1888 when its author, Frances Hodgson Burnett (1849–1924), won a lawsuit over the rights to theatrical adaptations of her novel. ***Arms and the Man*** premiered in London on 21 April 1894; Shaw's 'A Dramatic Realist to His Critics' appeared in the *New Review* in July. In ca. 1928 Shaw recalled **Heinemann** showing him 'the ledger account of **Pinero**, whose plays he published at **eighteenpence** a-piece'; he also recollected proposing that Heinemann publish his 'unacted and then-considered-unactable plays,' but nothing came of it (quoted in Whyte, *William Heinemann*, 166).

28 / To T. Fisher Unwin

29 Fitzroy Square W
24th February 1896

[TR: Yale; CL 1]

Shaw had written to Unwin on 16 February, 'I dont see my way at that rate to give the time to writing the preface [to Arms and the Man*] & seeing the play through the press; nor is there anything in the enterprise worth your bothering about. It is the usual difficulty: I can make more money by writing articles, and make better provision for the future by writing new plays' (CL 1, 598).*

Dear Fisher Unwin

If I ever publish 'Arms & The Man' I shall treat it to not only an introduction, but probably to an appendix as well. The American copyright is, if anything *more* important than the English, as the play has been much more widely made known there, and the Americans rather fancy me.

But what is the use of vexing our souls about it? It's evidently not worth publishing: you are at your old benevolent game of occasionally publishing a friend's book for amusement. I'll take the will for the deed until I have something for you with real business in it.

yours sincerely
G. Bernard Shaw

29 / To John Lane

29 Fitzroy Square W
3rd June 1896

[ALS: HRC]

Lane seems to have been pressing Shaw to publish a collection of his journalistic essays, which Shaw disparages below as 'old articles' and 'stale feuilletons.' They included book reviews in The Pall Mall Gazette *(1885–8), art criticism in* The World *(1886–9), and music criticism in* The Star *(1888–9) and* The World *(1890–4). The last would appear as* Music in London 1890–94, *volumes 26–8 of the* Collected Edition *(Constable & Co., 1930–8). There were posthumous comprehensive collections of the musical criticism (3 volumes, 1981), art criticism*

(1989), book reviews (2 volumes, 1991, 1996), and dramatic criticism (4 volumes, 1993).

Dear Lane

I flatly refuse to give you a vegetarian lunch. I am not yet rich enough to make an enemy for life of an influential publisher. Experience has taught me to avoid such freaks.

    For months past I have been carefully avoiding you, as I haven't time to bother over these old articles of mine. It doesn't pay: my business is to produce fresh stuff. Over and over again the subject has come up. Look at that mine of wit & wisdom, the musical page of 'The World' from 90 to 94! Three times a week I am asked why I didn't republish it. Three times a year I receive proposals which amount to my scraping the stuff up and sifting and editing & proof correcting – a harder and longer job than writing a new play – all for about £50. Very satisfactory for the gorged plutocrat of a publisher, who simply drops the book into the slot of his business & takes out the profit; but quite another pair of shoes for the author. No: as soon as my stuff is worth publishing, it will be published fast enough; but if you think I am to be tempted by the ecstasy of seeing stale feuilletons in print, you err, John Lane, you err most damnably. What is done is done, and what is read is read. When you feel disposed to offer me £1000 a year for the right to republish what you please of my journalistic contributions, then I shall begin to believe in the affair & to seriously consider the question of republishing them myself. At present – and here you have the economic situation in a nutshell – my spare time is worth more to me than it is to you ...

yrs ever
G. Bernard Shaw

30 / To John Lane
29 Fitzroy Square W
29th June 1896

[TLS: HRC]

Lane seems to have offered Shaw a mere £80, with royalties of 15%, to republish his journalism.

Dear Lane

On turning our project over in my mind, my hopes of being able to carry it out fall almost to zero. In less than three weeks I shall have to start for Bayreuth, rushing back in time for the International Socialist Congress. Both of these mean extra journalistic activity; and meanwhile I have a play in hand, and The Savoy and Cosmopolis putting the screw on me for articles which I want to write. How is it possible for me to hand you over the manuscript of a book in August at this rate? You think the job of arranging it a short one; but that is because you don't know my style of working. The thing will take a lot of thought and contriving and altering and shaping.

From the purely business point of view, there is nothing in the project for me – I forewarned you that there wouldn't be. £80 is nothing, or rather it is a minus quantity: I could make it more easily and congenially by writing fresh articles, which I should have in hand into the bargain as stock for subsequent republication. Fifteen per cent is a heavy comedown for me. Five or six years ago I had no difficulty in getting twenty per cent on half crown books; and, as you know, 20 on half a crown is better than 20 on five shillings, much less fifteen. If the job were one which I could hand over to a secretary or editor, it might be worth my while to let it be done without interrupting my own work; but as it is, I should lose my race like Atalanta if I stopped to pick up trifles. After all, economics are economics: if my articles were worth republishing, they would have been republished long ago. What's the use of offering £80 to a man who has bitten the apple of dramatic authorship?

I write this lest you should be counting on me, being conscious in the depths of my soul that I haven't the faintest intention of taking the work in hand seriously. I am always interested in what people talk to me about, especially when my own cleverness is in question; but you have no idea how much pressure it takes to induce me even to address an envelope in my full literary armor.

yours ever,
G. Bernard Shaw

Shaw would attend the annual **Bayreuth** Festival (established 1876), celebrating the work of Richard Wagner (1813–83), between 19 and 22 July, and the ninth **International Socialist**

Congress in London between 27 and 31 July. Shaw's **play in hand** was probably *You Never Can Tell*, completed on 18 May. Shaw had contributed 'On Going to Church' to the first number of **The Savoy** in January. His 'Socialism at the International Congress' appeared in the September issue of **Cosmopolis**. In Greek mythology, **Atalanta** lost the race (but in doing so won her suitor) because she stopped to **pick up** three golden apples.

31 / To Grant Richards   29 Fitzroy Square W
                                                              8th November 1896

[ALS: HRC; CL 1; PP: *Author*]

Richards had asked if he could publish Shaw's plays. The seven works mentioned below would appear on 19 April 1898 in a two-volume set entitled Plays: Pleasant and Unpleasant, *which included* Arms and the Man, Candida, The Man of Destiny, *and* You Never Can Tell *(pleasant), and* Widowers' Houses, The Philanderer, *and* Mrs Warren's Profession *(unpleasant).*

Dear Sir

As far as I have been able to ascertain – and I found my opinion on what I have been told by Heinemann, Lane & Walter Scott of their experience with dramatic works by Pinero, Wilde, George Moore, &c – the public does not read plays, or at least did not a very few years ago. Have you found any reason to suppose that it has changed its habits?

I have by me three realistic plays, including the one published by Messrs Henry, as to which there need be no difficulty, as it is as dead as a doornail. One of them is a frightful play; but it ought to be given to the world somehow: indeed, it may perhaps be performed by the Independent Theatre to an invited audience. At least they are always hankering after this.

I have also three plays which are works of dramatic art purely, and which include 'Arms & the Man.' But the other two have not yet been performed; and it would be better to wait until after their production before printing them.

Another little play, which is to be performed at the Lyceum, I will probably publish through the theatre; but there is no reason why its sale should be restricted to the inside of the house after the first run.

One quite indispensable condition is simultaneous publication in

America. Indeed there is much more to be made out of my name there than here at present.

> yours faithfully
> G. Bernard Shaw

The **frightful play** is *Mrs Warren's Profession*, about the societal causes and repercussions of prostitution (although the word is never uttered), written in 1893 and first presented by the Stage Society on 5 and 6 January 1902. The first public performances in England were in Birmingham (four performances) and London (twenty-one) in 1925, and in 1926 at the Strand Theatre, London (sixty-eight). Actor (and later manager of **the Lyceum** Theatre) Henry Irving (1838–1905) held the rights for *The Man of Destiny*, the **little play**. (None of the eight plays in *Plays: Pleasant and Unpleasant* was presented at the Lyceum.) **Simultaneous publication** took place with Herbert S. Stone of Chicago, who reported disappointing sales of only 374 sets (out of 1240) between April and December 1898.

32 / To Grant Richards

29 Fitzroy Square W
27th March 1897

[ALCS: HRC; CL 1; PP: *Author*]

Richards had suggested reprinting Cashel Byron's Profession, *which had been published in unauthorized editions by two American publishers, George Munro and Harper & Brothers, in 1886; other American pirated editions would appear with Brentano's (1899), Herbert S. Stone (1901), and The Stein Co. (1908), the latter bearing the title* Sporting Life or Cashel Byron's Profession.

It is my private belief that half the bookselling trade in London consists in the sale of unauthorised Cashel Byrons. However, I presume Scott has some copies of his stock left. I shall ask him how many presently.

I suppose the thing may as well be republished. I read the copy you sent me. The comedy in it amused me; but the fundamental folly of the thing sickened me.

I'll bring round 'The Philanderer' on Monday. I wish we could get six plays in one volume. I propose to call the issue 'Plays, Pleasant & Unpleasant.' Vol. I. Unpleasant, 3/6, Vol. II, Pleasant 5/–. Both together, half a crown. If we could get all six into one volume, I should have the unpleasant ones printed on light brown paper (Egyptian mummy color) in an ugly style of printing, and the pleasant ones on white paper (ma-

chine hand made) in the best Kelmscott style. Nobody has ever done a
piebald volume before; and the thing would make a sensation.

G. Bernard Shaw

Walter **Scott** had published a one-shilling edition of *Cashel Byron's Profession* in 1889; Richards reprinted the novel in 1901. Shaw was proposing an excellent bargain at **half a crown** (2 shillings 6 pence) for both volumes, as their combined price was 8 shillings 6 pence. **Egyptian mummy** bits were ground into powder to make a brown oil **color** known as 'Mummy Brown' or 'Egyptian Brown'; the Winsor & Newton Company (founded 1832) manufactured it as late as 1896. The **Kelmscott** Press was founded in 1890 by poet, artist, designer, and craftsman William Morris (1834–96) and produced fifty-three volumes between 1891 and 1898. Recalled Richards, 'I had, I thought, proved my own good taste in the design of books already published. But the Morris revolution, with Shaw as its fiercest fanatic, burst on us like a typhoon' (*Author*, 128).

33 / To John Lane   29 Fitzroy Square W
                                                        10th April 1897

[ALS: HRC]

Dear Lane

When we met yesterday I was due at the Haymarket in two minutes, so did not dare to make a fearful revelation to you concerning 'Cashel Byron.' My plans concerning it have been changed by a proposal which has been made to me for the publication of all my works (as far as they are presentable) – plays, essays & so on. It would not be very handsome on my part to take 'Cashel Byron' out of the pudding when it is one of the best plums in it. Besides, the percentage is a very perceptible advance on that which we discussed. Now as I am not very anxious to revive 'Cashel Byron' (which is a foolish affair – I have just read it through) and *do* want to put my plays on record in print, I had rather use the novel to sugar the plays for a publisher than exploit it separately. In fact, if it stood by itself I doubt if I could bring myself to let it out at all: as it is I shall preface it with a sufficiently abject apology for its horrifying folly.

yrs ever
G. Bernard Shaw

'I had to read "You Never Can Tell" to the **Haymarket** [Theatre] company today – two hours and forty minutes – it's too long: I shall have to spoil it to suit the fashionable dinner hour,' Shaw wrote to Ellen Terry on 9 April 1897 (CL 1, 740). 'It was the failure of his hope for this production which led Shaw to publish his plays so that they could be read' (Mander and Mitchenson, *Theatrical Companion to Shaw*, 51). *You Never Can Tell* was first presented by the Stage Society in London on 26 November 1899.

34 / To Grant Richards   29 Fitzroy Square W
19th May 1897

[ALS (tr): HRC]

Dear G.R.

I have just made a desolating discovery. 'Widowers' Houses,' instead of being published immediately after the performance in Dec. 92, was not published until Feb. 93. The agreement was for five years: consequently Henry & Co are in control until next spring. I daresay a fiver would pay them handsomely for their remainder both of the stock and the copyright. A boom began last year in the course of which they actually sold five (5) copies; but whether it has continued I do not know.

Now for your letter. The volumes should of course be saleable separately. If they prove commercially possible a third volume can be added: I have a third of it ('The Devil's Disciple' and 'The Man of Destiny') ready straight off ...

I shall find out about Clark. My impression is that he's all right.

I vehemently object to this 13 as 12 business. It is scraping the butter off an orphan's bread. My 20% five years ago was not subject to that. I prefer 12 as 13. Also I think the 10,000 limit prodigious. If you sell 2,500 I shall be astonished. Think of the time I shall have to wait – January next at earliest – to touch a farthing for my work! And whilst the grass grows the steed starves. How can so young a publisher be so rapacious!

As to America I cannot understand why the terms should be so much worse than for England. One gets a lot more for plays. Anyhow, you might try Putnams. When there was some question of Fisher Unwin publishing my plays Putnam approved and was willing to deal.

I enclose a draft agreement. If you want anything added, tell me what it is and I'll draft a clause. I do not yet understand the American arrangement, so have left it over until I do ...

yrs ever
G. Bernard Shaw

P.S.   The 'Quintessence of Ibsenism' agreement has expired.

Richards included **The Man of Destiny** in *Plays: Pleasant and Unpleasant* (1898); **The Devil's Disciple** was the first play in *Three Plays for Puritans* (1901). Shaw's books were printed by the distinguished Edinburgh firm of R. & R. **Clark** Ltd until his death. In the **13 as 12 business**, Shaw thought he was being taken advantage of by the **rapacious** Richards, who felt entitled to sell, for his own profit, one book (for every dozen on the ledger) without Shaw's usual percentage. Shaw cautioned Methuen & Co. in 1903, 'The terms which I am accustomed to ask & to receive in London are a royalty of 20%, 13 copies being reckoned as 13 & not as 12' (Letter 61). For G.P. **Putnam**'s Sons, see Letter 27.

35 / To G. Bernard Shaw   9 Henrietta Street, Covent Garden WC
20th May 1897

[TLS: Harvard]

My dear Shaw

Yes, I noticed about 'Widowers' Houses' last night myself when I got out the page in type. But will you communicate with them or shall I? I would rather you did, because they are much more likely to be amenable to suggestion from you than from me, as no doubt they won't be exactly pleased to have the chance slipping through their fingers – that I should have got your work, I mean.

I think it a pity that 'The Man of Destiny,' at least, can't find a place in one or other of the volumes, as people will be rather alert to see it and the paragraphs that have appeared about the business have suggested that they will contain all your work, both played and unplayed. 'The Devil's Disciple' doesn't so much matter, as nobody has heard about it to the same extent. 'The Philanderer' goes to you to-day ...

I notice what you say about thirteen as twelve and my rapacity. Believe me, I am most anxious that you should not think this seriously. For the first few months, of course, all my work here must be in a sense experimental. It is most difficult for me to know what terms pay, and to what extent they pay, until I have had plenty of trials. One of the things I went on was that Grant Allen for the 'Woman Who Did' signed first an agreement for twenty per cent, 13/12, and that Lane afterwards took considerable credit to himself for increasing the royalty voluntarily to twenty-five per cent. I have read your agreement. It is all right, I think. We will drop the thirteen as twelve and make the twenty-five per cent royalty commence at seven thousand, five hundred, if that will do. I enclose two copies. You can sign one & return it to me if it does.

In America terms are generally different, because the authors aren't so rapacious! Everywhere I am told that ten per cent on every copy is considered a very decent royalty, *there*, but I will go and see Putnam and see if I can get anything more out of him. When I know I will write to you ...

You say nothing in your letter or in the agreement about Introductions to each volume. I think that they are rather essential.

Will you bring 'The Quintessence of Ibsenism' up to date and let me publish that on the same terms?

I shall put your portrait for the volumes in hand at once ...

> Very sincerely yours,
> Grant Richards

The two alterations I made is to make the five years date from November 1, which will give me a clear five years with the books. Isn't that fair? & in adding a short sentence to clause IV.

Novelist **Grant Allen** (1848–99) was Richards's uncle and author of *The Woman Who Did* (1895), a notorious novel attacking the double standard of morality. Shaw brought *The Quintessence of Ibsenism* (1891) **up to date** only in 1913, when Constable issued a revised second edition, 'Now Completed to the Death of Ibsen' (who had died in 1906). A 'Preface: Mainly about Myself' to volume I (unpleasant) that was resumed in the 'Preface' to volume II (pleasant), both dated 1898, served as **Introductions**. (Letter 35, call number bMS Eng 954 (8), is published by permission of the Houghton Library, Harvard University.)

36 / To Grant Richards Lotus. Tower Hill, Dorking
21st May 1897

[ALS: HRC; CL 1; PP: *Author*]
Beatrice Webb had introduced Shaw to his future wife, wealthy Irish heiress Charlotte Frances Payne-Townshend (1857–1943), on 29 January 1896. From April to June 1897, the Webbs and Charlotte took a cottage at Tower Hill near Dorking, Surrey, and Shaw visited frequently.

Thanks for Philanderer.

Clark is all right – a first rate house. I enclose a letter which you can hold as your certificate of your compliance with my Fair Wages Clause.

Yes: separate introductions to the volumes by all means, and separate portraits if you like. Evans has an assortment which includes both tragic & comic masks.

The best people to give the portrait to are Walker and [Walter] Boutall, 16 Clifford's Inn. E.C. Emery Walker, the senior partner, will look after me like a brother. He is the guide, philosopher & friend of many publishers in the matter of illustrated books; and you ought to make his acquaintance anyhow. He is also a first rate authority on printing, and personally an almost reprehensibly amiable man.

If you have a copy of one of Walter Scott's volumes of Ibsen's plays you will see how the style of the thing I want works at three plays to the volume. In Scott's edition the block of letterpress is not properly set on the page; but otherwise it is not so bad.

In drafting the agreement I should have made the five years start from the date of publication.

Nov. will do as well. Probably we shall have to add something about the American business when we find out what can be done. In it I take it that you will not meddle in the publication there yourself, but virtually act as my agent and take a percentage on what you can get for me. Or have you any other plan?

'The Man of Destiny' is quite available if there is room for it.

'The Quintessence' has been skimmed a good deal. Hadn't you better wait and see whether I sell well enough?

I am writing by this post to Henry & Co.

yrs ever

G. Bernard Shaw

For Frederick H. **Evans**, see Letter 24. In 1890–1, **Scott** had published a uniform edition of **Ibsen**'s 'Prose Dramas' in five volumes. Sir **Emery Walker** (1851–1933) was associated first with the Kelmscott Press, then with the Doves Press (see Letter 74). The **American business** was the search for a U.S. publisher (see Letter 37). Shaw was writing to **Henry & Co.** for permission to reprint *Widowers' Houses*.

37 / To Grant Richards   The Argoed, Penallt, Monmouth
                                                          26th August 1897

[ALS: HRC; CL 1; PP: *Author*]

Richards was vacationing in Switzerland and 'spending a quiet fortnight at St Moritz' (Author, 129).

This letter of yours comes well, Grant Richards, from a man who has

been bounding idly up the Jungfrau and down the Matterhorn to an exhausted wretch who, after a crushing season, has slaved these four weeks
for four hours a day at your confounded enterprise. I have sent three
plays to the printer, transmogrified beyond recognition, made more
thrilling than any novel; and he has only sent me proofs of one, of which
it has cost me endless letters & revises to get the page right, to teach him
how to space letters for emphasis, and how to realize that I mean my
punctuation to be followed.

I had no idea of the magnitude of the job. Anything like a holiday is out
of the question for me. Must I endure in addition the insults of a publisher for whom I am preparing, with unheard-of toil, a gigantic triumph?
Read 'Mrs Warren'; and then blush for your impatience if you can.

Stone & Kimball's offer, as described to me in your letter of the 9th
Apl (doubtless negligently and lazily composed before going up the riv-
er) mentioned neither the price nor the royalty after 10,000 copies. The
latter I assume to be 20%: the former not less than 75 cents at least. A
princely affluence will accrue to S. & K. on these terms; but I desire to
make the fortune of one American publisher in order that I may spend
the rest of my life in plundering all the others.

Shall I draw them an agreement? If they prefer to do it themselves,
warn them that I wont assign copyright, but simply give them exclusive
leave to publish in the U.S. for 5 years.

yrs, overworked to madness
G. Bernard Shaw

The **Jungfrau** and **Matterhorn** are prominent Alpine peaks. Here (as elsewhere) Shaw uses
revises to mean revisions. Herbert Stuart **Stone** (1871–1915) & Hannibal Ingalls **Kimball**
(1874–1933) founded their Chicago publishing firm in 1893, parting in 1896. Stone then
formed Herbert S. Stone & Co., which published *Plays: Pleasant and Unpleasant* (1898), *The
Perfect Wagnerite* (1899), *Love Among the Artists* (1900), *Three Plays for Puritans* (1901), and
Cashel Byron's Profession (1901).

38 / To Grant Richards   The Argoed, Penallt, Monmouth
                                              28th August 1897

[APCS: HRC; CL 1; PP: *Author*]

By the way, a good many of the corrections so far (I have only sent back
one sheet, and that chiefly to get the page right and to settle about spac-

ing the letters for emphasized words instead of italicizing them) are corrections of Clark's departures from my copy, in spite of my straitest injunctions, in the matter of punctuation. However, I am now knocking righteousness into his head; and I shall feel deeply humiliated if my corrections are not under rather than over the Carlyle-Balzac average. I'll presently send you a sheet with the corrections of Clark's misdemeanors in red ink, and of my own in black. You may charge me for all corrections over and above 95% of the total cost of production.

G.B.S.

In addition to eliminating most apostrophes (see Letter 74), Shaw insisted on extra **spacing** of letters for emphasis, reserving italics for stage directions. Robert (1826–94) **Clark** founded R. & R. Clark in 1846; his son Edward (1864–1926) became a partner in 1887. Thomas **Carlyle** (1795–1881) and Honoré de **Balzac** (1799–1850) were notorious for their extensive proof revisions.

39 / To Grant Richards [The Argoed, Penallt,] Monmouth
25th September 1897

[ALCS: HRC; CL 1; PP: *Author*]

Grant Richards, my boy, do not deceive yourself. Ibsen's plays sell at three & sixpence [for] the volume of three plays. The first issue of a new play at 5/– by Heinemann fetches the rent of Ibsen's unique European position, which I have not yet reached. The point of a six shilling volume is the length of time it takes to read. The man who buys a six shilling book expects that he will not have to buy another for several Sundays; and he looks strictly to the quantity of matter supplied. Now a play is a very short business owing to the dialogueiness of it; and that is why every attempt to charge more than eighteenpence for a single play fails in England. The six shilling public will just go the seven shillings for our two volumes: make it ten, and you will not sell a thousand copies all told. At the three & six you will not lose; and you *may* land a really large circulation. An édition de luxe – two volumes in a case for a guinea – is the only real business alternative; and that would not pay *you*, as your interest does not lie in getting a reputation for that sort of thing, especially in connection with 'Mrs Warren's Profession.' Our original plan is the right one, and the only one in which there is any money. Sit tight therefore &

trust my judgment. I mean this book to break out far beyond 'my public': that is why I'm squandering hard work on it.

G. Bernard Shaw

Scott's edition of Ibsen's 'Prose Dramas' sold at **three & sixpence** per volume (see Letter 36). Here is Richards's reaction to the foregoing letter: 'I still believe I was right. The cost of each individual volume, after printing a first edition of twelve hundred and forty copies, was about two and sevenpence. All the experience I have since had leads me to suppose that if we had reduced the cost of production by doubling the number printed in the first edition and had made the books **three and six**pence each instead of five shillings, we should not have sold a much higher number within six months of publication. We did sell seven hundred and fifty-six copies in about that time, which may be said to have supported G.B.S.'s prophecy, but which I think proves rather that it took a long time for his kind of reputation to reach the book-buying public' (*Author*, 132).

40 / To Grant Richards
29 Fitzroy Square W
8th October 1897

[ALS: HRC; CL 1; PP: *Author*]

Dear G.R.

You have an india rubber mind: as fast as I stretch it to the TWO volumes, it contracts into one. If it were a question of 3/6 and 5, or even 6 shillings, I should not hesitate to go the larger figure; but it is a question between SEVEN shillings and TEN. Ten is a prohibitive price: you wont sell your 2000 copies at it – perhaps not even 1000; whereas at seven you will either sell upwards of 10,000 or the whole project will be a failure. I tell you the next price to seven shillings is a guinea for the two volumes in a case, which would get you a pornographic reputation.

My old circulation of 1000 was attained when I was comparatively unknown by an essay on 'Ibsenism,' with an unpopular title. And that was not a ten shilling circulation, but a half crown one.

I object strenuously to gilt tops.

If on thinking this over, you still feel suicidal, I am not sure that my best plan will not be to back my opinion by manufacturing the book myself, taking over Clark's contract from you and getting you to publish on commission. At any rate, it is a thing to be considered. There is an enormous section of bookbuyers who regard 10/– as a price absolutely outside their means, and 7/– within it. I believe in going for a large circulation, even if the paper is cheapened. Anyhow, Globe 8vo is too small for a big price, unless it is *de luxe*.

Do think it over a bit. The enterprise is really not worth undertaking at all if you limit your aim to 2000 circulation: at least not from my point of view. Allowing me the moderate tariff of £25 for the prefaces, I should get £25 apiece for the plays. It takes six months to write a play. Therefore the dramatic author would get less than £1 a week – say five shillings less than a dock laborer – 4½d an hour for writing masterpieces. It's sweating. Sell 10,000 at 7/– and I shall get 1/3¾ an hour. Do you grudge me that modest reward?

yrs arithmetically

G. Bernard Shaw

Books of Victorian erotica were often issued in expensive limited editions in slip**cases**, hence the allusion to Richards's **pornographic reputation**. Extant royalty statements show that the *Quintessence of Ibsenism* had sold about double **1000** copies in England by 1897 (CL 1, 811). Despite Shaw's **strenuous** objections, many of his works – including Constable's Collected (1930–8) and Standard (1931–51) editions – have **gilt tops**. Shaw reiterates the idea of **commission** publishing to Richards in Letters 49, 50, and 58. **Sweating** is the employment of labour at low wages, for long hours, and under poor conditions. 'Literature is also, unfortunately, a sweated trade. This is one of the reasons for the existence of our Society,' said Shaw in a 1906 speech to the Society of Authors (quoted in Bonham-Carter, *Authors by Profession*, 194). The Society of Authors (founded 1884 and still extant) is devoted to the protection of literary property.

41 / To Grant Richards

29 Fitzroy Square W

3rd January 1898

[ALS (tr): HRC]

In returning a few sheets on 23 October 1897, Shaw suggested Richards tell Clark 'that they need not justify to avoid dividing a word at the end – that it is better to divide a word than to have a loose line making a streak of whitey grey through the black. Caxton would have printed your name Gr-ant Richa-rds at the end of a line sooner than spoilt his page with rivers of white. The great thing is to get the color even. Besides, since we are substituting spaced letters for italic in underlined words, it is important that the spacing should be regular and rather narrow, so as to make the spacing distinctive' (CL 1, 816).

Dear Grant Richards

The villains have become desperate. The B-y is only one of their larks, to prove to you that I am a jumped-up idiot. The other one, which I like, they artfully printed on the wrong sized sheet to make it look tall and ugly. I return it to you cut down to the right size. The G-arden is not objectionable – rather enjoyable, in fact; but I have made an alteration on the black ink sheet which will avoid it. There is no hurry to decide, I suppose; but if you compare it with the other title page, with the too large capitals & the incurably ugly 'Ss,' you will see that it has points. But it seems to me that they have put a thin lead between the lines. Will you ask them if they have, and if so, to take it out and send it by parcel post to hell ...

G.B.S.

Printer William **Caxton** (ca. 1422–92) introduced the printing press to England in 1476. Although Shaw objected to **B-y**, the title page of *Plays: Pleasant and Unpleasant* reads 'Unpleasant' and 'Gard-en.' A **lead** is a space between lines of type (see 'leading' in Letter 42).

42 / To Grant Richards   Pitfold, Haslemere
                                                            20th August 1898

[CL 2; PP: *Author*]

Only four months after publication of Plays: Pleasant and Unpleasant, *Shaw had another work ready for press:* The Perfect Wagnerite: A Commentary on the Niblung's Ring, *which Richards would publish on 1 December.*

Dear G.R.

I send you herewith, by parcels post, the complete MS of the Wagner book. I compute it roughly at 35,000 words. This, in the type of the preface to the plays, would make 100 pages. I think, however, that it should be got up as a book of devotion for pocket use, and not bulked out as a treatise. I want to secure the American copyright: do you think Stone will venture upon it?

I have not made up my mind about the title. The Perfect Wagnerite seems to me the best. It might be *announced* as 'The P.W.; or the New Protestantism.' Quintessence won't do: it would be a weak repetition, and would suggest an explanation of all Wagner's works, whereas I have dealt with The Ring only. A sensible title would be 'Wagner's Ring: What it Means'; but nobody would read a book with a sensible title; and quite right too.

We had better have a specimen page or two. If we decide on a biggish book like the plays, the type should be small pica Caslon set solid, like the prefaces to the plays, in which, however, three lines might be knocked off with advantage to the lower margin. If we carry out the idea of a pretty little book of devotion, the type should be as in the plays.

 ˙ Get it into type as soon as possible, as I have no complete copy; and if the MS gets lost or burnt there is an end of it forever ...

yrs ever
G. Bernard Shaw

Shaw had married Charlotte Frances Payne-Townshend on 1 June 1898. On 1 June the Shaws set up house at '**Pitfold**,' near **Haslemere**, in Surrey. *The Perfect Wagnerite* (140 pages long) contains a section entitled 'Siegfried as **Protestant**.' The book discusses only the four operas in Wagner's *Der Ring des Nibelungen* (written 1848–74): *The Rhinegold, The Valkyrie, Siegfried,* and *Twilight of the Gods.* For Shaw's reaction to the **specimen page**s, see Letter 43. Shaw's preferred typeface was **pica Caslon set solid**. (A pica is a typographical unit of measure equalling ⅙ of an inch; there are 12 points in one pica. A type whose leading – a term derived from the lead used in hot-metal typesetting to adjust the amount of space between lines of type – is equal to the point size of the font used is 'set solid.') In subsequent letters to Richards that month, Shaw expanded (facetiously) on the **book of devotion** idea: 'a little Imitation of Christ affair about as large, at most, as the envelope of this letter' (25 August, *Author*); 'gilt edges, leather binding, clasps, and a bookmarker of perforated card with a text worked on it in wool. An edition de luxe in mother-of-pearl, in Russia leather case £2.2.0' (28 August, *Author*).

43 / To Grant Richards

[Pitfold, Haslemere]
9th September 1898

[PP: *Author*]

On 31 August, Shaw had written to Richards to 'Implore him [Clark] to believe that the lower margin simply cannot be too broad for the world's thumbnail, and that the top must be narrow, and that the top is the first line of the page and not the title' (Author). *And on 4 September he advised Richards, 'Don't be in too great a hurry to try these experiments [in type size]. You will learn from them the only part of a publisher's business that is real'* (Author). *In the following letter, Shaw elaborates on his strict aesthetic specifications, perhaps in an effort to avoid with* The Perfect Wagnerite *the problems he had had in printing* Plays: Pleasant and Unpleasant, *for which Richards charged him £10.6.0 for 'Author's Alterations & extra proofs.' Shaw responded on 30 September with a bill for £281.8.9 under the heading 'Services rendered as Typographical Expert by Author to Publisher,' deducting Richards's charge while adding £21 for 'Extra proof corrections in style of typesetting in the interest of the Publisher's reputation' (CL 2, 63).*

Dear G.R.

We have now got the two specimens right, one being as good as the other, in its own way: the question remains, which will we choose. Or rather, which will *you* choose; for far be it from me to force your inclinations when you have taken so much trouble.

Oddly enough, the larger type is the harder to read, partly because the line is too long to be taken in at an eyeful, partly because its size and clearness are positively dazzling. That is the only point to be considered between the two over and above their good looks. Now please yourself: I leave the decision to you. One will please me as well as the other.

(If you choose the big type [as I anticipate from your letter you are likely to] then you must impress upon Clark that every defect in the printing will be ten times more glaring with the larger than with the smaller. There must be no holes and rivers of white patching the page. As a first step to attain this, the huge gaps left at the beginning of each sentence on the sample page must be vehemently forbidden. The spaces between the words must be kept as narrow and even as possible: it is better to divide words at the end of the line with hyphens than to spoil the line by excessive spacing merely to 'justify' without dividing, as some printers make a point of doing. There should be no greater space between the point at the end of a sentence and the capital, than between the last letter of one word and the first of the next within the sentence. In short, the color of the block of printing should be as even as possible. The printing of the sample couldn't possibly be worse in this respect.)

For the big type, a rougher paper and cloth than we used for the plays will be advisable. I suggest tough holland sides and a blue back, with your favorite rough edges.

If you choose the smaller type, the format had better be the same as the plays, with perhaps a different colored cloth, to distinguish the volume of criticism from the volume of fiction ...

Yrs ever
G. Bernard Shaw

For Shaw's extended comments on **rivers of white**, **huge gaps**, and other typographical specifications, see Letter 74. To **justify** is to adjust the spacing so that a line ends evenly at a straight margin to the right of the text. **Holland** is a smooth, durable cotton or linen fabric used for bookbinding or upholstery.

44 / To Grant Richards   Blen-Cathra, Hindhead, Haslemere
                                                      2nd December 1898

[ALS (tr): HRC; PP: *Author*]

'Nothing worth talking about will ever come out of my books unless they are advertised,' Shaw had written to Sonnenschein in 1887 (Letter 12). The failure of Richards to adequately advertise Shaw's books would remain an ongoing point of contention between them; see Letters 46, 47, 56, 57, and 59.

Dear G.R.

The enclosed will get you prosecuted for obtaining money under false pretences. Your plan of publishing books without reading them is better than the usual one of reading them without publishing them; but it involves the necessity of getting the author to revise the advertisements. The P.W. contains nothing about Wagner's 'operas'; it deals only with The Ring, to describe which as an opera or set of operas is regarded as the shibboleth of hideous & abysmal ignorance by all good Wagnerites. People will expect a complete account of Rienzi, The Flying Dutchman, Tannhauser, Lohengrin, Tristan & Isolde, Die Meistersinger, & Parsifal, to which I dont even allude ...

yrs ever
G. Bernard Shaw

In mid-November, the Shaws had moved from 'Pitfold' to a larger house, '**Blen-Cathra**,' near **Hindhead**.

45 / To Grant Richards   Blen-Cathra, Hindhead, Haslemere
                                                      5th December 1898

[PP: *Author*]

The Perfect Wagnerite *was published on 1 December. Richards included the following letter in his 1934 autobiography* Author Hunting, by an old literary sports man; memories of years spent mainly in publishing, 1897–1925 *(see Letter*

149). Shaw censored himself for publication, writing in the margin to the galley proofs following 'this adulterated horror is not': 'Omit this. It is unfair to Clark. He was right about the paper,' referring to the following (excised) passage: 'The paper is miserable, and the folding and binding of the most commercially uncon-scientious kind. If Clark tried to persuade you that a change of paper would have involved special manufacture, refer him to the marines, who will peradventure believe such monstrous nonsense. The ruffian had a remnant which he has traded off on our youth and innocence' (Galley proofs, p. 35, HRC). The ellipses below are by Richards.

Dear G.R.

... The binding exhibits a hellish misconception of my suggestion. The holland should come right up to the back, leaving no margin of blue; and the blue should not be glistening ribbed sticky silk, but a kindred material to the holland, and really blue in color, which this adulterated horror is not ... I suggest a large paper edition at ten shillings, with a por-trait of Wagner.

If there is still time, I think it would be well to alter the cases and use thicker (or rougher and better) paper for the rest of the edition. That blue stuff is a most blasted fabric. Besides, don't you see how that ac-cursed margin makes the book look small and narrow and worth only a shilling? With the full 4¾" width of holland it would look worth five. Why, oh why, didn't you send me a case before deciding? ...

Yrs ever

G. Bernard Shaw

46 / To G. Bernard Shaw   9 Henrietta Street, Covent Garden WC

24th May 1899

[TLS (c): HRC; PP: *SHAW* 27]

Richards responds to a number of charges by Shaw relating to The Perfect Wag-nerite, *in particular that the book was insufficiently advertised.*

Dear Shaw

If I followed my first inclination I should say to you: 'Manufacture the books yourself; get Longmans to sell them, and be damned to you!' But instead I think I will point out to you how wrong in its main issues your letter is.

You begin by saying that you had all the trouble of choosing the format and directing the production of your book. You chose to take this trouble on yourself because you had your own ideas about what a book should be like. Whether you are right or wrong is beside the point. It is my business to make my books look well, and occasionally I satisfy myself with them, so that your superintendence of the production was entirely unnecessary.

Then you say: 'There has been *one* advertisement (gratuitous) of the book; and that I myself arranged for.' As a matter of fact, there have been twenty-three, costing in all nearly fourteen pounds. I shall be glad to show you the list if you like. As I labour under the necessity of attempting to make each book pay for itself I did not go on spreading money on advertising 'The Perfect Wagnerite' when it was perfectly obvious that money so spent would not return in a proportionate increase in circulation. Another thing: I cannot think how it is you write that there has been only one advertisement when I have a letter of yours in which you point out that advertisements appearing in two of the evening papers on the day of the book's issue were incorrect to some slight extent.

Early uncorrected sheets of your books *were* sent to America. You are quite right in that. It is usual to send early uncorrected sheets in order that the purchaser in such a case may see what he is going to have, but he is generally warned, and he was warned on this occasion, that in setting the book he was to follow the later sheets which were also sent. That he did not do so is his fault. I might have the more responsibility if I had carried through the arrangement, but I believe I am right in saying that the statement of sales and the money due to you were remitted direct.

Finally, when in the Winter of 1896 I first asked you whether you would not consider the publication of your plays in a collected edition, you warned me (certainly verbally, and I believe also in your letters: I will not stop to see) that I should ruin myself by the venture – that both Heinemann and Lane had assured you that plays did not sell. You had apparently at that time the sense to know that the public do not always want good work. I have noticed that authors with even more sense than you have, when the public show this indifference, visit it on the head of their publisher.

Sincerely yours,
Grant Richards

Although his work never appeared with **Longman**, Shaw mentions them on several occasions as potential publishers (see especially Letter 63). 'It is almost incredible that Longmans should be such a stupendous ass,' Shaw wrote on 24 March 1901 to Samuel Butler (1835–1902) upon learning that Longman had refused to publish *Erewhon Revisited*. On the 28th Shaw introduced him to Richards, who published the book in 1901 and *The Way of All Flesh* in 1903. The **uncorrected sheets** were sent to publisher Herbert S. Stone in **America**.

47 / To Grant Richards   [Blen-Cathra, Hindhead]
29th May 1899

[ADU: HRC; CL 2]

Shaw proceeds to respond to the justifications outlined by Richards in Letter 46 about his mishandling of The Perfect Wagnerite.

Dear G.R.

This is beyond all reason. You first write to me explicitly that you did not advertise the book; and because I politely accepted that statement you reproach me for forgetting that you spent £14 on advertisements & that they attracted my own special attention by their misleading character. How am I to keep my head among these reckless contradictions?

I dont deny that it is your business to make your books look well: on the contrary, that is the exact ground of my complaint that instead of doing it you go about amusing yourself & leave the job to me. I still have the ghastly proofs you submitted to me before I took the matter in hand. To say, as you do, that 'your [my] superintendence of the production was entirely unnecessary' is to proclaim yourself void of moral and artistic sense. I blush for you.

It is quite true that I warned you repeatedly that my plays would probably ruin you. Since you admit this, why do you complain that they have not sold? I never expected them to sell beyond the circulation I told you had been achieved by Scott & other publishers. I dont expect them to sell. It is you who reproach me with their limited sale, not I you. I propose to take the responsibility on myself in future, not to add it to your burdens. Personally I find you, like all thoroughly unbusinesslike people, a pleasant sort of ruffian, the kind of man I like to know. But why should I exhaust your capital & ruffle your temper by inflicting my books on you? If I take them in hand myself, the blame and loss will be mine. So long as you have them in hand, the blame & loss will be yours: that is what a publisher is for.

Any misunderstandings as to the arrangement with Stone are simply explained by the fact that you, not I, made it. I daresay they will send you particulars if you ask them. I never interfered in the business by a single word or line. If I had, it would have come out all right. Your plan, avowed by you from the first, of letting things slide, has its advantages; but you must not expect it to act exactly like the regular business plan of making explicit agreements. You admit that you did not carry out the arrangements; and as you know that *I* did not meddle, the conclusion is obvious there was no arrangement at all.

On the whole, it is not only certain now that you will be ruined, but that you will attribute your ruin to me. Why should I incur this responsibility? You had much better send me an exact account of the whole transaction, and let me readjust it on a commission basis as from the beginning. In this way I will make good all your loss; and you can sell the remainder of the edition for me on commission. Can I be fairer than that?

yrs sincerely
[G. Bernard Shaw]

The brackets around '**my**' are Shaw's.

48 / To Herbert S. Stone & Co.

Off Naples
4th October 1899

[ALS: NYPL; CL 2]

On 14 September the Shaws had left for a six-week cruise of the Mediterranean aboard the SS Lusitania *(not the RMS* Lusitania, *launched in 1906 and torpedoed in 1915). Shaw disliked the experience intensely, writing on 17 October that life aboard ship for the wealthy was 'a guzzling, lounging, gambling, dog's life' (CL 2, 111). The ellipses in the following letter are in CL.*

Dear Sirs

Your letter has just reached me here ... I see it stated that some American firm has issued an edition of an old novel of mine called 'Cashel Byron's Profession,' which is not copyrighted in the United States. As a matter of fact there is a mass of literary stuff by me which is in the same predicament ... Now I am aware that most authors regard the reprinting of their non-copyright works by American publishers as an act of piracy. You may therefore feel that your relations with me would be strained if you availed yourself on any occasion of the opportunity (such as it is) which is open to all American publishers. So I may as well tell you that I do not take the ordinary author's view. It may be hard on the English people that they have to bear the whole burden of supporting the English author whilst the American people read him as cheaply as they read Shakespear. I should substitute full international copyright to redress that injustice; but I should shorten its period, as the author may be presumed to get quite as much out of the right to levy on England alone as will pay him for his labor. Of course, like other authors, I will take what I can get; and since the new copyright treaty was made I have taken advantage of it; but I make no grievance of my old failure to secure American copyright, and see no reason why, because you now publish my copyright books, you should be cut off from the non-copyright ones which are open to your competitors in business. If you ever want to 'pirate' them, go ahead: I shall be only too glad if you find it worth your while.

Harpers paid me £10 many years ago to ease their silly conscience when they published 'Cashel Byron.' Not having thought the question out then, I took it. My friend Tucker the Anarchist published 'The Quintessence of Ibsenism' from a copy I sent him expressly for the purpose. A horrible fool trading under the name of Roycroft, expurgated & gentilified an essay of mine 'On Going to Church' and printed it, as he thought, *artistically*. The brute did not know the ABC of good printing. As far as I know these are the only reprints yet made in the United States except the Cashel Byron just announced as issued by a firm with a name like Brentano – I forget its exact form.

yours faithfully
G. Bernard Shaw

56

The **American firm** was **Brentano's**, which succeeded Stone as Shaw's U.S. publisher in 1904 with *Man and Superman*; their unauthorized edition of *Cashel Byron's Profession* was published in 1899. **Harper** & Brothers had published theirs in 1886, offering Shaw £10, despite the fact that the novel was not protected by U.S. copyright. Stone issued a **pirate** edition of *Love Among the Artists* the following year. For **the new copyright treaty** (of 1886), see notes to Letter 9. Benjamin R. **Tucker** (Boston), the first to publish Shaw in the United States – 'What's in a Name? (How an Anarchist might put it),' *Liberty* (11 April 1885) – issued an unauthorized edition of *The Quintessence of Ibsenism* in 1891. The **horrible fool** was Elbert Hubbard (1856–1915), founder of the **Roycroft** Printing Shop (1895–1938) in East Aurora, New York; see Letter 74.

49 / To Grant Richards　　　　　　　　　　10 Adelphi Terrace WC2
8th May 1900

[CL 2; PP: *Author*]

Shaw tries to lure Richards into commission publishing again (see Letter 40), this time with the promise that their new arrangement would remain confidential.

... And now, what about *Three Plays for Puritans?* It is going to involve a lot of composition, and at least three plates, at the old price. You have not done so amazingly well with *Plays P. and Unpl.* (an edition of 1200 in two years) as to feel certain that this book is going to be a treasure. I offer to pay for it (instead of Clark), and hold you harmless. The public and the press won't know. The honor and glory of the thing will be the same. You do not deign to reply on the point, possibly because your feelings are hurt. I don't care about your feelings, except in so far as they seem likely to ruin you, which would be extremely inconvenient to me. I want to know definitely and at once, because if it is to be commission, I must set about the printing at once; and if it is to be as before, I must draw up an agreement, which, this time, must be properly considered and executed in spite of your shrieks. If you won't be businesslike with other people, you *shall* with me: I'll make you, if only for the sake of your education. *Do* wake up.

G.B.S.

In early November 1899, Shaw moved his belongings into Charlotte's flat (over the London School of Economics, which Shaw had co-founded in 1894) in the elegant **Adelphi Terrace** (built 1768–72). He retained the Fitzroy Square house for his mother (and to qualify him to serve in the St Pancras Vestry; see Letter 73).

50 / To Grant Richards   10 Adelphi Terrace WC2
                                              31st May 1900

[PP: *Author*]

... I shall do just as much proof correction on this volume as on the last one – probably more. My corrections were in no way extravagant; and the few trial pages we had when I was doing your work of inventing a presentable format after the blighting failure of your own perfunctory attempt, cost you a few shillings and me many days in which I might have earned guineas. The extra proofs for the copyrighting performances I was perfectly willing to pay for with 150% profit for you. The price I did pay would have provided me with complete volumes on Japanese paper. Anyhow, this time I shall need no such copies; and I shall spare no expense (to you) in achieving the utmost accuracy and elegance of composition from Clark & Co. If you demur to the tiniest comma, I shall instantly offer to take over the whole cost of manufacture and revert to a commission basis. If at the last moment I think I can rewrite all the plays with advantage I shall do so on the proofs without a throb of remorse. So there!

Yrs resolutely
G. Bernard Shaw

51 / To Grant Richards   In the train – going to
                                       Blackdown Cottage, near Haslemere
                                              13th September 1900

[ALS: HRC; PP: *Author*]

Shaw wrote to Richards on 31 August that he had just drafted 'an Election manifesto for the Fabian Society' (Author), which Richards published on 2 October as Fabianism and the Empire *in 4000 copies. At Shaw's request, Richards printed 800 sets of galleys for exclusive distribution to Fabian members.*

Dear G.R.

There is no time to waste on preliminary proof corrections of that Manifesto. The Chiswick people must take the most violent measures to get

800 proofs delivered at the Fabian Office at the earliest possible moment
– say Monday midday at [the] latest.

The form of these proofs is most important: They ought to be galley
proofs, so that they may not be available afterwards instead of a copy of
the book. This can be managed by printing them in long forms & cutting
them galleywise. Margins should be wide enough for corrections. Further – and this is also vital – there must be no page heading or galley slip
heading to betray what the document is or where it comes from. Each
slip should be headed 'Copyright matter. Strictly private and confidential. All rights reserved.' This, I think, will prevent any editor into whose
hands a copy may fall, from making free with it.

The proofs should not be leaded. It will save paper and bulk to print
them solid & insert the leads (if any) afterwards.

yours, very tired
G. Bernard Shaw

Blackdown Cottage was the Shaws' country residence until mid-November 1900. *Fabianism
and the Empire* was printed by the **Chiswick** Press (which had also printed Morris's *Roots of the
Mountains* in 1892). 'Members apparently observed the "**private and confidential**" injunctions so scrupulously that not a single copy of either proof is known to have survived!' (Laurence 1, 44).

52 / To Grant Richards   10 Adelphi Terrace WC2
30th November 1900

[ALS: HRC; CL 2]

Dear G.R.

I want your immediate attention to the following bit of business, as it may
lead to the selling of some plays.

Hogg (Samuel French, 89 Strand) the theatrical publisher & amateur's guide & philosopher, says that he sells a hundred of Pinero's plays
whilst Heinemann is not selling five. He says the traditional price of a
play is sixpence; but he has got the price of really first class works up to
eighteenpence, as witness the enclosed *édition de luxe* of 'Jedbury Junior.'
Pinero's plays, as you know, are eighteenpence. Heinemann supplies
Hogg with as many as he can absorb at ninepence – half-price net –;

Hogg puts them in his list, which the amateurs devour; he collects the fees for each performance for the author and at the same time sells as many copies as there are parts in the play plus a couple for stage manager & prompter; and off they go in batches like hot cakes. He estimates generously that as you have the plates, you can supply the millions he will require at twopence a copy or thereabouts and retire presently on a competence. He is absolutely sceptical as to the possibility of selling a single copy of a six shilling volume of plays – knows all about it – can't be done. And he is issuing a new catalogue in six weeks & wants to have the eighteenpenny edition ready for it.

I have no doubt at all that this is good business. The notion of charging half a crown for single plays is absurd: it's like charging three halfpence for a newspaper. Hogg has a violent incentive to sell, because he not only gets eighteenpence in full for the book (at least so I presume, though perhaps the amateurs are sharp enough to demand discount) but he also gets a huge commission (20% he demands) on the fees, he having a practical monopoly of this huge & very specialized market which you can reach through him only. He keeps standing advertisements in a lot of big papers. Now these eighteenpenny editions could all bear an advertisement of the six shilling edition, with the prefaces, and would not interfere with the literary market, which is quite separate. Hogg will be enriched beyond the dreams of avarice; but you will get a hatful of the crumbs from his table. Make a better bargain for yourself if you can by claiming that half net is only business when a large number of copies are taken; but as a matter of fact it isnt so bad: you would send copies to America at that rate, or do a deal with Stoneham at it.

Besides, I shall want only twopence, which is a ridiculously nominal royalty.

Hogg says the cover must be *limp* & the book pocketable.

yrs

G. Bernard Shaw

Wentworth **Hogg** (1854–1940), managing director of London publishers **Samuel French**, had been licensing some of Shaw's plays for amateur performances. 'Shaw later balked at the 20% commission' (CL 2, 202). *Jedbury Junior* (produced at Terry's Theatre on 14 February 1896) was a comedy by popular playwright Madeleine L. Ryley (1859–1934). A **competence** is 'an income large enough to live on' (*Concise Oxford Dictionary*).

53 / To Grant Richards   Piccard's Cottage, St Catherine's, Guildford
30th December 1900
[ALS: HRC]

The following letter evinces Shaw's wide reading and his familiarity with more than one version of The Book of a Thousand Nights and a Night.

... The lady of this cottage has lent me an extraordinarily delightful set of eastern stories – a sort of exquisite Arabian Nights – entitled 'A Digit of the Moon,' translated with the frankness of Payne and without the robustious brutality of Burton, by F.W. Bain. Publisher James Parker & Co, 6 Southampton St, Strand, & 37 Broad St, Oxford, 1899. Now Bain in his preface says that this little cycle of stories is only part of a much bigger work. If so, somebody ought to get him at once to translate the whole & put it on the market as the biggest thing of the kind since the Arabian Nights. I haven't [*sic*] a copy of A Digit of the Moon, as it was only lent to me by special favor & taken away in cotton wool when I had finished it; but I daresay it is accessible at the Museum.

yrs ever
G. Bernard Shaw

The Shaws used **Piccard's Cottage**, in Surrey, as a country retreat periodically from mid-November 1900 to mid-April 1902. A bowdlerized version of the ***Arabian Nights*** (minus 'immoral' content) was published in 1838–40 by Edward William Lane. Poet John **Payne** (1842–1916) translated the tales in 1882–4 and explorer Sir Richard Francis **Burton** (1821–90) in 1885–8. For ***A Digit of the Moon*** (1898), British fantasy writer Francis William **Bain** (1863–1940) claimed to have translated them from Sanskrit (although it is believed he wrote them himself). Shaw refers to the British **Museum**.

54 / To Grant Richards   Piccard's Cottage, St Catherine's, Guildford
23rd January 1901
[ALS: HRC]

In the next three letters, Shaw expresses displeasure with the publication process of an acting edition of The Devil's Disciple *and of a new edition of* Cashel Byron's Profession *that would include its blank verse dramatization (*The Admirable Bashville*) and 'A Note on Modern Prizefighting.' 'There is enough stuff now,' Shaw wrote to Richards on 1 March, 'to excuse the monstrous price of 6/– for a book which has been on the market for years at a shilling' (ALS: HRC).*

Dear G.R.

The covers are most filthy and damnable & wont do at all.

1. The size is wrong. Let nothing tempt you to alter the size of the page. Not only is that long shape ugly in itself; but it wont go into the pocket as an acting edition must; and it takes up too much room on bookstalls & counters.

2. The paper is most loathsome; but all that is necessary is to turn it inside out and it will do well enough, except that the title must be printed on it in blue, not in black. Still, these blues have a sugarpapery look, and if you could get green on green as in the enclosed scrap, it would be better & more in touch with the 6/– volumes.

3. As to the arrangement of the title, I send you a rough sketch of what I would suggest. Send me more proofs; it is worth taking a little trouble to get this to look classy.

4. It is quite sufficient to put the title along the back edge without adding 'a comedy' & introducing a second size of type.

5. Make it a rule of your house once [and] for all that the printer is to use no rules. They are *always* ugly.

   'Cashel Byron'

Tell Clark that he has totally ruined the plays by leaving far too much margin at the top of the page & also down the middle. The whole edition ought to be cancelled & reprinted. He has done the same in Cashel Byron. I have marked roughly where the letterpress ought to come. This will enable him to make the page a line or two longer & the line an m wider if the blank verse version at the end & the introduction will make the book too fat. The blank-version by the way is far more amusing than the prose original; and it will make the edition unique.

Let me see proof of any advertisements concerning me that you put on the cover. The Manifesto, Cashel Byron, *everything* should be included!

yrs ever

G. Bernard Shaw

Rules are decorative lines used to separate or organize a page. An **m** (em) is the width of a typeface's widest letter (capital M).

55 / To J.E. Lyons   Piccard's Cottage, Guildford
                                                    [undated: ca. 4th May 1901]

[ALS: NYPL; CL 2]

J.E. Lyons was Grant Richards's manager. On 9 April, while the Shaws were touring France for a month, R. & R. Clark had printed the separate edition of The Devil's Disciple.

Dear Mr Lyons

I return the copy of D's D. You will see on examining it that it has been made up with utter carelessness. The cutting off of the imprint at the foot of the 4th page of the cover is only part of the neglect of the proper margins all through. On the front page of the cover there is a margin of ¾" at the top and ¼" at the bottom instead of vice versa. A printer capable of doing that should be boiled down into tallow forthwith & sold for what he will fetch. The inside is not quite so bad; but still the top margins are far too wide & the bottom ones too narrow; and some of the sheets have not even been folded or printed straight. Look at signature D, p 37, for instance. The letterpress slopes to the left like a shower of rain. These little things make all the difference between a respectable John Murray looking volume and a 'book of the words' at a charity concert; and it costs no more to have them right than wrong. All that is necessary is to call the printer names: when he learns that you know the difference and care about it, he will do his duty and dump his slovenliness on to somebody who knows no better. Kindly transmit to him the author's curse, with my compliments.

yrs
G. Bernard Shaw

For publishers **John Murray** (founded 1768), see Letter 64. A **signature** is 'a printed sheet ... folded to form a group of pages' (*Concise Oxford Dictionary*). Presumably, **a 'book of the words'** would be distributed to members of the audience to allow them to sing along during a concert.

56 / To Grant Richards   10 Adelphi Terrace WC2
                                                    21st May 1901

[ALS: HRC]

A new copyright bill had been passed in 1900, although the most important one would be the Copyright Act of 1911 (effective 1 July 1912) because it revised and repealed most earlier acts. Shaw had excerpts printed on a 'stereotyped' postcard entitled 'THE COPYRIGHT ACT, 1911' (see Laurence 2, 848 and Introduction).

Dear Grant Richards

There is a fatal omission in the eighteenpenny edition of The Devil's Disciple, just received. *Not a single copy must be let loose until this omission is remedied.* The book must contain the statement that all rights are reserved. I gave particular instructions about this, as the new copyright Bill contains a clause the effect of which will be that anybody can perform the play & refuse to pay fees if he can produce a copy without this notice in it. It should run 'This play has been publicly performed within the United Kingdom. It is entered at Stationers Hall and at the Library of Congress, U.S.A. All rights reserved.'

Further, there is no printer's name, an omission which subjects you to frightful legal penalties.

You should make it a stern standing rule of the house that *nothing* is to be issued without the printer's name, and that nothing but Tolstoy's propagandist works are to go out without 'All Rights Reserved.'

The advertisement on the back of the cover is printed too low down & cut through at the bottom. And the advertisement of Cashel Byron should have the 'and' on the second line deleted &, on the fifth line ' – *Unrewarded*, and a Note on Modern Prizefighting.' And it should be described as 'In the Press' as it cant come out now until next season. I gave instructions about all these things except the last; so dont blame

yrs

G. Bernard Shaw

From 1554 until 1924, British copyright was secured by registration with the **Stationers'** Company in London. Novelist and fellow vegetarian Count Leo **Tolstoy** (1828–1910) began corresponding with Shaw in 1908, following Shaw's gift of a copy of *Man and Superman. Constancy **Unrewarded*** was the subtitle of *The Admirable Bashville.* Richards published the third English edition of *Cashel Byron* the **next season** on 23 October 1901.

57 / To Grant Richards   10 Adelphi Terrace WC2

22nd October 1902

[ALS: Virginia; CL 2]

Dear G.R.

I rejoice in getting in a post ahead of you. Ha ha! Ha ha!

First, hand me over another pound and elevenpence. I have not had time to go carefully through the a/cs yet; but on the face of them they knock 25% off my royalty on the eighteenpenny books. The royalty agreed on was twopence, not three halfpence.

The general criticism of these a/cs is obvious: you dont advertize. I have never yet had my attention called to the existence of my own works except by a review. The sale is the old sale to my disciples: I could almost name all the purchasers. I have never seen an advertisement, never met any human being who had ever seen one, never expect to meet one. Cashel Byron is a dead failure in consequence, because all the disciples have cherished it for years; and there has been nothing to tell them that the new edition adds anything to the old. But for the pleasure of talking to you occasionally I might as well publish with Simpkin. You dont even put me in your own lists.

Observe, I dont complain. I am aware that when an author has got far enough to make a book of his secure against actual out-of-pocket loss, his only chance of getting it pushed up to the hilt is to exact an advance which the publisher can recover only by pushing as hard as he can. You are not really free to push without this pressure: you are forced to fight at the dangerous places, not at the safe ones. So dont understand me as reproaching you.

On the other hand dont you reproach me if I take my next book to Pinker and say, 'Get me what you can for that; and let me have no bother about it.' At present I dont know what I am worth in the literary market; and as I like bargaining more than a Jew does, I rather want to find that out.

Are you available for lunch one of these days?

yrs ever

G. Bernard Shaw

Shaw often abbreviates 'account' as a/c and 'accounts' as **a/cs**. Richards had countered Shaw's **you dont advertize** remonstrance in Letter 46. Shaw took his **next book** (*Man and Superman*) to successful literary agent James Brand **Pinker** (1863–1922); see Letter 60.

58 / To Grant Richards · 10 Adelphi Terrace WC2
7 November 1902

[TLS (c): UNC; CL 2 (e)]

CL 2 omits the second paragraph.

Dear G.R.

I wrote to Lyons at his request about the royalty. As the eighteenpence was supposed to be net, he naturally thought the royalty was at least fivepence. I regarded my consent to twopence as a Quixotic sacrifice.

The balance due on the account is so small that only a man in whom romance had obliterated every business instinct would propose to upset his book keeping by holding it over for a year. I have been holding over the entry in my own accounts. I want my books to show how much each book is worth a year to me; and all this is upset if anything is held over: in fact I shall pay the balance out of my own pocket if you dont send it to me.

I am at work revising the Superman. It will be a longish job. I seriously think I will, by way of experiment, simply sell it to whoever will give me the biggest advance. You will still have me on your list of authors, which is all you require, as you do not push the books past the point at which they replace their cost to you. *I* dont get the wages of a head clerk out of them; and I never will, and never can (such is the nature of business, though you dont understand it) unless I put the publisher in such a position that he will be ruined unless he makes the book a success. Now I dont want to ruin you, or keep you awake at nights; consequently, if I make a hard bargain I had much rather make it with somebody else, and be guiltless of the bread of your infants.

However, sufficient unto the day is the evil thereof. Send me that extra halfpenny; and let us put off the Superman until he is ready for birth. I may publish him myself on commission & do my own advertizing, especially if I can induce my wife to take charge of the details.

yrs ever
G. Bernard Shaw

The bread of your infants may allude to Lamentations 4:4, 'the young children ask bread, and no man breaketh it unto them' (KJV). **Sufficient unto the day is the evil thereof** is from Matthew 6:34.

59 / To Grant Richards Maybury Knoll, Woking
3rd January 1903

[ALS: HRC]

Until 25 April 1904, the Shaws rented a cottage in Woking (Surrey). The coastal town of Overstrand (Norfolk) was a playground for the very rich (known as the Village of Millionaires). In nearby Cromer, Shaw read Man and Superman *to Sidney and Beatrice Webb.*

Dear G.R.

Pinker is on the warpath: I have put the book into his hands experimentally.

I am rushing off to Overstrand (Overstrand Hotel, Norfolk) for a week's holiday & have only a moment's time to scrawl this note.

Since I saw you I went carefully through the accounts; and they were beyond all reason. Plays for Puritans has been a failure even in comparison with the very moderate standard fixed by Plays P & Unp. And yet no volume was ever so beparagraphed. It only needed that advertisement that I urged upon you often – the names of the three plays under the general title – to reap the harvest of all those paragraphs and performances. The Mrs. Warren preface was even worse: it fell so flat into the void of your silence that even the members of the Stage Society have no idea that it exists. Do you seriously ask me to go on with this sort of thing? If you advanced me £10,000, it would be just the same; except that I should ruin you instead of merely amusing you, as at present.

I must rush for my train – Methuen, I hear, is negotiating with Pinker; but nothing is settled.

yrs ever
G. Bernard Shaw

See Letter 60 to literary agent J.B. **Pinker**. As *Three Plays for Puritans* had 'sold slowly [**a failure**] there were several binding orders, resulting in a number of variants' (Laurence 1, 47). To **paragraph** is to write a brief notice or announcement. Shaw's new **preface** for the first separate impression of *Mrs Warren's Profession* (published by Richards in 1902) included the cast (and twelve photographs) of the **Stage Society** production of 5–6 January 1902.

60 / To James Brand Pinker   [no address
undated: ca. February 1903]

[ADU: Bucknell]

On 18 December 1902, Pinker wrote Shaw telling him that Methuen & Co. were interested in Man and Superman. *Shaw informed Pinker on 2 February 1903: 'as I am always in a hurry to get a book into type so as to run as little risk of possible of losing it through the loss or destruction of the MS, I shall not wait long for the publishers to make up their minds ... Failing any offers I shall take the matter into my own hands and publish on commission' (CL 2, 307).*

Dear Mr Pinker

Bless you: all those unreasonable conditions were merely to save your time. What a publisher is afraid of is a civil action for libel brought by an individual. In my books this practically does not arise: *my* libels are blasphemous libels, seditious libels & obscene libels, which could only become the subject of criminal prosecutions. Against these an author cannot indemnify a publisher or printer any more than he can indemnify them for a murder committed jointly by the three. Even in civil actions, how can an author indemnify a publisher legally? People put these silly clauses into agreements because they have no idea of law. Suppose, for example, I made an agreement with Methuen to pay any costs or damages he might incur for libeling you! You would simply put us both into Holloway for conspiracy. My statement that if a man, whether author, publisher, or printer, chooses to utter a libel he must take the consequences, is simply the law (and a very good law too); so you need never fear that any serious negotiation will break down over that point.

Next, as to the refusal to shew the MS *beforehand* (of course he can read it as much as he likes before he sends it on to the printer) that is the only way in which I can guard myself against having any time wasted by mere politeness. No publisher or editor ever refuses anything of mine straight out. If he means business he makes an offer, and far from wanting to send the MS, nothing will persuade him to take that trouble: he always comes to me in a state of enthusiasm about the book when it has been out about six months, & confesses that he has just been reading it for the first time. But when he doesnt mean business, he says that he will be most happy to consider any MS which I may send him for perusal. It is perfectly understood that this is a polite refusal, unless he happens not to know anything about me, in which case, of course, I should not think of dealing with him, as he would not give me my terms.

Thus my apparently outrageous conditions are really a series of rough tests – the outcome of my practical experience – by which I can at once pick out the men who know my work and are really keen on getting it. There is nothing so annoying as to delay real business & waste time & correspondence on publishers who are either merely exchanging literary civilities, or else keeping themselves open for picking up something cheap on the chance of the author being a duffer in business. Of course a publisher should read before actually publishing, as he is legally responsible; but what publisher ever does with a known author? No agreement can bind him to go on if he finds that publication would expose him to civil or criminal proceedings; and this is why I like to be on pretty sure ground, because a publisher undoubtedly could at the last moment repudiate a contract with me on the ground that my books are not orthodox.

When you really find your man, there will be no trouble. He will not want to have my MS 'on sale or return'; and he will not dream of expecting me to sign the sort of printed agreement that is kept in stock for those unfortunate scribes who are really nothing but outdoor employees of the publisher. He will bargain over the royalty, the advance, and the size of the edition or the term of years, and over nothing else. As for me, you would be astonished to find how reasonable and considerate I can suddenly become when real business begins. I am really not such a fool as I look.

In short, you may regard my conditions as a sort of sieve which will let all the lukewarm or hostile publishers through at the first shake. I believe that if you applied them systematically in the case of all known authors, they would save you hours of intervening & sheaves of correspondence every year.

Nothing is yet concluded with Longmans, either for England or America; so the field is still open. Only, I dare not delay the printing any longer. However, that could no doubt be arranged in case of any fresh developments.

yrs faithfully
[G. Bernard Shaw]

Sir Algernon **Methuen** (1856–1924) founded Methuen & Co. Ltd (1889–1972). **Holloway** Prison (opened 1852), briefly home to Oscar Wilde in April 1895, became female-only in 1903; it was rebuilt (1970–85) and is still in use. For more on **libels**, see Letters 117 and 128.

61 / To Methuen & Co.   [10 Adelphi Terrace WC2
undated: ca. 17th February 1903]

[ADU: BL; CL 2]

When Shaw informed Pinker that he was proceeding on his own with Methuen, Pinker replied (on 16 February): 'I am sorry that I should have shattered your faith in literary agents, but of course it is quite possible for you to do things which could not be done by a literary agent, who has to treat these things seriously' (CL 2, 309). To the daunting list of conditions below, Methuen replied on 23 February that they did 'not feel disposed to make an agreement on the terms which you suggest. We hope that you will believe that we perfectly appreciate the brilliant reputation which you have achieved, but in carrying on our business we always endeavour to avoid any occasion for friction and controversy and we feel pretty sure that we should never, as author and publisher, see with the same eyes' (TLS: HRC).

Dear Sirs

Some time ago, being very hard pressed for time, I asked Mr James Pinker to undertake the negotiations for the publication of a book which is at present ready for press. Mr Pinker informed me that you were willing to consider the matter; but he now tells me that you decline on the ground that my terms are unreasonable, an opinion in which he concurs.

As I have never had any difficulty of the kind before – perhaps because I never employed an agent before – it seems possible that there may be some misunderstanding. I should therefore like, before I dismiss the matter as finally closed, to put before you exactly what I would like a publisher to do for me.

In the first place, you will want to know why I am changing publishers. I am doing so solely because I am not satisfied that my present publisher is getting as much as can be got out of my books. Strictly speaking, he does not sell any copies at all; he is content with the number of copies which the public buy spontaneously on the appearance of the reviews – say from 1500 to 2000 copies. This sees him through without any expenditure (the printer no doubt advancing the printing); and under these circumstances he naturally concentrates his advertising powers on the books which will not sell at all without pushing, and leaves mine unaided. I believe that a sale of at least 5000 copies could be obtained by ordinarily energetic handling; and accordingly I want to find a publisher who will advance me £250, not because I am in need of ready money, but because I do not know how else to give my books a fair chance in competition with those which force the publishers to nurse them carefully. I am aware that 5000 copies would not be a large circulation for a popular novel; but I am assuming that you, like all leading publishers, are willing to deal to a certain extent with work of the higher literary class which appeals to a comparatively select circle of readers; and I am also assuming that you recognize me as an author of established reputation for the production of work of that class. Otherwise it would be absurd to touch my books at all.

The terms which I am accustomed to ask & to receive in London are a royalty of 20%, 13 copies being reckoned as 13 & not as 12. The ordinary covenants about remainders are unnecessary, because there never are any remainders. My books do not die after the first demand drops: they dribble away slowly but steadily. I expect the publisher to bear the entire cost of printing. I am willing to correct the printer's errors & to put in as much work on the proofsheets as may be needed to make the book as good as I know how to make it. I always send in a practically finished – and highly finished – typewritten MS (the present book [will] be printed from a *third* typed fair copy of my actual draft); so you need not fear a Balzac or Carlyle bill for corrections. Further, as I occasionally contest elections, any contract that I make must contain a 'fair wages' clause. This does not in practice lead to any difficulty, as it is unfortunately rather a political formula for the defence of parliamentary authors against hostile electioneering agents than an effective restriction. It would debar you from employing some three or four houses which you can quite easily do without, and a number of small printing shops to which you would never dream of resorting. Probably, however, you are familiar with 'fair wages' clauses by this time. To the political author they are an absolute necessity: seats have been lost by the imprint on a poster; and I myself was much inconvenienced many years ago by the fact that my first book was printed by Hazell Watson & Viney at a time when they were a 'closed house' to the London Compositors (they are no longer so).

My license to publish (I never assign copyright or stageright) is for the United Kingdom & the Colonies only, and should, after the expiration of 5 years, be terminable at any time on six months notice. But simultaneous publication in America is indispensable. The book must be copyrighted in America, because it contains a play with valuable stage rights; consequently the common plan of exporting copies is out of the question.

These are practically all the conditions I have to make. There is really nothing in them except the question of terms: nothing ever arises on them. No doubt they are not the conditions you make with everybody; but I am not everybody and you are not everybody: if I were everybody, you would not deal with me at all, and if you were everybody, I should not publish with you. At all events I should be glad to have your decision direct from yourself, if you will oblige me so far, as Mr Pinker probably never heard of a fair wages clause in his life, and is too much shocked by it to conduct my business with his usual self possession.

yrs faithfully
[G. Bernard Shaw]

Shaw's **present publisher** was Grant Richards. Printers and bookbinders **Hazell Watson & Viney** Ltd were located in Aylesbury, Buckinghamshire.

62 / To Grant Richards   [Maybury Knoll, Woking]
30th March 1903

[ALS: HRC]

Shaw wrote to Pinker on 5 March that Methuen 'simply wanted more than I was prepared to give him. I proposed no condition that is not to be found in thousands of contracts today' (CL 2, 314–15). Shaw sent Man and Superman *to Clark on 23 March with instructions to print it at his own expense (CL 2, 314).*

Dear G.R.

What will you sell me the plates of those three volumes of plays for? I am not in a hurry for an answer; but I think I will presently see whether I cannot do something with a cheap edition. I have made a contract with Clark for printing the new book; and if I make a good thing of it on the commission plan with Longmans or somebody (or perhaps the local stationer at Woking) I shall go into the business regularly & work all my books that way, making one sell the other.

I have been a good deal bothered by this publishing business. I thought for some time of sticking to the old system & going to the man who would make me the largest advance; so that he would be ruined if he didnt advertize. It occurred to me that I could probably extort as much from you as from anybody else; but somehow I feel scruples about robbing your children. Finally I decided that if I changed at all, I had better change the system & really get some experience. Clark's estimate leads me to believe that for an author with my particular sort of circulation, commission is the best plan: besides, I can then play what tricks I like with the books without having sense of trifling with your career. If I make anything out of it I will tell you how it's done.

For the moment, however, I only want to suggest that at some convenient point in the future you should transfer the books completely to me. I think the agreement about Puritans was that you were to have an edition of 2,000; and that agreement was probably modelled on the first one, of which you only signed the draft or something unbusinesslike of that sort.

yrs ever
G. Bernard Shaw

Richards had published *Three Plays for Puritans* on 15 January 1901 at **2,000** copies.

63 / To Grant Richards

Maybury Knoll, Woking
4th April 1903

[ALS (tr): HRC]

Unwilling to offer Richards his 'new book,' Man and Superman, *Shaw proceeds to lecture him on the consequences of his lackadaisical business practices.*

Dear G.R.

Your letter is conclusive. You have ceased to give your mind to new books by new authors. In the days before you had found your line, you thought a little about Plays, Pleasant & Unpleasant, as a new book that you were interested in, and as part of the new & momentous venture in Henrietta St. But when Puritans came, you never gave a moment of your real business attention to it. And you would treat my new book exactly as you treated Puritans & Cashel Byron & Mrs. Warren.

Please remind yourself here that I am not reproaching you. You were quite right: new books are not your line. You did not know that at first: you were a beginner with everything to find out about yourself; and it seemed first rate to be the publisher of Grant Allen, Bernard Shaw &c &c. But now the experiment has been completed. What is the result? I'll tell you.

There are two sorts of publishers. There are the publishers who produce & publish new books, from Murray & Smith & Elder to Hutchinson & Digby Long. And there are the publishers who keep the rising generations supplied with new editions of standard non-copyright works, from Routledge to Dent. Now it is my opinion that your line is Dent's. You admit that you can make nothing out of new books: you doubt whether anybody does. You probably care as much to get my new book as to get any other new book in the market; yet you have never been able to care for it enough to make me an offer for it. You have let it stand at this: that if I choose to drop it into your letterbox as I dropped Puritans you will do with it what you did with that. Even now, when you see that commission is inevitable since I have actually concluded my bargain with the printer, you cannot rouse yourself to make me an offer. You make a sentimental remark about your uncle, and suggest vaguely that I might as well publish on commission with you as with anyone else. That, of course, is not true; for you must cram all your selling power – that is, your travelling – on to stationers who sell the Unit Library & the Temple Shakespeare, and who have never seen a six shilling book in their lives. You are in earnest about selling those reprints; and therefore you sell them. You are not in earnest about me: you only want me for ceremony. Come: face the situation; and then advise me, if you dare, to give this book to you instead of to, say, Longmans. Follow up your line & dont fool over the other line. I am delighted that you are going strong in it, and that my books helped you over the experimental period. But if you havnt noticed what the experiment has proved, I have; and accordingly off I go to Longmans. Probably I shall eventually transfer the whole lot to him; for I notice that

74

you make no proposal as to cheap editions: probably you havnt taken in my letter. Decidedly – not your line. Forgive me.

G.B.S.

Richards's offices were at 9 **Henrietta St.**, in Covent Garden, until 1902. Shaw submitted *The Irrational Knot* to **Smith, Elder** & Co. in 1881. **Hutchinson** & Co. Ltd (1887–1985) and **Digby, Long** & Co. were London publishers. George **Routledge** (1812–88) and Sons Ltd (founded 1843) achieved immense success with its series of Railway Library shilling volumes. J.M. **Dent** (see Letter 110) published the **Temple** Library, which included a pocket edition of **Shakespeare**'s works in forty volumes. Publishing houses often made use of **travelling** sales-people. Rather than **Longman**, Shaw decided upon Constable & Co. (founded 1890), which Frederick H. Evans had suggested in response to Shaw's 6 May query about finding a publisher for *Man and Superman* (CL 2, 321–2).

64 / To John Murray 10 Adelphi Terrace WC2
2nd June 1903

[ALS: NLS]

Shaw had written to Murray on 22 May to sound him out about publishing Man and Superman (now printed), concluding with 'I wish to change my present publishing arrangements because the business of my present publisher is, in my opinion, gradually developing off my lines. The separation is quite a friendly one' (ALS: NLS).

Dear Sir

Thank you for your letter of the 22nd of May. Since then I have been waiting for a set of corrected proofs from the printer.

I was not so unreasonable as to expect you to publish a book without reading it – though I must say that my usual grievance is that the publisher will *not* read my MS, and comes to me six months after publication full of the unexpected news that the book, which he has just looked at for the first time, is quite interesting. But my position is rather a difficult one. No publisher or editor will tell me flatly that he wont publish anything of mine (because of his Church connexion, or Nonconformist connexion, or whatever it may be): he says he will be happy to consider anything I send him. I always take this as a polite form of refusal. To save loss of time and misunderstanding I have to find out first whether the field is really open; and that was the object of my previous letter.

Will you now do me the favor to read the book *yourself?* A professional reader cannot help you in the matter, as the mere question of literary presentability has been settled long ago in my case. You do not, I presume, want to pay somebody to tell you that I am a 'paradoxical & brilliant writer,' and all the rest of the clichés about me. But the *character* of the book is very considerably in question. It deals with the most controversial questions and with the most delicate subjects; and there are people who will forgive John Murray for Byron who wont forgive John Murray for this. Perhaps I am making too much of the affair: indeed, I hope I am. But I may not have carried off the dangerous passages quite so cleverly as I suppose; and I therefore, even at the risk of overdoing it, beg you not to touch the book on anybody else's recommendation, but to read it yourself.

I enclose sheets B to P inclusive. Sheet A, which I will send when it arrives (probably tomorrow or next day) consists of a long preface in the form of an epistle dedicatory to A.B. Walkley, who suggested the play to me – 'a Don Juan play' was what he proposed. He has read the dedication, and consents very willingly to its publication. Sheet P will contain a set of aphorisms in the manner of La Rochefoucauld. These will also follow presently. So the public cannot complain of scant measure for their money.

I am anxious to know your decision because I want to publish before parliament rises; and I want to find an American publisher. American publishers are very timid; and if I can send the book as accepted by John Murray for England, it will perhaps save me the trouble and expense of having the book printed in America at my own expense & formally published in time to save the copyright.

yours faithfully

G. Bernard Shaw

Shaw uses **Nonconformist** here to mean an advocate of religious freedom. The ancestor of Sir John **Murray** (1851–1928), publisher to Queen Victoria, was John Murray (1745–93). Following the death of George Gordon, Lord **Byron** (1788–1824), on 19 April 1824, Murray and five of Byron's friends and executors burned the two volumes of the poet's manuscript memoirs in Murray's office fireplace on 17 May. The sardonic aphorisms of François, duc de **La Rochefoucauld** (1613–80) were published as *Réflexions ou Sentences et Maximes morales* (1665).

76

65 / To G. Bernard Shaw   50 Albermarle Street W
9 June 1903

[ALS: HRC; CL 2 (e)]

John Murray read Man and Superman *in short order and sent Shaw the following rejection letter.*

My dear Sir

I have put aside other work in order to read your 'Man and Superman.' I have been much interested and in parts amused by it – but I will not weary you with any comments on the literary side of it, which, as you very properly remark are superfluous in your case, and in other respects would be of little value.

You have appealed to me for a personal opinion on the question of publication, and this I will give – valeat quantum – always assuming that you wish me to deal with you so frankly as you have dealt with me.

The book consists of more or less connected parts: the Introductory letter – the Play – the Revolutionists Handbook – & the apophthegms.

It is perhaps going beyond the limits which I have laid down above to say that the Introductory letter is somewhat long & laboured, and loses effect in consequence – but this is the opinion forced upon me.

From the publishers point of view the question is, as you have plainly said, whether he would care to give his imprint to such a book. To this question I am afraid that I, personally can only answer 'no' –

The object of the book is to cast ridicule upon – or perhaps I should say to assail – marriage and other social & religious institutions.

Now however much a man may disapprove of these institutions it seems to me that respect for the very deep seated feelings which hundreds of thousands of educated people entertain in regard to them should induce him to make the attack in a somewhat reverent form: setting forth the arguments on both sides and stating clearly what is to be the substitute & how it is to be attained.

In such cases as these, I venture to think that the argument from ridicule will not touch the thoughtful and tends to do more harm than good among the thoughtless.

I daresay you will say that I am old fashioned & conventional. I am fully prepared to accept the description. However imperfectly I may express my meaning I write from a very sincere conviction for which I am sure you will make all proper allowance.

At least I am equally sincere in again thanking you for having consulted me in this matter, & remain my dear Sir

Yours faithfully

John Murray

Valeat quantum valere potest: 'Let it pass for what it is worth' (Latin). *Man and Superman* opens with a **long & laboured** 12,000-word **Introductory letter** ('Epistle Dedicatory') to A.B. Walkley and closes with 'Maxims for Revolutionists,' a series of **apophthegms**.

66 / To John Murray

10 Adelphi Terrace WC2
10th June 1903

[ALS: NLS]

Dear Sir

I am greatly obliged to you for reading 'Man & Superman' so promptly, and for the memorandum of errors. Also – and this more deeply – for your friendly treatment of me.

I am sorry, being an incorrigible preacher, that the book has no message for you. I assure you there is in it what is to me a perfectly serious religion, a perfectly practicable and urgently needed policy, a view of heaven and hell that is quite real, and a criticism of life that drives most modern men either to what I have depicted as hell, or to the pessimism of Ecclesiastes. *I* propose a tertium quid.

You say I should punch an Archbishop's head reverently because hundreds of thousands of educated people regard him with awe. But if I am to take their point of view, why punch his head at all? Of course I *could* do it reverently. Since my opinion of marriage is that of the apostles, I could express it in the words of St Paul instead of making Don Juan call it 'the most licentious of human institutions.' I could, without rousing the slightest suspicion of Nietzschianism, convey my opinion of morality by the unexceptionable remark that righteousness is filthy rags. I am, like you, an old fashioned and conventional man, confronted by a mass of stupidity, ignorance, want of social conscience, rationalism, materialism, and lascivious aestheticism. Nothing easier then for me to save unpleasantness (since I have an 'independent' income) by saying my creed in the old fashioned phrases which nobody now understands. But I am afraid you would object just as strongly to a string of platitudes as to a string of blasphemies. And my business is to shock people into thinking, not to soothe them into apathy. I am an assayer of people's beliefs; and I have to do it with hydrochloric acid, not with sugar and water. Do you remember what Newman said when they told him that he should try to be controversial without being offensive. 'I have tried it,' he said, 'and nobody listened to me.' Profiting by his experience, I have never tried it, and dont intend to. As to ridicule, I value it above most social solvents. The world has not been particularly reverent to my convictions; and I am extremely obliged to it, as it has refined them considerably by that process.

You must read Man & Superman again in ten years time. It proposes as well as exposes. Again, sincere thanks.

yours faithfully
G. Bernard Shaw

'Vanity of vanities; all is vanity' (KJV) is the most frequently cited example of **the pessimism of** the Book of **Ecclesiastes** (1:2). **Tertium quid**: 'third thing' (Latin). **St Paul's opinion of marriage** (in 1 Corinthians 7:9) is 'But if they [the unmarried and widows] cannot contain, let them marry: for it is better to marry than to burn' (KJV). **Nietzschianism** (more accurately, Nietzscheanism), from the ideology of Friedrich Nietzsche (1844–1900). In 1906 Shaw dispelled the misconception that 'on the strength of the single word Superman (Übermensch) borrowed by me from Nietzsche, ... I look for the salvation of society to the despotism of a single Napoleonic Superman' (Preface to *Major Barbara*, CP 3, 20–21). The **controversial** John Henry Cardinal **Newman** (1801–90) was an Anglican convert to Catholicism (1847) and author of *Apologia pro Vita Sua* (1864).

67 / To Macmillan & Co.

10 Adelphi Terrace WC2
19th June 1903

[ALS: NYPL; CL 2]

Dear Sirs

Thank you for your cable message just received. I presume you have received the proof sheets of my book 'Man & Superman' from Messrs Harper. I am sorry I have had to hurry my proposal by cabling; but I am in a difficulty with the book owing to the fact that the best time for me to publish in London is July, before the rising of parliament for the August recess; and I must either lose that season or else get my book printed at once in the United States for simultaneous (formal) publication there. In consequence of a certain exchange of courtesies between myself and Messrs Harper some time ago, I felt bound to offer them the refusal of the book; but I knew that it was not at all the sort of thing they wanted; and I asked them to cable their anticipated refusal, which they did yesterday. Mr. Thring, the secretary of the Authors' Society here, recommended me strongly to submit the book to you; and as your very enterprising & catholic activity had already disposed me to meet this recommendation more than half way, I cabled you forthwith.

My books have hitherto been published in America by Messrs Stone of Chicago, except the novels issued by Brentano, which are unauthorized non-copyright editions of which I know nothing except that I sometimes buy copies from a London firm which smuggles them extensively. I have not quarreled with Messrs Stone; but I do not intend to publish with them again, because they seem to me to be content to sell enough copies to see them through – which can always be done with my books without advertisement – and leave the matter there. I may be wrong in this; but at all events I shall try whether I am or not by changing.

Roughly, I think any book of mine ought to sell a thousand copies in America without much pressing, on the strength of the reviews and paragraphs, which I generally draw from the press in greater profusion than is at all personally convenient to me. Beyond that, it would be a matter of pushing; but I should probably never attain a large popular circulation. From the purely business side, I doubt if I am worth dealing with, as it seems to me that the necessary capital could always be invested in a book that would bring a larger return.

As to terms, I have given up the royalty system in England. I manufacture the book myself, and publish on commission. But I find that publishers prefer the royalty system; and in America I prefer it myself, as I cannot easily manufacture books at such a distance. I ask (and get) from America a royalty of 12½% on the nominal price for the first thousand copies, and 15% for the rest. In England I get 20%. The agreement, in the form of a license, not of an assignment, to be limited to a period of five years (or to be terminable thereafter at six months notice) or to an edition of a stated number of copies. This is important to me, as my books never die completely: a dribbling demand keeps on continually even when the novelty is worn off & the advertising dropped. My earliest books still sell a little.

The English edition will be published by Archibald Constable & Co.

yours faithfully

G. Bernard Shaw

P.S. Should you decide not to publish the book, will you be so good as to keep it until I cable a request as to its disposal; so as to save the great delay of two journeys across the Atlantic. Will you also let me have a yes or no cable message as to your decision.

George Herbert **Thring** (1859–1941) was secretary of the Society of Authors 1892–1930. The **unauthorized novels issued by Brentano** were *Cashel Byron's Profession* (1899) and *An Unsocial Socialist* (1900). Constable & Co. dropped the '**Archibald**' in 1910.

68 / Grant Richards

[Maybury Knoll, Woking]

21st June 1903

[TLS: HRC; CL 2]

Constable published Man and Superman *in August. There was no 'frantic competitive struggle' between the two British publishers: Richards went bankrupt in April 1905.*

Dear G.R.

... I have at last come to terms with your rival Constable; and I now look forward to a frantic competitive struggle between the two firms as to which can sell most copies. You really owe me some reparation for the perfectly damnable trouble and disturbance you have brought upon me in my old age, when I might have reasonably hoped my publishing arrangements were settled for life in the hands of a man likely to survive me by a quarter of a century. The new edition of The Perfect Wagnerite is excellent. When I went to The Ring cycle in May I had to fight my way through crowds of men offering other Wagner books for sale; but I only saw one Perfect Wagnerite in the stalls; and I afterwards found out it was my wife's.

Have you ever considered the question of a cheap edition of my works – something on India paper at 1/– or the like? – At worst it is a way of making the books advertize one another. I do not press for a reply, as the thing will probably be done by Dent or somebody else; but dont say, when you finally drive me to desperation, that I did not appeal to you repeatedly to think over the matter.

yrs ever
G. Bernard Shaw

Five hundred copies of a **new edition** of *The Perfect Wagnerite*, with a new preface and 'extensive and significant' revisions (Laurence 1, 38), had been printed in January 1902. Given the small print run, combined with Richards's inept advertising (see Letter 57), it is not surprising that Shaw, sixteen months later, would bemoan the book's absence at a performance of Wagner's **Ring cycle**, using the word '**excellent**' sarcastically.

69 / To Harper & Brothers 10 Adelphi Terrace WC2
10th July 1903

[ADU: HRC]

In rejecting Man and Superman *on 17 June, Harper & Brothers had written to Shaw that the book 'would not meet with a sale in this country sufficiently large to warrant as a business venture the expense of setting it up afresh and manufacturing an edition. We are inclined to think that the importation of copies of the English edition might be sufficient to satisfy the natural demand in this country'* (TLS: HRC).

Dear Sirs

I am much obliged to you for reading the book for me. The importation of the English edition is not an available resource for a dramatist, whose stage rights are usually enormously more valuable than his copyright. For example, out of one of the three plays in my last volume, of which only a thousand copies were sold in America in the first six months (this 1000 copies is practically certain with my books, as it represents what can be sold to my regular clientèle at a dollar & a half without advertisement) I received $12,500 in theatrical royalties from its first tour in the United States. Any expert could cut a popular comedy out of Man & Superman if its copyright (which carries stage right in America) were not secured.

I confess I am rather taken aback by your refusing to publish on the ground of financial risk. I see no reason to suppose that any other American publisher of your standing will have any higher opinion of my book commercially; so I shall settle the matter by getting it printed in America myself & registering to secure copyright. Then, if the book has any success in England, I can deal with the question of American publication at leisure, and without asking the American publisher to risk any capital in the enterprise.

yours faithfully
[G. Bernard Shaw]

70 / To George P. Brett   10 Adelphi Terrace WC2
                                                  10th July 1903

[TLS: NYPL; CL 2]

Macmillan's president George Platt Brett (1858–1936) had written to Shaw on 30 June that 'we almost never undertake the publication of any book on which a time limit is placed; and we could not make an exception for a book of this character, which we would expect to be longer in finding its public than if, for instance, it were a novel' (CL 2, 335–6).

Dear Sir

Your letter of the 30th June has just reached me.

It is a pity that we have not been able to conclude a perfectly straightforward piece of business, convenient for me, safe and profitable for you, and likely to lead to permanent relations between us unless you handled the book very badly indeed. But as long as you persist in treating me like a literary idiot whilst I treat you as an intelligent man of the world, nothing is likely to come of our negotiations. Anyhow, I have no time to prolong them; so I have settled the matter by sending the book to an American printer, who will set it up and effect normal publication and registration of copyright. I can then wait for the effect of the English publication and arrange for the American publication at my convenience at reasonable terms ...

yours faithfully
G. Bernard Shaw

71 / To George P. Brett   [Maybury Knoll, Woking]
                                                    13th July 1903

[ALS: NYPL; CL 2]

Shaw had cabled Brett, whose 3 July reply reiterated his earlier position on a time limit.

Dear Sir

Your letter of the 3rd July arrived yesterday. I shall send it to the Secretary of the Authors' Society here, as it was he who advised me to offer you the book. He may as well know your terms for his future guidance.

I am quite aware that authors, under pressure of money difficulties, often do very unthrifty things for the sake of an advance, and that publishers are not slow to take advantage of their impecuniosity. But I must confess that in a case where no advance is asked or offered, where the author is a man of established reputation and independent means, where there is practically neither a risk nor even a temporary advance of the cost of production involved (I am assuming that you can get a few months credit from your printer), and where the royalties are ordinary and reasonable, a demand that the author shall also bind himself to you for life for better for worse, takes away my breath. I shall always be interested in your success, because I am sufficient of an economist to watch with curiosity how far so spirited a commercial policy can go; but our relations must in future be purely friendly ones: my publishing will be done elsewhere.

Why on earth dont you put your cable address on your notepaper and invoices? Have you shares in one of the cable companies? Think of all the dollars you have cost me by this omission!

                                                    yours faithfully,
                                                    G. Bernard Shaw

72 / To Constable & Co.   10 Adelphi Terrace WC2
                                                    15th July 1903

[ALS: HRC; CL 2]

On 5 July Shaw had written to Otto Kyllmann (1860–1959), senior partner at Constable & Co., 'When it comes to hustling, the American is simply not in it. If I had time to explain their business to them, and allow them a fortnight to take in

84

the explanation, there would be no difficulty, as the idiots all want *the book; but I am forced to dash from one to another until I find one who is awake. I had it practically settled with the Macmillan Co; but their intelligence gave out on a minor point (for* them*) on Friday.' (CL 2, 335).*

Dear Sirs

After expending some two or three millions on cable messages, and convincing the American publishers that they could name their own terms because I was tied to time, I have at last cut the Gordian knot by printing the book myself in the United States. The University Press of Cambridge Mass. have just cabled to me that they are at work on Man & Superman, and that they will effect a formal publication for copyright purposes on the 25th instant: that is, on Saturday in next week. I have just sent a card to warn Clark. Will this suit you? All that is necessary, of course (in case the day is inconvenient) is formal publication, meaning exposure of a copy for sale, and entry at Stationers' Hall, a purely antiquarian custom which I keep up because it settles the date of publication for the benefit of the inheritor of the copyright and the enlightenment of future literary historians.

May I pass the title page for press? I have passed everything else. By the way, I wish you would change your name: it does not fit my page at all. An alteration of Archibald to Osbaldiston would just do it; and Archibald, though again at large, probably wouldnt mind. As it is, to avoid that horrible gap after the colon I have had to shorten the line by an em, and print Ltd at full length as Limited, omitting the commas, so as to close up the type. My title fits beautifully.

As to advertisements, the list you sent me might be enlarged. The Saturday Review is of more use to me than to other people because I was one of its bright particular stars for some years. And I am prepared to submit to blackmail from The Academy: it must live, poor thing! What about the Queen, the Lady's Pictorial, and the Free Lance? The Outlook & the Speaker probably dont count for ordinary business; but if their charges are at all modest, their reviews are (to me) worth the bribe of an ad. To whom do you propose to send review copies?

yrs faithfully
G. Bernard Shaw

P.S.   The main thing to advertize is 'new book by Bernard Shaw.'

For **The University Press of Cambridge Mass.**, see Letter 74. With the exception of *The Lady's Pictorial*, Shaw had published (or would publish) articles in the *Saturday Review*, *The Academy*, *The Queen*, *The Free Lance*, *The Outlook*, and *The Speaker*. Shaw was one of *The Saturday Review*'s **bright particular stars** from 1895 to 1898, when it published his dramatic criticisms, reprinted as *Dramatic Opinions and Essays* by Brentano's in 1906 (unauthorized) and 1907 (authorized), and by Constable in 1907. (Shaw quotes from Shakespeare's *All's Well That Ends Well*, 1.1: "'T were all one / That I should love a bright particular star, / And think to wed it.')

73 / To T. Fisher Unwin
10 Adelphi Terrace WC2
23rd July 1903

[ALS: NYPL; CL 2]

Novelist Sir Walter Besant (1836–1901) was founder and first president of the Society of Authors. Shaw joined in August 1897 and was a highly influential member, serving on its Dramatic Sub-Committee from 1906 until late 1915, 'when his wartime unpopularity after the publication of Common Sense About the War *[1914] led him to withdraw for the sake of amity within the Society. He continued to serve without formality until his death' (Exhibit, item 82). The issue of copyright was one of the Society's paramount concerns.*

Dear Fisher Unwin

I quite understand, of course, that you have no interest in the dealings of the American publishers. Lord forbid that you ever should; for they are shocking duffers.

It seems to me that the grievance involved by the absence of copyright, as it existed formerly between England & the U.S., and as it partly exists today, is the grievance against the American public for not sharing the expense of keeping the author alive. Besant's complaints were frankly anti-social: he said that with universal copyright a successful book would be 'a silver mine' for the author – that is, that the author should get paid over and over again for the same job, once for every country in which he has copyright. As soon as this is understood, copyrights will be shortened every time they are widened. Possibly also books will have to be registered in different classes with different terms of copyright; for it really is ridiculous to treat, say, Smith & Elder's Dictionary of National Biography, representing an enormous investment of capital, exactly as you treat a flashy novel representing a few pints of whisky and a couple of months of a third rate writer's time. In short, copyright is a public question, and not an author's question. Can anything be more absurd than to give fortytwo years monopoly of an obscene book to a literary blackguard and only fourteen years to the inventor of the steam engine?

My new book is on the verge of appearing: I am only waiting to secure simultaneous publication. Constable is publishing it. You will find an interesting article by me in the current number of The Author on the real want of the age, which is, not more publishers but more bookshops. I can sell 1800 copies of a new 6/– book without advertising; but when I want to improve on that, I am stopped in two ways, 1st, the publisher *wont* advertize because the 1800 copies have landed him safely, and 2nd, there are no shops where people can see & buy anything except five quires of notepaper for a shilling and a Bible, with a 6d reprint or so.

yrs faithfully
G. Bernard Shaw

Constable published Shaw's **new book**, *Man and Superman*, on 11 August 1903, but there was no American **simultaneous publication**: Brentano's published it only on 1 June 1904. In his **article** in the July issue of the Society's journal, *The Author*, entitled 'Book Distribution: Not More Light, but More Shops,' Shaw asserted that there was not one bookshop in the London borough of St Pancras (of which he was a councillor). When told that the London Directory listed sixteen, he countered that these were merely stationers who stocked 'Bibles and prayer-books, photographs, picture frames, purses, artists' colors, and fancy goods of all cognate kinds' (quoted in Bonham-Carter, *Authors by Profession*, 196). The sixty-three volumes of the **Dictionary of National Biography** – brainchild of publisher George Smith (1824–1901), of Smith, Elder & Co. – were issued between 1885 and 1900.

74 / To William Dana Orcutt   [Springburn, Strachur]
28th August 1903

[CL 2; PP: Orcutt]

The Shaws had begun a two-month visit to Scotland on 1 August. Book designer William Dana Orcutt (1870–1953), of the University Press in Cambridge, Massachusetts, was preparing an American copyright edition of Man and Superman *(which Constable had just published). Shaw had sent him a copy set by Clark, with instructions to duplicate the volume. Orcutt sent his attempt to Shaw, who returned it with the following 'treatise' on book design in which he outlines his aesthetic principles at length and pays homage to his mentor, William Morris.*

I send you by book post 'Man and Superman' with the necessary corrections. I have made no attempt to deal with the apostrophes you introduced in 'don't,' 'you've,' etc., etc. But my own usage was carefully considered; and the inconsistencies were only apparent. For instance, Ive, youve, lets, thats are quite unmistakable; but Ill, hell, shell for I'll, he'll, she'll, are impossible without a phonetic alphabet to distinguish between long and short e. In such cases I retained the apostrophe: in all others I discarded it.

Now you may ask me why I discarded it. Solely because it spoils the printing. If you print a Bible, you can make a handsome job of it, because there are no apostrophes and inverted commas to break up the letterpress with holes and dots. Until you force people to have some consideration for a book as something to look at as well as something to read, you will never get rid of these senseless disfigurements that have destroyed all the old sense of beauty in printing.

Whilst I am on this subject, let me beg you not to be offended if I tell you that whilst I am astonished at the way in which you have followed my proof sheets line by line, and grateful for the promptitude with which you have put the work through, the book, as you have produced it, is a perfectly shocking piece of printing – almost as bad as the work of the Roycroft Shop, which is the worst in the world. Dont be angry; just turn to p. 130. Look at the last ten lines. I have marked the blemishes. The enormous quads at the end of each sentence are bad enough; but when it comes to allowing two of these gaps to occur at the same point in two successive lines, it amounts to a misdemeanor. Now your compositor has actually put four of these gaps in a straight line down the page. Four! He ought to be boiled!

If you look at one of the books printed by William Morris, the greatest printer of the XIX century, and one of the greatest printers of all the centuries, you will see that he occasionally puts in a little leaf ornament, like this ❧❧❧, or something of the kind. Your Roycroft idiots, not understanding this, pepper such things all over their 'art' books, and generally manage to stick an extra large quad before each to show how little they understand about the business. Morris does not do this in his own books; he rewrites the sentence so as to make it justify without bringing a gap underneath another in the line above. But in printing other people's books, which he had no right to alter, he sometimes found it impossible to avoid this. Then, sooner than spoil the rich, even color of his block of letterpress by a big, white hole, he filled it up with a leaf.

Now that is 99% of the secret of good printing. Dont have patches of white or trickling rivers of it trailing down the page like raindrops on a window. At the top of p. 131, I have marked these rivers. Are they not horrible? *White* is the enemy of the printer. *Black*, rich fat, even, black, without grey patches, are, or should be, his pride. Leads and quads and displays of different kinds of type should be reserved for insurance prospectuses and advertisements of lost dogs.

If your type were genuine Caslon, like that of my Scotch printer, you might have followed him line for line without doing any worse than he has done. But your fount has narrower letters: eleven of them occupy the same space as ten of the Caslon; so that you have had to put 10% more white into every line than the Scotch printer; and that 10% is fatal. You should have saved 30 pages out of the Glasgow printer's 244. Of course he has not been able to live up to William Morris (in fact he thinks me stark mad); but then he had the disadvantage of having to suffer all the damage to his original setting made by my corrections.

Now for the minor points. Your margins are very far from being those of the Mazarin Bible. Your top margin is a full inch – *much* too wide (perhaps your man made the mistake of measuring it from the running title up instead of from the top line of the text) – and the lower only 1¼". The difference is only enough to make them look equal. Try ½" from the top margin, ignoring the title and pagination and measuring from the top line of the text, and the top and bottom margins will come about right. The inner margins are monstrous – ¾" each, making a Broadway of 1½" down the middle of the book, so that it looks like two tombstones side by side. The rule here is simple: the book, when open, should look as if there were no division at all

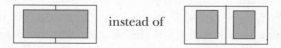

The best looking margin would be from ¼" to ⅜" – total Broadway ½" to ¾".

On the title page you have only used two different founts of type. For that I bless you, as most printers would have used at least sixteen. But why two when one would have been so much better? I send you my Glasgow title page, and invite you to note that there are no rivers in it (there is a Mississippi and a Missouri in yours), and that the measure of the publishers imprint has been contracted to avoid a big quad after the colon. See how nice and fat and black and solid it looks!

I am only too painfully aware that when all is said and done that can be done, a play, with its broken lines of dialogue, its mixture of roman and italic, and its spaced out words for emphasis, can never enable a printer to do full justice to himself. But something can be done. You can hardly imagine how atrocious you could make that play look by simply leading the page and putting large initial capitals to the names of the speakers. We can at least make the best of a bad job.

Tell the compositor that in spacing out letters for emphasizing the word, German fashion, he must be careful to make the space at the beginning and end of the word still wider than the spaces between the letters. It means more white, unhappily; but it cannot be helped.

That, I think, is all. Do not dismiss it as not being 'business': I assure you I have a book which Morris gave me – a single copy – by selling which I could cover the whole cost of setting up the 'Superman'; and its value is due *solely* to its having been manufactured in the way I advocate: there's absolutely no other secret about it; and there is no reason why you should not make yourself famous through all the ages by turning out editions of standard works on these lines whilst the Roycroft people are exhausting themselves in dirty felt end papers, sham Kelmscott capitals, leaf ornaments in quad sauce, and then wondering why nobody in Europe will pay twopence for a Roycroft book, whilst Kelmscott books and the Doves Press books of Morris's friends Walker and Cobden Sanderson fetch fancy prices before the ink is thoroughly dry.

By the way, the Roycroft people may have learnt a little since I last saw their work. They once reprinted something of mine, with literary improvements by Mr Elbert Hubbard. He sent me a copy; and I have seldom written a more candid letter than the one in which I acknowledged it. It ought to have taught him something; but I fear he is incorrigible.

After this, I shall have to get you to print all my future books, so please have this treatise printed in letters of gold and preserved for future reference.

[yours sincerely
G. Bernard Shaw]

90

A **quad** (or 'mutton,' 'mutton quad,' and 'em') is the width of a typeface's widest letter (capital M). The Shavianism **Broadway** presumably alludes to Manhattan's wide avenue. The **Doves Press** (1900–16) was founded by Emery **Walker and** bookbinder Thomas J. **Cobden-Sanderson** (1840–1922). Shaw's **Scotch printer** was R. & R. Clark. The **Mazarin Bible** (after Cardinal Jules Mazarin), better known as the Gutenberg Bible, was one of the earliest books printed from movable type. The **book which Morris gave** Shaw is most likely the magnificent Kelmscott edition of *The Works of Geoffrey Chaucer* (1896), with 87 illustrations by Edward Burne-Jones. Morris printed 425 copies at £20 each and 13 (on vellum) at 120 guineas (£126); 48 were specially bound in white pig's skin with silver clasps. (Shaw later inscribed his copy to sculptor Auguste Rodin, for whom he sat in April and May 1906.) Hubbard's **literary improvements** to the unauthorized **Roycroft Shop** edition of Shaw's 'On Going to Church' (1896) included taking 'numerous liberties with the work, to the extent of juggling or altering opening words of sentences to accommodate himself for the use of his ornate initial letters' (Laurence 1, 29). Shaw recalled his **candid letter** (not located) on 7 January 1900: 'My epistolary eloquence has seldom soared so high as it did in my reply to him' (CL 2, 130).

75 / To Otto Kyllmann [Springburn] Strachur, Argyllshire
9th September 1903

[ALS: HRC; CL 2]

Dear Kyllmann

The copyright of Man & Superman in the U.S. is now secured; & no importation of sheets can affect it in any way. But the book has been set up & printed & (technically) published in America; and the electros are flying here, duly insured, at my disposal; so that on coming to an arrangement with an American publisher, I can at once order an edition to be printed on the spot. The legal position, as I understand it, is that English copies are now contraband in the United States; and even if imported with consent of the holder of the copyright (myself) would be subject to the protective tariff, which would presumably be heavy enough to make it cheaper to manufacture in America.

My own intention, now that I have made myself master of the situation at a cost of about £70 cash, is simply to wait and let America wait. I gave the American publishers – at least a representative few of them – their chance; and they wasted my time, put me out of temper, compelled me to spend a lot of money rather than be cornered or else delay publication here, and finally landed me in perfect security as regards copyright, and in a thoroughly mulish and vindictive humor as regards publishing.

Mahomet having gone to the mountain in vain, the mountain may now come to Mahomet. My bargain will depend, of course, on the success of the book here. I am in no hurry; and if anybody wants to handle it on the royalty system, he will have to begin by buying my electros from me at a satisfactory profit. Of course, having the electros, I am open to a proposal to publish on commission; but on the whole I am disposed to wait. The book will lose nothing by keeping.

Do you see all the reviews of the book? I see you quoted Chesterton in one of the advertisements; but there was a review in the British Weekly that could be quoted far more effectively in the religious papers. I will give my mind to the whole business of advertising one of these days – when the rain has stopped long enough to allow me another holiday in addition to the three fine days we have had since I arrived here on 1st August.

yrs faithfully

G. Bernard Shaw

Copyright deposit for *Man and Superman* was made on 12 August 1903; Brentano's issued the book on 1 June 1904. **Electros** (electroplates or electrotypes) are printing plates formed by using electrolytic deposition of copper on a mould. The saying 'If the hill will not come to **Mahomet**, Mahomet will go to the hill' is found in 'Of Boldness,' one of the *Essays* (1625) of Francis Bacon (1561–1626). The review by Gilbert Keith **Chesterton** (1874–1936) appeared in the *Daily News* (22 August); the one in the **British Weekly** (3 September) described Shaw as 'that most modern and unfettered of thinkers' (CL 2, 367).

76 / To Grant Richards

10 Adelphi Terrace WC2
30th March 1904

[ALS: HRC; CL 2]

'Have you any royalties for me?' Shaw asked Richards on 13 March 1904 (ALS: HRC). Richards replied on the 14th promising statements and adding, 'I wish you would tell me what sort of sale you had for "Man and Superman"' (TLU: UNC), Constable's first Shaw book published seven months previously.

My Dear G.R.

Three Plays for Puritans appeared on the 15th of Jan 1901. Up to June 1901 you sold 1204. Net royalty to author £80.5.4.

Man & Superman appeared in August 1903. Up to 31 Dec. Constable sold 2707, three hundred more than double. Net profit to author £148.2.10 + 634 copies in hand completed for sale, on which I shall get about £111.

What is more important is that future editions will be printed from my plates; and then my takings per copy will considerably exceed a one & fourpenny royalty.

Consider also this frightful fact. In the 18 months ending 30 June 1902 – the latest account to hand – you had sold only 1421 Puritans all told. At the first issue, when the reviewing acted as an advertisement, you sold 1204. In the second 6 months (no advertisement) only 137. In the third 6 months, 80!

Mind: I dont blame you in the least for not advertising. It is absolutely inevitable in the struggle for life that you should bring all your ammunition to bear on your risks & leave your certainties to take care of themselves. But it would be perfectly silly in [*sic*] me to continue our arrangement for ever & ever. You are now an established institution; and my books are of no real consequence to you. You sometimes fancy they are; but that is an amiable delusion. If you had made me a serious offer for the Superman I should have taken it. You virtually shifted me to Constable, and changed my system; and it is now inevitable in the course of business that I should get all my books into my own hands & work the thing myself. I am growing old & avaricious & fond of handling capital instead of being nursed like the ordinary author-duffer. What about my accounts? I expect an ENORMOUS cheque.

yrs ever

G. Bernard Shaw

For Shaw's **shift to Constable** (with whom he established his **system** of commission publishing), see Letter 67.

77 / To Brentano's

10 Adelphi Terrace WC2

15th June 1904

[TLS: Cornell]

Brentano's, in its heyday one of the largest retail outlets for books in the world, was formed in 1853 (as Brentano's Literary Emporium) and declared bankrupt

in March 1933. Simon Brentano (1860–1915) was president 1877–1915, when
his brother Arthur (1858–1944) succeeded him. Simon's son Lowell (1895–1950)
was editorial director and first vice-president 1918–33. Brentano's had published
Man and Superman *on 1 June, while the Shaws were touring Italy (1 May–10*
June). *On 30 May, Shaw wrote to literary agent J.B. Pinker that he had 'closed*
with an offer from Brentano of 25% for five years' (CL 2, 420). In 1928 Shaw
had refused to sign an agreement because Brentano's had omitted to state the five-
year period (see Lowell Brentano to Shaw, 10 February 1929, TLS: HRC).

Dear Sirs

I have only just returned from a holiday in Rome. That is why I have neglected the business of the agreement so long.

I now enclose a draft agreement in ten clauses which will satisfy me
and which contains, I think, all you require. It explains itself; so I need
only mention that the date of payment mentioned in Clause 5 is imposed
on me by the Income Tax authorities. I have to make a statement of my
income every year in April.

If you approve of the draft, please have it faircopied on a single sheet
of paper; sign it in the presence of a witness; and send it to your agents
Messrs Stevens and Brown with instructions to them to exchange it with
me for a counterpart duly executed by me. It is better to leave the date to
be filled in by them, as I am allowed only fourteen days to get it stamped
here.

I send you the draft direct to save time. Messrs Stevens & Brown cannot approve or execute an agreement for you: they can only take care
that it is not delivered to me until I give you the counterpart. As Messrs
Stevens & Brown are not my agents, and will not collect my royalties, I do
not wish to give them any trouble that can be avoided.

Man & Superman looks better than I could have hoped; but nothing
can be done to make it a really well set up book. In fact I had actually ordered electros of the English edition to be sent out to you when I recollected that the dialogue of the American in the play had certain
peculiarities to represent the difference between English and American
pronunciation. These would have had no sense in America, where the
pronunciation I desired to indicate is normal; consequently I used the
customary spelling in the American edition, and so had to stick to the

Cambridge plates. What is wrong is that the printer imitated the English edition line for line, but instead of using a genuine Caslon type made from the same punches as the Edinburgh printers used, he used a very inferior imitation with a ten % narrower face. Handsomely set, this would have reduced the book by 25 pages; but he made a point of honor of following the Edinburgh copy line for line, and so had to make up those 25 superfluous pages by spacing, with horrible results. However, the public is not educated enough to complain: in fact it rather likes a streaky page, all leads and rivulets. A country which stands the Roycroft Printing Shop will stand anything.

I[n] future call me Bernard Shaw instead of G. Bernard Shaw. Twenty years ago I had to use three names to distinguish myself from other Shaws and Bernard Shaws; but now I have a practical monopoly, and I only use the G. in private.

I most violently object to having 'Author of An Unsocial Socialist and Cashel Byron's Profession' after my name on the title page. They are naturally your favorite works, because you have filled the American continent with unauthorized editions of them; but I am not particularly proud of them; and in any case I never use the formula. Besides, the italics and inverted commas utterly ruin the title page. You should never have two different sizes or styles of type on the same page when it can possibly be avoided. My English title page beats yours into fits.

I have also received your unauthorized resuscitation of my old Quintessence of Ibsenism. Next time you do it, tell the printer not to use leads, but to use a larger type and set solid, also to make his top margin much narrower, and contract the center margin somewhat. The proof reader has missed some errors – Lasselle for Lassalle on p. 16, Spinx for Sphinx on 55, desparately for desperately on 93, utmoct for utmost on 120, idealists for idealist on 130, revolutionist for revolutionists on 132, hyphen omitted on 135, Molièr for Molière on 153, munifcence for munificence on 155, and probably others which I have not glanced at. If you are stereotyping or moulding, better correct these. Some day I shall cut you out with an up-to-date edition. On page 100 you call my worthy friend Mr Benjamin Tucker 'the original publisher.' This is really too bad. The original publisher was Scott of Newcastle. Why not simply say 'Note by Mr Benjamin Tucker.'

By the way, you had better send review copies to Wilshire's Magazine, The Conservator (Horace Traubel) and Liberty (Benjamin Tucker). They are all crank papers; but my following is strong among cranks and their subscribers. I mean, of course, review copies of Man & Superman.

yours faithfully

G. Bernard Shaw

Shaw alludes to the **unauthorized** *Cashel Byron* (1899) and *An Unsocial Socialist* (1900). There was an October 1913 Brentano's edition of *The Quintessence of Ibsenism* (Laurence 1, 18), but no earlier **unauthorized resuscitation**. Shaw had published in *Wilshire's Magazine* (Toronto) as recently as November 1902. *The Conservator* (1890–1919) was edited by Walt Whitman disciple **Horace Traubel** (1858–1919); the anarchist periodical *Liberty* was published by **Benjamin** R. **Tucker** (1854–1939), a leading proponent of what he termed 'Anarchistic-Socialism.'

78 / To Brentano's

Ross shire – travelling
12th August 1904

[ALCS: Colgate]

The Shaws were visiting Scotland beginning in early August. Shaw began redrafting his publishers' contracts as early as 1885 (see Letter 7) and over the years helped many less business-minded authors with their agreements (see Introduction).

Dear Sirs

Your letter of the 1st Aug. has just reached me. There is no hurry about the agreement, as I shall not be in London until October.

I strongly advise you in future to sign any agreement I send you without incurring the expense of a legal opinion. Your attorney is bound to propose some alteration whether one is needed or not, just as a doctor is bound to prescribe for you when you call him in, whether you are ill or not. As he cannot alter my agreements for the better, he has to alter them for the worse in order to give you something for your money, which you might just as well have saved. All the changes you mention are pure imbecilities from your point of view, except the alteration of the figures, which has nothing to do with the law. As to the redrafting, I shall probably alter it all back again, as nothing in the world is quite so improbable as that your attorney can express himself better than I can. If he could, he wouldnt be an attorney, but an author. I fully expect to find

that he has muddled the whole thing; but it doesnt matter: our understanding will keep itself as long as it is of service to us.

yours faithfully

G. Bernard Shaw

79 / To Grant Richards   Old House, Harmer Green, Welwyn

18th December 1904

[TLS: HRC; CL 2]

*The 'private letter' mentioned below was written to Richards on 30 November and
included a request to see him 'in comparatively private life' (rather than at the
office) to obtain 'a little first hand information' (ALCS: HRC).*

Dear Grant Richards

Matters have now reached a point at which I must now take action. I have
lost and am daily losing considerable sums by your failure to keep the
market supplied with my plays, which are just now in special demand.
And my royalties are some years in arrear. I take it that as you have not
answered my private letter asking how you were situated, you prefer to
leave our affairs to the ordinary course of business.

You at present have the plates of the books you have published for
me. I must either get those plates into my hands at once, or else have
the volumes which are out of print set up again. Under our agreements
your license to print them is limited to 2500 copies; and there is a provi-
so that this license lapses if the books are not continuously on sale, or
the royalties not paid within a certain period. In short – since all the
conditions have been disregarded – you have practically no license to
print my books now at all. Therefore the plates are useless to you. To me
they would save time and expense in getting my books on the market
again. I therefore ask you at what price you would let me have them. If
the price is reasonable, it can be deducted, for the benefit of your other
creditors, from the royalties due to me; and I can wait for the balance
until after your affairs are sufficiently recovered to enable you to make
some settlement.

Failing an arrangement of this kind, I shall proceed to recover my royalties, and force a definite bankruptcy; for the present position (as I un-

derstand it) in which you are neither bankrupt nor solvent, and in which booksellers are complaining that they cannot obtain copies of my books to meet a special demand for them, is intolerable. A glance at my account will remind you that I have not been an unfriendly creditor; but as you gave me no notice of the meetings which have taken place, and have not responded to a friendly inquiry, I conclude that your affairs have reached a point at which you do not care what I do.

Unless I have a satisfactory reply in the course of next week I shall put the matter into my solicitor's hands, and instruct him to go ahead with all possible expedition and vigor.

I shall be in London for a part of Tuesday; but for the rest of the week I shall be here at Harmer's Green.

Yours faithfully
G. Bernard Shaw

The Shaws began leasing The **Old House, Harmer Green** on 2 July 1904.

80 / To Grant Richards

10 Adelphi Terrace WC2
31st December 1904

[ALS: HRC; CL 2]

Although Richards had twice written to Shaw during this period, his letters were delayed (see Letter 81). In any case, it was too late to remedy the damage done by Richards's inaction, and bankruptcy was imminent.

Dear Grant Richards

As I have had no reply from you to my last letter (though some infatuated person has sent me a circular meant for your trade creditors), I must join with your other author creditors on the 4th to have you adjudicated a bankrupt. I am quite unable to understand why you have let things come to this pass. Has the crisis paralyzed you? Our position as authors is absolutely desperate, not so much – in my case not at all – because of the arrears of royalty, but because our books are out of print and tied up, and your business in the hands of the trade creditors whose interests are quite different from ours. We must have somebody to deal with; and if you sit down and refuse to move or act or even answer a civil question – confound you! – we MUST substitute a trustee in bankruptcy.

I cant help thinking the situation might have been saved; for your business must be sound enough to go on; and it is the interest of *all* your creditors that it should go on. Yet you force us to wreck it by simply letting things slide. I conclude that on turning it over you have concluded that you had better ride for a fall than face the economics that would be needed to allow the shop to clear itself; and you may be right; but I wish I could feel sure that you have not simply lost your nerve. At least tell the Sheriff, with my compliments, that you have no power – nor can your trade creditors derive any – to sell any book of mine on any other terms than those specified in my license.

> yrs as ever
> G. Bernard Shaw

81 / To Grant Richards

The Old House, Harmer Green,
Welwyn, Herts.
6th January 1905

[ALS: HRC]

In the following letter Shaw tries to goad Richards into action, especially into approaching G.H. Thring, secretary of the Society of Authors, which Richards finally did (see Letter 83).

Dear Grant Richards

We have left Woking; so both your letters were delayed. But anyhow what could I have done? I held back until the last moment, and in fact did not hand over my agreements & accounts to the Authors Society until they demanded them from me to complete their case (which would have gone on just the same whether I was on their list of not) for the 4th. Unless you can square Thring, matters must take their course. As I explained to you, what has driven the authors into a corner is the fact, first, that they were not invited to the meeting of your creditors, and, second, that their books are tied up and they can get nobody to deal with owing to your unaccountable inaction. Take my own case! You say that your travellers are offering my books to the trade; but what the blanketywanketyblank is the use of that when the booksellers who have been clamoring for my plays all last month cannot get copies for love or money? The trade creditors do not care a rap about this, naturally enough: what they want is to keep things going with their receiver in, until they get as much as there is to be got from the sale of the stock in the ordinary course. But I know from what they are saying that they do not think, after the publicity that has now been given to your difficulties, that the situation can finally be saved. Only by the most energetic & persuasive action on your part – by talking to Thring, by talking to all the creditors, by studying the holes they are in & giving them relief from their more immediate dilemmas, by convincing them that you are still alive & advancing, by making the most of your illness of last spring & saying flatly that it completely disabled you & finished you for several months when trade required your fullest competence & most strenuous vigilance & activity, can you retrieve matters enough to get breathing space.

As for me, I must get out of your hands in any case. I have given up the royalty system definitely: it does not pay me nor suit me. My business has settled down definitely into one of the Ruskin or Spencer type. Henceforth I manufacture for myself & publish on commission. I repeat, the royalties can wait; but I must have the plates. And you do not say one word about this in your letter. Oh Grant Richards, Grant Richards, *what* a chap you are!

yrs ever

G. Bernard Shaw

For John **Ruskin** as self-publisher, see note to Letter 24. When Herbert **Spencer** (1820–1903) came into some money in 1853, he resigned as sub-editor for *The Economist* and began publishing his own work.

82 / To Grant Richards

The Old House, Harmer Green,

Welwyn, Herts.

15th January 1905

[ALS: HRC; CL 2]

Dear Grant Richards

Listen to me attentively if you can; for you are in the most deadly peril of spending irrecoverable years as an undischarged bankrupt through your poetic inaptitude for business.

You never proposed any agreement for Plays, Pleasant & Unpleasant. I drafted one, much against your will; and you wrote at the foot of it 'approved, Grant Richards.' That agreement has expired: it was for a period of 5 years from 1897.

I forced you, in your own interest, to execute an agreement for Three Plays for Puritans. Very likely you have lost your copy. Mine is in the hands of Thring or Field & Roscoe; but it does not matter, as it was for 2,500 copies only; and you have had that number printed; consequently it is only valid now as to the royalties due me.

For the other books we had no agreement, though I warned you repeatedly that the absence of an agreement left you defenceless. I did not press the matter because the Puritans agreement was there to shew the nature of our verbal understanding as to 'the usual terms.' You wrote me a letter as to the royalty on the separate plays.

You are therefore right when you say that I am at liberty to take the books away and stop you publishing them at any moment and to arrange with anybody else to publish them without reference to you or to the Receiver.

Unfortunately this liberty includes the liberty to pay for the setting up of the books all over again, and the ruinous expenditure of time in correcting the proofs, whilst all the time you are sitting calmly on a set of plates which are of no use to you, and which would save me all this. You are the proprietor of those bits of metal; and though you may not print copies of my books from them, you may mend your saucepans with them, or melt them down, or hammer them up, or sell them at the nearest marine stores for scrap iron. Clark holds them at present because he has a lien on them for what you owe him; but that gives him no power to print from them; and meanwhile my books, just now in brisk demand through the Court performances, are out of print.

I have explained this to you very carefully some 17,000,000,000,000,000 odd times, and offered to buy the plates at a reasonable advance on their value to anyone else except myself; and I cannot get the explanation into that solid head of yours. You betray no consciousness of having ever heard of my difficulty; and you shew not the faintest intention of helping me out of it. In desperation, therefore, I have had to take steps to transfer those plates from you to somebody whom I *can* deal with, however slowly and expensively and officially: namely, a trustee in bankruptcy.

And this, mind you, whilst it is my interest as well as yours that you should *not* be made a bankrupt, and that your business should be kept up as a going concern, either for disposal to a new firm, or even in your own hands. I am doing what I can to make Thring endeavor to release the other authors from messes similar to mine, and then to avert the bankruptcy by withdrawing the petition. But you persist in frustrating my efforts. The unanswerable reply of Thring is 'We must have someone with whom we can deal; and the only way of securing that in the face of Richards's airy apathy and the inertia of the Receiver, who cares for nothing but seizing what comes in from day to day for the mortgagee, is to force a bankruptcy.' Your solicitor cannot help you, because you are in the absurd position of having a solicitor with whom you are not on speaking terms. Mr Adam Walker consents to do your solicitor's work, only to discover, at his first interview with me, that you have told him nothing about my position, and have probably not even read my letters, much less shewn them to him. What is to be done with you under such circumstances? I am anxious to save you from bankruptcy; Walker is anxious to save you from it; your trade creditors are strongly interested in saving you from it; it is inconceivable that you and the trade creditors and the receiver could not in two days give Thring all the MSS, plates, rights &c that he wants, and so make it his interest also to save you; but the one person who baffles all these salvage corps is Grant Richards himself (and perhaps his hostile solicitor).

Do you realize what bankruptcy means for you? You wont get your discharge easily: as far as I can ascertain there is not an extenuating circumstance connected with it. You will be stranded for years, unable, under penalty of prison, to order a pair of boots without warning the bootmaker that you are an undischarged bankrupt, unable to spend a five pound note without carefully considering whether it is not a fraud on your creditors, and impossible as a publisher or anything else that requires a clean bill of health. Dont, in the name of common sense, run yourself into all this when all the forces that are driving you into it can be so easily disarmed, and all the forces against it so easily united.

However, I write all this with the conviction that it will be utterly lost on you. *Quem Deus vult perdere &c*

yrs ever
G. Bernard Shaw

Richards published *Three Plays for Puritans* on 15 January 1901. **Field & Roscoe** was a firm of solicitors that handled much of Shaw's legal work. **Adam Walker**, most likely a Richards employee, apparently possessed legal expertise or responsibilities. Eleven Shaw plays (701 performances) were presented at The Royal **Court** Theatre (London) 1904–7 under the management of Harley Granville Barker (1877–1946) and J.E. (John Eugene) Vedrenne (1867–1930). An **undischarged bankrupt** is someone who has been declared bankrupt but who is not yet in possession of the 'order of discharge' that would cancel any outstanding debts. *Quem Deus vult perdere*: 'Those whom God wishes to destroy, he first makes mad' (Latin).

83 / To G. Bernard Shaw   [no address
undated: ca. 16th January 1905]

[TLS (c): HRC]

My dear Shaw

I have read your letter very carefully and Walker has read it (by the way, you are incorrect in saying I have not read your previous letters or shown them to him; I have both read them and shown them to him: he read them all on the day preceding your visit).

As for the plates: it is very doubtful whether Clark has any lien over them, nor do I know that they have laid claim to any lien; in any case if – I say 'if' – we get a further adjournment to-morrow I will see immediately what can be done towards selling the plates to you.

Now as to Mr. Thring. You tell me, and I suppose you are quoting him textually, that he speaks of my 'airy apathy and the inertia of the Receiver.' I had no correspondence with Mr. Thring of any kind, nor had the Receiver, until I wrote to him a few days ago at your suggestion and asked if he would make an appointment to see me. He refused pointblank to see me except with his solicitors, to whom he suggested I should write. I did so at once. They replied that they could only consider any suggestion of mine or any information in writing, 'through my solicitors in the usual way.' Mr. Thring in the information he gave you has not been candid, and in his treatment of me he has been far from straightforward. If even now, and if the question of the Receiving Order is again postponed, Mr. Thring will give me a list of the authors for whom he acts – I know only of Aylmer Maude and yourself in this connection – I will very willingly and at once do all I can to give his clients, or principals, or whatever you would call them, what he wants.

And as for doing what I can to avoid bankruptcy, of that you can be perfectly sure. Because I have not all the time been suppliant at Mr. Thring's door and I have not been humanly able to do exactly what you have wanted, it does not mean, as you seem to think, that I have been either nerveless or apathetic.

> Believe me, my dear Shaw,
> Very sincerely yours,
> Grant Richards

Aylmer Maude (1858–1938), translator (with his wife Louise) of Tolstoy, was on the Fabian Executive 1907–12.

84 / To Grant Richards   The Old House, Harmer Green, Welwyn
17th January 1905

[ALS: HRC]

Dear Grant Richards

Thring said nothing: he wrote to me and explained his position, which is exactly as I stated it, though the expressions you quote were not used by him. He *ought* to have used them; and he meant them; but he has not my habit of vivid expression. And good heavens! what does it matter what he said or didnt say? Is this a time to devote to the momentous question of whether he is a straightforward man or not? You ought to have been a suppliant at his door until you had made him safe. If Maude is the only other person concerned, there ought to be no difficulty: all he wants is to get loose.

I have had no answer from my letter to Thring on Saturday; and I dont know what is going to happen today. But I urge you not to waste priceless time in standing on your dignity with Thring or with anybody else. 'Inertia' is the mildest of words for your suicidal inaction. You know very well that you should have squared me and Maude months ago; and your only chance now to get at people is to gaily confess that you have been shockingly remiss, and ask your creditors to get you out of the mess. Remember, people can forgive anything except being humbugged; and they are always conciliated by being asked for advice. If you stop to fight, or to deny, or to excuse, or even to apologize, you are lost. Make yourself pleasant, no matter what provocation you may get; and you will not only be doing what you do best usually, but you will be pursuing the only possible policy under the circumstances.

Clark will certainly hold the plates until it is settled whether he has a lien on them or not. I know this; for of course I have been in communication with Clark & with everybody else from whom I could get any information.

yrs ever

G. Bernard Shaw

As a result of his **suicidal inaction**, Richards went bankrupt in April. He managed to remain afloat by reinventing himself as E. Grant Richards (1905–8), Grant Richards Ltd (1908–27), and the Richards Press (1927–63).

85 / To R. & R. Clark   10 Adelphi Terrace, London WC2
                                          11th March 1905

[TLS: NLS]

On 24 April Shaw sent Clark £42 for Richards's plates and blocks, with a request to insure them. 'In delivering future orders of mine to the binders, please be careful to consign them for me, and not for the publishers. My object in this is to leave the binder no excuse for claiming a lien on my property for debts due him by the publisher' (ALS: NLS).

Dear Sirs

I enclose my cheque for £24-7-6 in settlement of your account.

Can nothing be done about those plates which you hold against the debt of Mr Grant Richards? I am now forced to make up my mind to order supplies of my books from America; and it seems to me absurd that you should drive my printing business out of the country for the sake of a few shillings worth of scrap metal. Hitherto the pressure on authors to manufacture their books in America has been strong enough in all conscience (I should have saved nearly a hundred pounds by importing Man & Superman from Cambridge, Massachusetts, instead of having it set up twice); but to ask me to get my books set up a third time, with a complete set of plates locked up in your warehouse, is beyond all reason.

Surely there must be some way out of the deadlock, though the lawyers do not seem able to find it. The plates, without my license to print, are worth only their weight in metal. They are not indispensable to me, because of the existence of the American plates. Yet I am willing to pay something for them in order to give the creditors some motive to release them and enable me to give you an order.

As you claim a lien on the plates, you are holding them for value against the estate of Mr Grant Richards, who, by the way, has no right to print a single impression from them, his license to do so having expired. What value do you set on them? I should like to know exactly what your position is, so that I may be able to judge how far your lien will stand in the way of any arrangement; for though I must order from America very soon now – probably in the course of next week – I shall make a final effort to ascertain whether there is any legal means of extricating us from our dilemma. I should save at least a fortnight by getting the supplies from you.

yours faithfully,
G. Bernard Shaw

86 / To Brentano's

Derry, Rosscarbery, Co. Cork
1st August 1905

[APCS: Cornell]

The Shaws were in Ireland 6 July–29 September, Shaw's first visit since leaving in 1876. Although Dodd, Mead & Co. became Shaw's American publishers only in 1933 (following Brentano's bankruptcy), they had recently made him an offer, which Shaw rejected.

... My last book I promoted myself to secure the copyright, and then fought the publishers at my ease. I got 25% for the license to publish for some years (not more than 5 – I forget whether 5 or 3) and for the use of my plates. Now Dodd's offer is not very far off this. The 5000 copies at 20% would bring me £75 less than at 25%. I should save the cost of printing (say £60); but I should not own the plates and should, if I wished to change my publishers later on, have to buy them from Dodd. So I shall not take his offer. The fact is, Dodd keeps offering what I do not want, an advance of capital for manufacturing the book and an advance on royalties. The ordinary author wants both and must give a quid pro quo in concessions. I dont want either: what I offer is a no-risk enterprise; and it is the publisher who must make the concessions.

G.B.S.

Moses Woodruff **Dodd** and John S. Taylor had founded 'Taylor and Dodd' in 1839 as a publisher of religious books. The name was changed in 1870 with the arrival of Dodd's nephew Edward S. Mead (d. 1894). On 24 July 1933 Shaw referred to Dodd, Mead as 'an old firm of unchallenged piety and respectability' (CL 4, 347) and in 1945 as a 'highly respectable old business' (Letter 176).

87 / To Otto Kyllmann   [10 Adelphi Terrace WC2
                                               undated: ca. 24th March 1907]

[ALS; CL 2]

The Times Book Club (founded 1905) offered discounts on recently published and remaindered books. Their low prices and publicity methods in The Times *infuriated publishers, who (backed by their authors) refused to supply books. Shaw voiced his disagreement at the annual general meeting of the Society of Authors on 20 March: 'The business of the publishers is to make as much money as they can in the easiest way to themselves; that is also the business of* The Times *newspaper; and it is also our business in our business capacity' (CL 2, 677). To show that publishers' fears of a booksellers' boycott were unfounded, on 31 August he issued 500 copies of a special impression of* John Bull's Other Island and Major Barbara: also How He Lied to Her Husband *(which had appeared on 19 June) with the imprint of the Times Book Club replacing that of Constable. 'On 23rd September Shaw informed readers of* The Times *that, far from boycotting the book and thus protecting the publisher against the loss created by Shaw's sales direct to the Times Book Club, the booksellers had ordered and sold larger quantities of this book than of any of his earlier ones, cashing in on the publicity created by the action and by the Book Club's advertisements, at Constable's expense' (CL 2, 678). Nonetheless, the Society voted to back the boycott, and publishers placed heavy restraints upon the Club. It took two years for the Club and the Publishers' Association to resolve their differences, with the Club agreeing to a time lapse before selling second-hand or remaindered copies.*

Dear Kyllmann

I am desperately anxious to get John Bull & Barbara through the press; and you may depend on it the delay is not my fault. I confess I am less concerned about the novels; but they also will be dealt with as soon as I can spare the time.

As to the Times Book Club, I object strongly to differential treatment of customers; and I shall give the Times no more discount than anyone else as long as, like anyone else, they simply buy as they go, sending the boy round for half a dozen when they are short. But of course if they give an order for a thousand copies, that is another matter. Special terms for special orders are reasonable; but special terms for normal orders is a black offence to all other buyers, who are each clearly entitled to a 'most favored nation' clause. This is so, isnt it? It used to be, anyhow.

yrs ever

G. Bernard Shaw

During the **Times Book Club** debacle, Shaw wrote four letters to *The Times* totalling about 8000 words: two entitled 'Publishers and the Public' (25 October and 17 November 1906), 'The Society of Authors' (25 March 1907), and 'Books and the Public' (23 September 1907). 'At all events,' wrote Shaw on 23 September, 'there has been no boycott of my book; and the sole sufferers in the transaction are the publishers' (Ford, *Letters of Bernard Shaw to The Times*, 77). The four letters are printed in Ford, 61–8 and 71–80.

88 / To Constable & Co.   [10 Adelphi Terrace WC2]
                                        26th March 1907

[TLU (c); CL 2]

Shaw told T. Fisher Unwin on 8 July that 'The Times Book Club is not publishing for me. What it is doing is collaring the whole sale of the book whilst my publisher and the half dozen timid shopkeepers who call themselves the book trade sit looking on at it and saying what a wicked institution it is' (TR: UNC).

My dear Constables

Your letter does not get us any further; and if we were to start talking about the matter we should go back six months before the end of ten minutes.

The first thing to grasp in this matter is that you are hopelessly and entirely in the wrong, and that I am absolutely and solidly in the right. The booksellers and libraries want to extinguish a new and dangerous competitor. It is the interest both of the publisher and the author to have as much competition in book selling as possible. The booksellers assure you that if you sell one hundred copies of my 'Dramatic Essays' to the Times Book Club, they will take as few copies of that work from you as possible. Now you know perfectly well that they are already taking as few copies from you as possible, and that they would not take one copy more or less if you supplied forty thousand million copies to the 'Times Book Club' (which I presume you would heroically refuse to do if you got the order, in your existing frame of mind). By refusing to supply those copies, you are depriving yourselves of another, Brentano of another, the 'Times Book Club' of the equivalent of another; and you are doing no mortal good to any of the parties.

The great difficulty which confronts us all is that the bookselling trade in England is so absolutely incapable and insufficient. Although I, who am not a book-buyer, buy at least 30 books for every pair of boots I buy, I can find a thousand boot-shops for you more easily than a single book-shop. What is wanted is a great extension of the big general shop with a counter for books; that is to say, a bringing to bear on book-selling of large capitals and of combinations in retail trade as opposed to the old-fashioned separate shops for separate articles.

This way of doing business involves a good deal of speculative buying, and of periodical clearance sales – what you and I call remaindering. And this means the scrapping of all your net book agreements and such like reactionary rubbish. If you allow a big distributor unlimited powers of remaindering, or even of giving away your books with a pound of tea if he likes, he will order from you in hundreds or thousands. If you limit him, he will simply send round a boy to you for one copy as is asked for; and he will not do even this until he has done his utmost to persuade the customer that the book is one which no real lady or gentleman would read, and that some other book, published by sensible people like Routledge or half a dozen others who stand outside the ring, is the proper food for a respectable mind.

Then there is the inevitable division between the publisher's interest and the author's. You make your livings out of a whole body of authors. Consequently, your interest is, not to do your best for each individual author, but to get the greatest result out of the whole mass of them taken in a lump. The notion that the two interests come to the same thing – a notion much exploited by literary agents – is quite illusory. If you are ever reduced to selling umbrellas at corners of streets by auction, you will find that the way to thrive at that is not to stand out for the highest price for each umbrella, but to sell as many umbrellas as possible at a comparatively modest profit. Now if each umbrella belong to a separate owner for whom you are acting, these owners would clearly all be sacrificed to enlarge your income. I do not admit in the Times business, this particular separation of interests comes in. I am quite convinced that in boycotting the Times you are injuring yourselves as much as you are injuring me, and limiting your future prospects very much more than you are limiting mine; but I put the point merely to show you that an author is fairly entitled to make an individual bargain as to the handling of his books, and to bar certain conditions, or to admit certain other conditions, which the publisher would not bar or admit if left a free hand.

The condition which has sprung up to meet this boycott, is quite simple and effectual. It is, that the author shall have the right to buy as many copies of his book at trade price as he chooses, to be delivered to his order at any accessible address he many give, without any question as to what he purposes to do with them. No matter what settlement may be arrived at in the 'Times' case, every author who is worth his salt as a man of business will for the future always make this stipulation. I have never in all my experience heard of a publisher refusing to let an author have copies of his own book at trade price until the present difficulty arose. No doubt the publisher who wants to boycott a particular distributer [*sic*] at the author's expense as well as his own, would rather be able to force the author to support him in the boycott. But it is really difficult to find polite language to express one's contempt for the imbecility of an author who would allow himself to be used in that way when there is no lack of alternatives open to him.

The whole question between us then comes to this. Will you supply the Times' Book Club with my books or not. I am quite willing to save your face with the Publishers' Association, if you desire it, by taking the order from the Club itself, and giving the order as from myself. But as you will know perfectly well what the transaction means, it would be far more sensible for your Association to decide that in cases where the book is under the author's control and he disapproves of the boycott, his wishes must be fulfilled, however deeply his opinions may be deplored.

The only other sensible thing to do is to refuse to publish my books; for what can be more absurd than to boycott a hostile bookseller and at the same time act for a hostile author.

The matter of my new book is really very urgent, as I am dispatching the last corrected sheets to America today; and I want to publish here the moment the book is set up in America.

Also the question of the hundred copies of 'Dramatic Opinions' presses. I asked the Book Club people to hold hard until I tried to settle the matter amicably; but their subscribers are bothering them, and, naturally, they are bothering me. If they cannot dodge you in some way (and I warn you that I will abet them in any game that they can devise for that purpose), they will have to buy their supply at full price from the nearest book-shop, whilst you and I will only get trade price subject.

Let me hear from you as soon as you can bring yourselves to face the situation.

yours faithfully
[G. Bernard Shaw]

Shaw had lamented the lack of **book-shop**s in 1903 (see Letter 73). The 1899 **Net Book Agreement** divided books into 'net books' (sold without discount) and 'subject books' (discounted subject to each bookseller's discretion). 'Books under six shillings (what came to be the typical price for Shaw's early volumes) did not fall under the Agreement' (Kelly, 'Imprinting the Stage,' 39). *Dramatic Opinions and Essays* were published by Bréntano's (1906) and Constable (1907).

89 / To John Lane

10 Adelphi Terrace WC2
2nd June 1908

[TLS: CL 2]

Lane had begun publishing a uniform edition of the works of essayist and novelist Anatole France (1844–1924) – whom Shaw had met in Rome in 1904 – that would run to thirty-five volumes.

Dear John Lane

This notion of yours about a preface by me or by Walkley or by Gosse or by any other Englishman is a mistake. Such a preface can be nothing but an impertinence. A solemn impertinence would be insufferable; and a vivacious impertinence would be like flat ginger ale compared with Anatole's champagne.

You will observe that I, who say this, am a great writer of prefaces – that I have in fact revived the preface for the first time since Dryden made it classical. But this does not mean that there were not in the meantime plenty of prefaces which nobody ever read. What it does mean is that Dryden wrote his own prefaces and that I do the same. What you want is a preface to the English edition by Anatole France himself – a preface which must be an entirely frank statement of his impressions of the English and of his attitude towards them. There must be no standing on ceremony, no playing to the entente cordiale, any more than there is in my preface to John Bull's Other Island. Tell Anatole France that such a preface is expected from him in England and that the substitution of a sort of literary chairman's speech for it would be an insufferable banality.

He will not need much explanation. His preface to a pamphlet by Combes first sold up an enormous edition of the pamphlet and was then reprinted without the pamphlet. Such a preface as I suggest, if there were enough Anatolian pepper and salt in it, would give your edition such a send off both in the way of reviews and sales, that you could afford to pay Anatole France handsomely for his trouble.

Anyhow, *I* wont write the preface; and in my opinion anybody else who does will thereby shew himself very highly qualified to do it unsuccessfully.

yours faithfully

G. Bernard Shaw

For A.B. **Walkley** and Edmund **Gosse**, see Letter 21. **Ginger ale** was created in Ireland around 1851. The preface to *Fables, Ancient and Modern* (1700) by John **Dryden** (1631–1700) is considered one of the finest essays in English. France had written a **preface** to Émile **Combes**'s *Une campagne laïque (1902–1903)* – at 460 pages, hardly a **pamphlet** – published in 1904.

90 / To Curt Otto [no address]

24th October 1908

[TLU (c): Cornell]

Curt Otto (d. 1929) was director of Bernhard Tauchnitz (Leipzig), which began publishing English-language titles in Continental Europe and the rest of the world (but not the British Empire) in 1841. Edward Bulwer-Lytton's The Last Days of Pompeii *(1834) was its first publication in 1842. Tauchnitz published twenty-six*

Shaw titles between 1913 and 1954, the first being Man and Superman *(for a complete list, see Todd and Bowden,* Tauchnitz International Editions, *1012). Tauchnitz paperbacks were inexpensive volumes aimed at anglophone travellers in Europe.*

Dear Doctor Otto

Your letter of the 11th August arrived here while I was travelling abroad; and my secretary did not send it on to me as I was supposed to be having a holiday from all business.

I am not wholly convinced that my English editions would not suffer by the competition of a Tauchnitz edition. If I were an author with a large public consisting for the most part of people who do not travel, then of course I should not hesitate for a moment. But as far as I can ascertain, my special public is in the main a travelling public; and I know by my own experience that people who have once learnt to travel, and who read real literature only during their holidays, put off buying that literature until they reach Paris, when they go straight to Galignani's and load themselves with Tauchnitz. To Rudyard Kipling, Mrs Humphry Ward, and Sir Arthur Conan Doyle, this does not matter: the proportion of travellers among their readers is so small, that your editions increase their public by acting as samples; but I doubt whether readers of these popular authors are to any great extent my readers.

However, I am quite willing to experiment with Man and Superman to begin with. Only it must be an experiment and not a permanent contract. I must have the power to discontinue at the end of, say, five years, if I find that your edition is doing my English business more harm than good.

If you have no objection to this stipulation, send me a draft of the contract you propose; and I will then give you a definite answer.

Yours faithfully,

[G. Bernard Shaw]

Shaw reiterates his fears that his **English editions** would **suffer** in **competition** with his Tauchnitz ones in Letter 96. The famous **Galignani** bookstore in Paris is still active. According to Shaw, **Rudyard Kipling** (1865–1936), **Mrs Humphry Ward** (1851–1920), and **Sir Arthur Conan Doyle** (1859–1930), as **popular authors**, had a different reading public from his.

91 / To Curt Otto [no address]
12th November 1908

[TLU (c): Cornell]

Dear Doctor Otto

If the Creator of the Universe, surrounded by all his archangels, and introduced by the fathers of the Church with the full retinue of Saints, were to ask me to make an agreement with a publisher for longer than five years, I would refuse him point blank.

If you are right in your belief that the republication of Man and Superman in your series will be advantageous to me, then there will be no reason for my withdrawing it; so the number will not be left blank. But suppose you were wrong. Suppose that after two or three years experience I become convinced that the Tauchnitz publication was a mistake, you surely will not expect me to go on suffering a loss until the expiration of my copyright, merely because it would be inconvenient for you to mark a certain number in your catalogue as out of print. You say that you are quite willing to accept my proposal and to consider the republication of Man and Superman as an experiment on my part. But there is nothing experimental about an irrevocable arrangement. You must either accept the restriction or else give up the idea of ever publishing anything of mine, because I never under any circumstances make an agreement of the kind you suggest and, as a member of the Committee of the London Society of Authors, I am continually trying to prevent other authors from making these arrangements. I do not know any other instance in which one party of a contract is asked to bind helplessly and irrevocably for life, without any effective guarantee on the other side that the relations of the party will continue satisfactorily. I should like to see Baron Tauchnitz's face if I asked him to enter into such an agreement with me.

If our negotiation breaks down on this point, that need not, I hope, alter the friendly character of our relations.

Yours faithfully,
[G. Bernard Shaw]

Man and Superman became **number** 4436 in the Tauchnitz **catalogue** only in 1913. Shaw could be referring to **Baron** Bernhard **Tauchnitz** (1816–95), who founded the firm in 1837, or to his successor, his son Christian Karl (also a baron).

92 / To Constable & Co.   10 Adelphi Terrace WC2

7th June 1909

[TLS: UNC; CL 2]

My Dear Constables

When are you going to send me my money? I have just sent in my income tax return, the preparation of which has revealed the most alarming facts as to my financial condition. My income is considerably less than half what is was in the previous year; and yet I have had to set up a motor car solely to keep up the credit of your list of authors.

Just consider a moment. I have had to pay in the course of the year £557.17.5 hard cash out of pocket to supply you with books to sell. On the 31st December last you owed me in round figures £1600. Had you paid me I could have invested it with complete security at 4%; and I should by this time have had £32. No doubt you have been able to employ it at 300% at a considerable risk (to *me*) of the entire loss of it; but you do not propose to give me any of that money, nor am I getting any interest on my £557. Add to this that your printers probably give you six years credit sooner than risk losing your custom and leaving their plant unemployed. You will tell me that you cannot get the money yourselves from the booksellers; that Kyllmann is now married and has to be very careful; that Meredith is an orphan; and that you lose so much by my books that if it were not for the County Guides, you would have to give them up altogether. I reply that I also am married; I also am an orphan; and my creditors very often do not pay me at all, whilst the market value of the time that I spend in advertizing for your benefit by my public activity would be under-estimated at £10,000 a year. Under these circumstances, would it be too much to ask you to let me have a couple of pounds to go on with until you are thoroughly solvent again? I do not wish to be too hard on you; but a man must live. And if when you have fully consolidated your position, you could guarantee me a reasonably prompt annual settlement, it will make matters much easier for you when I die, and you suddenly find yourselves in the hands of some shark without a ray of personal affection for you and with some elementary knowledge of business.

yours, almost destitute,

G. Bernard Shaw

Shaw had purchased his first **motor car**, a De Dietrich, in December 1908. According to
Dan Laurence, Shaw was 'a shockingly careless driver' (CL 2, 822); see Letter 139. **County
Guides** alludes to Constable's expensive, illustrated (with maps, plates, and photographs),
multi-volume series *The Victoria History of the Counties of England*. Founded in 1899, the VCH
(as it is known today) has been based at the Institute of Historical Research in the University of London since 1932.

93 / To Simon Brentano

10 Adelphi Terrace WC2
6th November 1912

[TLS: Cornell; CL 3]

*According to the envelope, the following letter was sent to 37, avenue de L'Opéra,
Brentano's Paris bookstore since 1895 (and still extant). Shaw had reason to complain of poor returns. For example, according to Brentano's 'Royalty Accounts' for
1908, Shaw earned $335.94 on sales of* Man and Superman *and $159.50 for*
Three Plays for Puritans, *Shaw receiving 25¢ on each $1.25 book (letter to Shaw
of 5 January 1909, TLS: HRC). Shaw now offers a threefold solution to Brentano's poor sales: counteract ineffectual press reports, publish his plays in separate
editions, and advertise his works in those editions.*

My dear Mr Brentano

Whatever the reason may be, it is beyond all question that the return
from my books in America is so disproportionate to the returns from England that I am not satisfied to leave things as they are. I believe I should
have no difficulty in inducing some of the American publishers who are
keen on my work to guarantee me larger annual returns, sales or no
sales, than I get now.

I suggest to you that there are three points which need reconsidera-
tion on your part.

First, as to the press. It is quite true that an enormous number of allusions are made to me in the American newspapers. For some years I had
a contract with a press cutting bureau to supply me with these. There
were so many of them that I insisted on a special rate of two cents a clip-
ping. I sampled them very thoroughly; and my opinion is that the great
majority of them may be divided into those which are quite useless as advertisements of my books, and those which are positively injurious.
There was nothing in them to inform any reader that I was an author
whose books could be procured at the stores. They presented me partly

as an eccentric character making occasional pronouncements in English newspapers, or as a playwright whose plays were performed at theatres but not necessarily published, or as a freak or a lunatic. This mass of publicity is a hindrance, not a help: far from needing to be exploited, it needs to be counteracted.

Second, in spite of the great success in England of my method of publishing plays separately as well as in the collected volumes, you have steadfastly refused to consider my repeated suggestions that you should do the like in America. I enclose you, as a sample, a letter that reached me only the other day.

Third, though I am no very great believer in extensive newspaper advertisements for such books as mine, except as a means of paying for reviews, I am all the keener on making my books advertize one another. I do very little in the way of press advertizing in England; but I never let a book go out without a full list of my works at the end, with prices and descriptions complete. I am not content with putting these on the jacket, which is almost always thrown away unread: I put it at the end of the book, and print it up and down the page instead of across it; and I put it not only in the collected volumes, but in the single plays. Now if you consider that you dont do this, and that even if you did you would circulate much fewer of these catalogues through your refusal to sell the plays separately, you will see that you are not availing yourself of your opportunities of publicity to anything like the available extent.

However, I have said all this before without making any impression on you. In short, you dont believe it; or else this small scrap of your big business is not important enough to alter your routine for. Well, as it is of considerable importance to me, I should like to let our agreements expire, and to take the manufacture of the books into my own hands, and to ask you to do no more than to sell them for me on commission. In this way the experiment of issuing separate editions would be entirely at my risk and not at yours. I could adopt and maintain my own methods as to making the books advertize one another. You would have nothing to do but warehouse the stock as it came from the printers and bookbinders, and sell them across the counter or to the trade. You will have no risk and no responsibility; and if I succeed in increasing the circulation, you will probably make as much out of the commission as you do now out of your profits.

I am sorry that it has not been possible for me to publish at the psychological moment; but that disadvantage has been common to both the English and American editions, and doesnt account for the very remarkable difference in the results.

I am sorry we have missed you this season; but you are right not to risk a visit to London. My wife has been suffering for a long time past from obstinate bronchitis; and London is about the last place I should recommend you to visit at this season if you can possibly avoid it. Next time, try and catch us on your way out, before there is any chance of fog. We have had more fog in London during the past month than I have seen here for several years past.

yours sincerely,
G. Bernard Shaw

The American **press cutting bureau** was Burrelle's (today Burrelle's/Luce); the letter cancelling their service appeared in the *New York Times* on 24 January 1906 (see CL 3, 123). Nothing came of the idea that Brentano sell Shaw's books **on commission**; their royalty arrangement remained in force until the firm's bankruptcy in 1933. It is unclear why Shaw laments that it was not possible for him **to publish at the psychological moment** (the time at which something is best done to achieve the desired effect).

94 / To Simon Brentano   10 Adelphi Terrace WC2
                                            19th April 1913

[TLS: Cornell; CL 3]

Perhaps to counter Shaw's accusation below that Brentano's were 'from the point of view of driving a circulation ... the most inefficient publishers in the entire universe,' in December 1913, as a Christmas promotion, an eighteen-volume 'Collected Edition' of Shaw's works was issued at $20 per set; only 350 sets were printed (Laurence 1, 36).

Dear Brentanos

On going through your accounts I find no mention of the volume containing John Bull's Other Island and Major Barbara. Also, I find that Dramatic Opinions and Essays seems to have dropped out of your accounts after January 1910. Consequently, you must owe me by this time some millions of dollars.

In view of this omission, and of the fact that neither of us noticed it until it was discovered by accident, I think we may now drop all affectation of being men of business. My own pretences in that direction have always been of the hollowest; and I am greatly relieved to find that you are worse than I am. I cannot just at present remember any other publications that we have forgotten; but I daresay three or four will occur to us presently. You will observe that all your profit and loss accounts for the last few years are now knocked into a cocked hat, and that you have probably been living considerably beyond your income, whilst I have been suffering corresponding privations by living considerably inside mine.

But I am really much more concerned about the books we have remembered than the ones we have forgotten. The sum that you remit me for all my books is less than I get in England by the publication of the cheap separate editions of my plays alone. It is hardly one fourth of what I receive on other items. Considering that the American reading public is so much bigger than the British public; having regard also to the fact that in England there are so few booksellers that it is hardly an exaggeration to say that there is next to no circulating machinery for literature, it seems to me that either my works must be extraordinarily repugnant to American taste, or else that from the point of view of driving a circulation you must be the most inefficient publishers in the entire universe. What is your own view of the matter? I think I ought to make at the very least a steady and certain 12,500 dollars a year out of my American copyrights. Anyhow, I ought to make more than 2,500: in fact I feel sure that any other publisher in America would jump at an offer to take over the whole concern for double that sum. I may mention that besides the separate editions of my English plays at 1/6, which are in my own hands, I have accepted offers from my English publishers to publish John Bull's Other Island and Man and Superman in a still cheaper form at sixpence a copy, with a royalty to me of one penny. This experiment seems to have been a success, and has enabled me to reach a very large circle of readers who are cut out by the higher prices. I have not yet received any copies of your separate cheap editions. I confidently expect to find them marked five dollars a copy.

Yours faithfully
G. Bernard Shaw

Laurence points out that, having declined (in 1906) royalties for an edition consisting of public-domain materials, it is curious that Shaw requested payment on sales of *Dramatic Opinions and Essays* (CL 3, 165), which was unauthorized. The expression **knocked into a cocked hat** means thoroughly beaten, altered beyond recognition, rendered useless. Constable's **sixpence** editions of *Man and Superman* (1911) and *John Bull's Other Island* (1912) were a sales **success**: 71,800 and 31,200 copies respectively by the end of 1912 (Laurence 1, 55, 79).

95 / To Curt Otto

Ayot St Lawrence, Welwyn, Herts.

14th January 1914

[ALS: Colgate]

In 1906 the Shaws began leasing the New Rectory (built 1902), a ten-bedroom home in the tiny Hertfordshire village of Ayot St Lawrence (near Welwyn). The house, which they purchased in 1920, is known today as Shaw's Corner. Letters 95 and 96 confirm Shaw's initial reservations about dealing with Tauchnitz (Letter 91).

Dear D[octor] Otto

There are two mistakes in the Superman agreement; and one of them occurs again in the Wagnerite agreement. Clause 6 in both agreements says that the agreement is 'not peculiar' (nicht eigentümlich) to your firm. But the point of the clause is that it *is* peculiar, and cannot be assigned. I have therefore struck out the 'not.'

In Clause 2 of the Superman agreement 'edition' should be 'addition.' I have altered that also.

These alterations should be initialled in the margin. I have initialled the copies you are to keep. Will you kindly initial the other and return them to me.

I see no reason why Plays Pleasant & Unpleasant & Cashel Byron's Profession should not be Tauchnitzed. The Admirable Bashville had better be appended to Cashel, as the addition to the cost of production is negligible, and the attraction of the volume increased ...

yours faithfully

G. Bernard Shaw

Tauchnitz published **Plays Pleasant & Unpleasant & Cashel Byron's Profession** in 1914.

96 / To Curt Otto   10 Adelphi Terrace, London, WC2

23rd May 1914

[TLS: Colgate]

Misalliance *and* Fanny's First Play *had just been published by Constable on 18*
May; they did not appear with Tauchnitz until 1921. After receiving the follow-
ing letter, Otto forwarded copies of his previous letters to Shaw, who replied on 27
May that they 'were quite clear; but my head was not, as I was very busy with the
production of Pygmalion. I withdraw my reproach with many apologies' (ANS:
Colgate).

Dear D[octo]r Otto

I did not notice that you had knocked £10 off the usual advance in your
proposal for the last two books. As you made no allusion to any changes,
I did not scrutinize the figures and concluded that the advance was to be
as before. It seems clear to me that if you make the reduction without any
apparent reason, and I accept it, you will advance only £20 on the next
book, £10 on the one after that and nothing on the following one. After
that, you will expect me to advance you £10, then £20, then £30 and so
on. This prospect is so depressing that I had much rather you sent me another £20, making the advance on the two books up to £40 as before; for
I really do not see why you should treat me worse than you did at the beginning.

As to Misalliance and Fanny's First Play I cannot let that go yet. The six
shilling volumes in which I publish my plays, have a certain sale on the
continent; and inquiries for English books of this kind are always accompanied by the question is there a Tauchnitz? If the reply is in the affirma-
tive no order follows. My publishers therefore urge me strongly to leave
them in a position to reply in the negative for a year or so. So for the
present Misalliance and Fanny are not available.

I enclose the agreements with the alteration of the advance from thirty
pounds to forty. This alteration should be initialled in the margin: I
therefore return all four copies to you for this purpose.

Yours faithfully

G. Bernard Shaw

97 / To Brentano's   10 Adelphi Terrace WC2
15th January 1916

[TLS: Cornell]

Dear Brentanos

... The book is all but through the press: nothing remains but to pass the final revises and tell the printer to go ahead. As the war has taken away so many of our workers, printing is slow, like everything else; and communication is precarious. Two successive copies of a play for stage use and the agreement relating thereto were torpedoed; and the same fate may overtake this volume; but with reasonable luck you may expect to have the stuff in your hands before the end of February. You can then set your printers to work on it and let me know how soon you can effect publication and thus let me get the book out on this side.

The New York Times has long since allowed my war stuff to go out of print. Is there, as far as you know, any demand for it? I am very tired of it, and not anxious to stir it up again; but I have stuff to make up a little volume if there would be anything in it.

Yours faithfully
G. Bernard Shaw

The book was *Androcles and the Lion, Overruled, Pygmalion*, issued on 21 April. Shaw's **war stuff** was *Common Sense About the War*, published in *The New Statesman* on 14 November 1914 and in the *New York Times* on 15, 22, and 29 November, and reprinted in the *New York Times Current History of the European War* on 12 December. It appeared (with thirty-two other pieces) in *What I Really Wrote About The War* (1930), volume 21 of *The Works of Bernard Shaw: Collected Edition* (Constable, 1930–8).

98 / To Brentano's   10 Adelphi Terrace WC2
22nd August 1916

[TLS: Cornell]

Dear Brentanos

In your last accounting to me dated 31 March, no mention is made of three books of mine: namely, The Quintessence of Ibsenism, The Perfect Wagnerite and The Sanity of Art. Can you tell me anything about them?

If you dont publish them, you ought to. In fact, you must have published them, because I must have secured the copyright of the 1913 edition of The Quintessence of Ibsenism through publication by you. The Sanity of Art was copyrighted in America in 1895 and reprinted with a preface in 1908. The 1913 edition of the Perfect Wagnerite contained a new section, which I must have copyrighted. Are they are out of print, or have you forgotten all about them? I had forgotten them myself; but my attention has been violently recalled to them by the discovery that The Sanity of Art is going out of print in England and the plates have been lost.

Yours ever

G. Bernard Shaw

Brentano's published *The Quintessence of Ibsenism* in 1913 and 1500 copies of *The Perfect Wagnerite* in 1909 (which included the first publication in English of the 'Preface to the First German Edition' and a new chapter, 'Why He Changed His Mind'). The **new section** of the **1913** Constable impression of *Wagnerite* was a 'Preface to the Third Edition,' an abridgment of the German preface. The New Age Press (London) and Benjamin R. Tucker (New York) published *The Sanity of Art* on 8 February 1908, and Boni and Liveright (New York) in 1918; there was no Brentano's edition.

99 / To Constable & Co.   10 Adelphi Terrace WC2
                                          11th May 1917

[ALS: BL; CL 3]

My dear Constables

Where's my money? How do you expect a poor author to live? I consider my cheque due on the 25th March; and on referring to an expensive ready-reckoner which I have purchased I find that tomorrow the interest on my balance at the moderate war rate of 5% will amount to £10–1-1. I do not mind the £10 as between gentlemen; but I feel strongly about the one and a penny. I lose a great deal more, by the way; for I always wait for your cheque to arrange for my years [*sic*] expenditure & income by buying exchequer bills and the like short loan securities; and by the delay I lose the interest on the lot. And throughout the year I idiotically pay the printing and binding bills out of my private account instead of out of sales. As I grow old and avaricious, and see you rolling in wealth, this state of things makes me feel martyred.

I appeal to Nathan. Kyllmann has no conscience about money; Meredith has no head for business; Nathan, I feel, will understand me. After all, what is £1500 to you all? Think of what it is to me!

ever

G. Bernard Shaw

Interest-bearing **exchequer** (or promissory) **bills** were issued by authority of Parliament. Otto Kyllmann, William Maxse **Meredith** (1865–1937), and George Emanuel **Nathan** were founding directors at Constable & Co.

100 / To Brentano's   10 Adelphi Terrace WC2
25th April 1918

[TLS: Cornell]

Dear Brentanos

I have this day received from you a cheque for seven hundred and eighty-six pounds three shillings and ninepence (£786-3-9 = \$3742.26) on account of book royalties due to me.

But your deduction of Income Tax for the year 1917 raises a difficulty. I have already paid that Income Tax direct to the United States revenue authorities through my lawyer, Mr Benjamin H Stern, 149 Broadway, New York. What is to be done? Will you make good the deduction, or will you send me a certificate that you have made it and leave me to recover it, which will probably cost me more than the sum is worth? The whole business is in a muddle; and I am inclined to contend that Stern, and not you, should be considered my 'proper representative.' It is evident that if all managers, publishers and editors dealing with me are to deduct 2%, and I am thereby absolved from making any return in respect of their payments, I shall escape the higher tax payable on larger incomes.

Yours faithfully

G. Bernard Shaw

Benjamin H. **Stern** (1874–1950), of Stern & Reubens (New York), an authority on international copyright law, was American attorney for Shaw and for the Society of Authors.

124

101 / To Brentano's Ayot St Lawrence, Welwyn, Herts.
7th June 1918

[APCS: Cornell]

Your letter of the 14th May suggests that you understood me as accusing you of acting incorrectly in deducting 2% for Income Tax. That was not my intention. I was quite aware that you are, equally with myself, the victims of a law which obliges me, under heavy penalties, to make a full return of my income and pay the tax on it, and at the same time obliges you to make a partial return of my income and pay on it over again the tax already paid by me. The same thing occurs with my theatrical fees; and several copies of the Act have been sent me to instruct me in the state of the law.

I presume that what will happen is that you will give Mr. Stern a certificate that you have paid the 2% on my behalf, and that he will then obtain a refund; but when the present muddle straightens itself out it is possible that this roundabout method may be altered.

Meanwhile I hope you are charging the U.S. Government a commission for collecting their taxes for them. There is no reason, as far as I can see, why you should be forced to perform any of the executive duties of the Government without adequate remuneration.

G. Bernard Shaw

Shaw may allude either to the 'War Revenue **Act** of 1917' or the 'Revenue **Act** of 1918,' both of which raised taxes to help the United States defray war-time expenses.

102 / To Brentano's 10 Adelphi Terrace WC2
22nd January 1919

[TLS: Cornell]

Shaw had contracted to write five articles on the Paris Peace Conference (18 January 1919 to 21 January 1920) for the New York American, *one of publishing tycoon William Randolph Hearst's (1863–1951) newspapers, for $2500 apiece. Having supplied seven articles for that price, Shaw received full payment of only $3000. He returned the cheque (see CL 3, 616) – and another for $7000 that came as a result of his demand for the agreed fee. Hearst himself intervened, apologized profusely, and Shaw was paid £2800, the equivalent of $12,500. 'I find myself*

relapsing into ephemeral journalism because it means ready money from America,'
Shaw wrote to Otto Kyllmann on 12 January 1920 (CL 3, 654). Shaw compares
the Hearst windfall to Brentano's paltry sales for the year 1918.

My Dear Brentanos

Your accounts dated the third January 1919 have just reached me. They
are the final crusher. Not counting separate plays there are thirteen volumes on the market. You sell one copy per day of each, Sundays included. The net result to me for the whole year and for all America is $1895,
subject to British and American income tax at war rates. This is being a
classic with a vengeance. Is it worth going on at such figures?

What is to be done? Shall I publicly announce that as America is not
doing its duty, I shall solemnly discontinue publication in that benighted
land? Shall I put my whole publication business to auction among the
publishing firms with a reserve price of a flat royalty and a guarantee of
$12,500 a year, sales or no sales?

Just consider the case. I have just had from the Hearst press an offer
for 20,000 words of eight times the sum you have for me as the result of
the year's trade in all my books!

You will say very rightly that the explanation is that you have nothing
to sell but stale stuff. No new books. Yet there are millions and millions
of people in the United States who have never read a line of mine and
whom you cannot reach, or rather who cannot reach you. There must be
some way of getting at them. I shall look up these people who sell complete sets of Mark Twain at two dollars a month.

Mind: I am not blaming you: I expect no better results within the circle
of your operations, and in view of the fact that my books will just pay
their way without any shoving. But they wont pay *my* way with double taxation taking away considerably more than a third of my income, and an
inflated currency reducing the purchasing power of the rest to less than
half of its pre-war value. I have never had to think of money before, either because I had none or because I had enough. Now I am becoming
the greediest of sharks out of sheer dread of dying in the workhouse.
Hence this outburst of avarice, a vice of old age.

ever

G. Bernard Shaw

The **Hearst** articles appeared in the *New York American* 19 January–23 March 1919. Constable published them on 12 March 1919 as *Peace Conference Hints.* Harper & Brothers had issued a **complete set** of the works of **Mark Twain** (1835–1910) in 1917.

103 / To Curt Otto   10 Adelphi Terrace, London WC2
                                            4th October 1919

[TLS (c): Colgate]

Prior to 1914, the German mark had been linked to the gold standard and during the war remained valid largely to finance cross-border trade. In the following letter, Shaw is probably asking for a draft drawn on a German bank that could be settled with an English bank that would have required gold backing for the English bank to disburse on it. The value of the domestic mark was volatile and backed only by the good faith of a bankrupt government.

Dear Herr Otto

It is with great pleasure that I find myself able to correspond with my German friends again. I need hardly say that the war did the most painful violence to my personal feelings, and that I was unable to make any distinction between the German casualties and those of the Allies in respect of the loss they inflicted on European civilization.

My answer to your letter is belated, I am sorry to say, by two months; but I was travelling in Ireland when it arrived; and a variety of circumstances with which I need not trouble you prevented me from dealing with my correspondence until my return to London and to my regular routine.

It is clear that your omission to give me the notice of renewal and obtain consent to it, as stipulated in our agreements, was not wilful. I now hereby consent to the continuance of the agreement in all respects, save one, as if my consent had been obtained before the expiration of the terms of the agreements.

The exception I make refers to the royalty of 16 Pfg. That royalty was not intended by me to be an absolute fee per copy, but a tantième of 10% on the selling price. On a selling price of Mk 3, it would be less than 6% – indeed at the present valuta less than 1½ %. I cannot afford to reduce that percentage. On editions issued by my London publisher at one shilling I get 20%. Ten per cent is the very lowest I have ever accepted for even cheap books; and our Society of Authors would consider me a blackleg if I ran down the market any farther. If our agreement had been for books selling at three marks I should have demanded 20%. If I now accept 10% on Mk 3 I may seem to you to be rapacious; but I assure you I regard myself as acting with almost thriftless consideration for your post war difficulties. Remember that I, too, though I am supposed to be the victor in the struggle, am as hard hit by it. The Government takes more than a third of my income in taxation; and prices are more than double what they were before the war whilst the Berlin valuta is Mk 100 against £1.

I therefore stipulate that you pay me 10% on the selling price for the present, whatever it may be, and that you make the payments in blue Marks and not in British currency. But as to this last point, it is not pressing, because I may not receive any payments 'from German nationals resident in Germany in respect of pre-war transactions or contracts, as these should be dealt with in the Clearing House scheme.' These words are quoted textually from the orders given me by the Board of Trade in July last. But if and when you are permitted to pay me, and find it convenient to do so, please send me blue Marks. They are being bought and hoarded here to wait for a rise in the valuta; and this you may take as a proof of the faith of our financial speculators in the recuperative powers of your country.

It is worth considering whether we should not make new contracts to replace the old ones. We should be free from all official restriction in respect of them.

What other books of mine have you in mind for inclusion in your addition [*sic*]?

> With friendliest Hochachtung
> G. Bernard Shaw

The Shaws had spent July and August at Parknasilla, Co. Kerry, **Ireland**. There were 100 pfennings (**Pfg.**) to one Deutsche Mark. **Tantieme** (unaccented) are 'royalties' (German). The **valuta** is the comparative value of one currency with respect to another. A **blackleg** (British slang) is someone who continues to work during a strike (a 'scab'). The Reichsbank began issuing blue 100-mark notes, known as 'blaue Hunderter' (blue hundreds), in 1908. Shaw probably wants to distinguish these pre-war **blue Marks** from the sepia-coloured Papiermark, mass-produced starting in 1914 and, with hyperinflation, near worthless by 1923. **Hochachtung**: 'respect' (German).

104 / To Otto Kyllmann   Ayot St Lawrence, Welwyn, Herts.

29th January 1920

[TLS: BL; CL 3]

Kyllmann had persuaded Shaw to undertake what would become The Works of Bernard Shaw: Collected Edition, *published in 30 volumes between 1930 and 1932, with three later volumes (one in 1934, two in 1938), for a total of 33 volumes. William Maxwell (1873–1957), secretary (1914–20), director (1920–6), and (after Edward Clark's death in 1926) managing director at R. & R. Clark, has convinced Shaw to switch from handsetting to monotype, a keyboard-operated typesetting machine. In 1929 Shaw would write: 'I prefer machine setting: its results are now superior to those of hand setting' (Letter 126). Shaw inscribed a copy of* Everybody's Political What's What? *(1944) 'to William Maxwell my most important collaborator in bookmaking' (Laurence and Leary, eds,* Flyleaves, *35).*

My dear Kyllmann

... I enclose the page of the Collected Works as approved by me after consultation with Maxwell. I was greatly astonished to find that though I was quite right about the pseudo-Caslon, yet by far the best looking page he brought me was the work of the monotype machine. I pounced on it at once. A day or two after, Emery Walker, whose authority on the subject is toppest hole, wrote to me and told me not to decide until he had shewn me a specimen page of the Life of Abbey now being set up by the Arden Press. He brought it along; and lo! it was Monotype Caslon.

This getting of the book on the machine will be a great matter.

Although Clark is in a hurry to begin, I doubt if it is wise to start now with the certainty that I shall hang up the job if it begins ahead of me instead of with a good batch of copy in hand. I have to come up to town on Tuesday to see a play at Hammersmith in the afternoon. If you can stand a vegetarian lunch I shall be feeding alone at one; and there will be enough for two. If that is impossible, give me an appointment in the forenoon not earlier than ten thirty, and I shall come and explain my difficulties, chief among which is the fact that I must devote the whole month of March to the production of Heartbreak House if certain arrangements now under discussion come off, as they probably will.

Clark has just sent me in a bill for £682, which I have no means of paying. For God's sake stop selling my books, or I shall be ruined.

ever

G.B.S.

For **Emery Walker**, see Letter 74. The **specimen page** was from E.V. Lucas's *Edwin Austin Abbey: The Record of His Life and Work* (1921). **Hammersmith** (since 1965 Hammersmith and Fulham) is a west London borough. Shaw may allude to preparations for the world première production of *Heartbreak House* by the New York Theatre Guild that opened on 10 November 1920 at the Garrick Theatre (New York) and ran for 125 performances.

105 / To Curt Otto

10 Adelphi Terrace WC2
[ca. 20th March 1920]

[TLS (c): Colgate]

Shaw replies to some of Otto's questions about Shaw's war-time writings. The comment about an 'annual settlement' implies that Shaw received royalties from Otto only once a year.

Dear Mr Otto

How unlucky that I was out of town when you called! I live in the country now as much as possible, as I am so much interrupted in London that I find it almost impossible to do any literary work there.

As to the agreement, it is very good of you to offer to make an exception in my case by rendering half yearly account but it is really not necessary. I proposed it only if it could be done without breaking your routine. As it is, the 30th. June will suit me very well: in fact it was in order to have a payment in the middle of the year that I raised the question. I can always manage at the end of the year; so let the annual settlement stand.

As to the bound copies, I presume any bookseller can, if he likes, have your volumes bound in cloth cases by any binder and that if he chooses to have them bound by you, you are binding for him in full competition with the bookbinding trade in general and therefore cannot charge him more for the sheets than for the sewed edition. On that understanding I am quite willing that the percentage shall be 'on the retail prices of the volumes as volumes.' I think that will meet the case.

As to the group of short plays entitled Great Catharine, O'Flaherty V.C., The Inca of Perusalem, Augustus does his Bit, and Annajanska, they were included in my last published volume with Heartbreak House, the whole being entitled Heartbreak House, Great Catharine, and Playlets of the War. Heartbreak House in the Constable edition occupies 100 pages, Great Catharine 50 pages, and the four playlets 106 pages. Annajanska has no literary importance, and need not be published at all unless you have a few spare sheets to pad out a volume with. The three others are interesting as *jeux d'esprits* on the war; but as the Inca of Perusalem is the Kaiser, and the play therefore touches German ground, you had better read it carefully before you print it.

As you have not followed my volumes in your issue, you are at present left not only with these new ones to dispose of, but also with Misalliance and Fanny's First Play. Misalliance is a long play, and has a thundering great preface entitled Parents and Children. It will make a volume by itself quite as well as Major Barbara. Fanny is shorter, and has only a couple of pages of preface. You could, I think, make a sufficient volume of Fanny, Catharine, and Annajanska. Then you could make another volume of Heartbreak House with its famous preface, and The Inca, O'Flaherty and Augustus. You would then be completely up to date. The agreement can be modified accordingly if necessary; but I have drawn it in such a way that we can at any time make it cover a new publication by an exchange of letters.

I am not quite sure that it would be wise to publish Androcles in a volume that does not mention it in the title. Pygmalion is better known to playgoers; but the preface to Androcles has a vogue among people interested in religious questions which is continually increasing; and I believe that for the purposes of a permanent edition like yours Androcles will prove a better seller in the long run. Besides, 'and other plays' is the most depressing title known in the bookmarket. Never, if you value your solvency, risk your capital on 'and others.' It is always taken by the public to mean 'and others not worth mentioning.'

I think this covers all the points in your letter.

Faithfully,

G. Bernard Shaw

The Shaws purchased their **country** home in Ayot St Lawrence (they had been leasing since 1906) in 1920. *Heartbreak House: Great Catherine: Playlets of the War* (1919) is volume 15 (1930) of Constable's *Collected Edition*. (Shaw writes '**Catharine**' – 'Katharina' in German – presumably for Otto's benefit). The playlet *Annajanska, the Bolshevik Empress* was written in 1917. The **preface** to *Heartbreak House* (also 1917) is dated June 1919. The Inca in the playlet *The Inca of Perusalem* (written in 1915) is based on Kaiser Wilhelm II (1859–1941), ruler of the German Empire from 1888 to November 1918. Shaw concludes his 1919 introductory note to the play with: 'But I should certainly put the play in the fire instead of publishing it if it contained a word against our defeated enemy that I would not have written in 1913' (CP 4, 952). *Misalliance, The Dark Lady of the Sonnets, and **Fanny's First Play**. With a Treatise on*

Parents and Children had been published by Constable and Brentano's in 1914. The **thundering great preface** to *Misalliance* is much longer than the play itself, as is the preface to *Androcles and the Lion: A Fable Play* (written between 2 and 6 February 1912, published in 1916). The 'Preface on the Prospects of Christianity' (dated December 1915) addresses such **religious questions** as atonement, salvation, miracles, transubstantiation, and Hell.

106 / To Otto Kyllmann

Ayot St Lawrence, Welwyn, Herts.
31st December 1920

[APCS: BL; CL 3]

On careful examination I find that the new page is wrong; and I am now taking it up with Clark myself, as the matter demands a degree of invective which would be unbusinesslike if it came from you. I am knocking an em off the width and two lines off the length. And the type is NOT Caslon: it is a Miller pseudo-Caslon: that is, Caslon smartened and spoilt. The difference in the capitals is quite horrible. I have demanded another specimen page in the real thing.

G.B.S.

Miller is a 'Scotch Roman' font slightly more ornate than **Caslon**.

107 / To Arthur Brentano

10 Adelphi Terrace WC2
17th January 1921

[TLS: Cornell]

When Simon Brentano died in 1915, his brother Arthur succeeded him as president.

My dear Brentano

My new volume of plays will very soon be ready. It is all in type, and awaits only my final revision. Before we settle about the publication, however, I want to make a certain reservation. I have arranged with Constable & Co here for the publication of a complete edition of my works. This will be a very big business, as it may run to thirty volumes. I shall probably supply introductions of an autobiographical kind to most of the volumes; and there will be a lot of stuff that is now buried in the files of old newspapers and magazines. Therefore I must reserve from future agreements the right to include everything in this complete edition; and I want to include the contents of the Heartbreak House in it.

I have not yet arranged anything in America; and I should like to know whether you have any views concerning it. As booksellers, your firm would come in on it no matter who published it; and as the cost of the new edition (it will all have to be set up afresh) will be very considerable, the bookseller may have the best of the deal: still, you may as well know what is going to happen.

I am much disturbed by your threat of retiring from business; though of course at my time of life I am becoming accustomed to such shocks. But it raises the whole question of whether I ought not to transfer my whole American literary business to a publisher who is nothing but a publisher. I do not care a dump about Brentanos apart from Arthur Brentano. If you retire my blood will cool to the lowest business temperature at once. You know, there is something to be said for publishers pure and simple – if only they were not so *very* simple. The interests of Brentanos are enormously scattered: I cannot expect so much individual attention from you as I could get from quite a tiny publisher: I never have the comfortable feeling that if you never sold a copy of Shaw, you would be ruined. I doubt if you would notice it. If you are really going out of the business why don't you advise me to change my plan; and if not, why not? I pause for the reply.

Ever,

G. Bernard Shaw

The **new volume** of five inter-connected **plays** was *Back to Methuselah*, published by Brentano's on 1 June and Constable on 23 June 1921. Brentano's **enormously scattered interests** included bookshops in New York, Philadelphia, Cleveland, and Paris, as well as a popular international book-finding service. Arthur Brentano's **reply** (if any) has not been located.

108 / To G. Bernard Shaw   One West Forty-Seventh Street, New York
24th March 1921

[TLS: HRC]

Critic and publicist Joel Elias Spingarn (1875–1939) was founder and literary adviser to Harcourt, Brace & Company (founded 1919 as Harcourt, Brace & Howe) 1919–32. The firm is known today as Harcourt Trade Publishers.

Dear Mr Shaw

I have just re-read the preface to 'Androcles and the Lion'; and the Shavian (and sometimes very Christian) discussion of the life and teachings of Christ suggests to me the following proposal. Would you care to write for us a volume, large or small, on the subject of Anti-Semitism? This has become an important problem everywhere, in England and America, no less than in the countries which gave it birth, if one may judge by the latest utterances of Belloc, Chesterton, and (by contrast) Henry Ford. I haven't the slightest idea in the world what your attitude may be, and I simply don't care; for whatever your message may be, it will be illuminating, and will bear the impress of sincerity. It would be idle to mention terms to you until we know whether the idea interests you; but if it does, you may rest assured that we should do our utmost to meet your suggestions ...

Very sincerely yours,
J.E. Spingarn

G.K. **Chesterton** published *The New Jerusalem* in 1920; Hilaire **Belloc** (1870–1953) published *The Jews* in 1922. **Henry Ford** (1863–1947), father of assembly-line automobile mass production, aired his anti-Semitic views from 1920 to 1927 in his own weekly newspaper, *The Dearborn Independent*.

109 / To J.E. Spingarn   [Harlech, No. Wales]
7th April 1921

[APCS: NYPL; CL 3]

Shaw was taking a two-week holiday at Harlech in North Wales from 6 to 19 April.

Somebody ought to write a powerful counterblast to the Anti-Semites; and the somebody had better be an intelligent Gentile. Nordau and Zangwill will not be listened to on this subject as Wells or I would be. But it would be a very big job, and a difficult one, as a criticism of the Zionist experiment in Palestine (which is very open to criticism) would have to come into it – also a criticism of Nationalism generally, which might appeal to Wells.

I daren't even think of it at present: I am old; and all my bolts are shot.

Perhaps if I wrote a play about a Jew, it might be published with a preface; but I have no intention of doing so.

Many thanks for the proposal.

G. Bernard Shaw

Max Simon **Nordau** (1849–1923) co-founded the World Zionist Organization in 1897. In 1895 Shaw had published a critique of Nordau's *Entartung* (1892–3), *Degeneration* in the 1895 English translation, entitled 'A Degenerate's View of Nordau,' in Tucker's *Liberty*; it was reprinted (with revisions and a new preface) in 1908 as *The Sanity of Art: An Exposure of the Current Nonsense about Artists being Degenerate.* Novelist Israel **Zangwill** (1864–1926) founded the Jewish Territorialist Organization (1905–25). By **the Zionist experiment in Palestine**, Shaw may allude to the Balfour Declaration of 2 November 1917 stating Britain's support of the establishment of a Jewish 'national home' in Palestine. Shaw's friend, novelist H.G. **Wells** (1866–1946), would write about Zionism and Palestine in his 1933 science fiction work *The Shape of Things to Come* (see 'Book the Fifth: The Modern State in Control of Life').

110 / To J.M. Dent

10 Adelphi Terrace, London, WC2
22nd June 1921

[TNS: Colgate]

Joseph Malaby Dent (1849–1926) founded the publishing house J.M. Dent & Co. (London) in 1888, which became J.M. Dent & Sons in 1909. He had written to Shaw on 20 June requesting permission to include a Shaw play in a volume of modern English plays in his Everyman's Library series (launched in 1906): 'I cannot pay you at all an adequate fee, but I do not want it for nothing, though frankly I want to sell the book at the same price as Everyman's Library, namely, 2s.6d.' (TLU (c): Colgate). Shaw's plays appeared in the Everyman series only in 1960 (Rose and Anderson, Dictionary of Literary Biography, 88).

Dear Mr Dent

I do not see how I can manage it. My plays are all on the market in separate editions at low prices; and you will understand that it is not possible as a matter of business to sidetrack one of them by putting it into the Everyman Edition. Constable would think I was mad – not without reason.

I am much obliged to you for the proposal, all the same.

faithfully,
G. Bernard Shaw

111 / To Curt Otto   10 Adelphi Terrace WC2
                                              28th July1921

[APCS (c): Colgate]

It is a little too soon to let the new book go. A good many of my clients travel on the continent; and if they find they can buy a Tauchnitz they will give up buying the English edition, which now costs ten shillings. I have just discovered that the profit on all the English editions of all my works for the two years 1919–20, without including any charge for the author's labor, amounted to exactly £29-0-11. This is the result of moderate prices in the face of high wages and cost of paper. I must raise my prices and nurse my circulation more attentively.

Do you mind waiting until January next? It will be all right then.

                                              G. Bernard Shaw

The new book was Constable's *Back to Methuselah*, published on 1 June 1921. Tauchnitz published the play in 1922.

112 / To Otto Kyllmann   10 Adelphi Terrace WC2
                                              17th December 1921

[TLS: BL; CL 3]

My dear Kyllmann

If you can do no better for me than the bills, let me have them. They will console my bankers, on whom I shall have to overdraw heavily at the end of the month.

But I can't go on unless I get half yearly settlements to March and September, payable at Midsummer and Christmas. Unless you can do that for me I shall quite seriously have to chuck the whole business, because the credits involved at present are too long. You see, on the account it appears that I have to stand out of my returns from eighteen months to 6; but this represents only the time that elapses from the placing of the book on the market, whereas I am forced to consider the time that elapses from the writing of the book. For example, part of the Methuselah preface was written in 1906: the rest has been in hand for the last few years. This inevitable condition of literary work intensifies the overcapitalization which is now outrunning me seriously. My paying the manufacturing bills does not after all very much matter: you would pay them at longer intervals than I do; but they would have to be settled up every half year in any case; and my personal relations with Clark are in many ways very convenient. Leighton sends me bills for millions of books which he claims to have bound: what becomes of them, God knows: I suppose I should send you his bills to check. But the iron fact remains that I have to find £4000 on the 1st. January; and although 10,000 copies of a ten shilling book of mine have been sold, I have not half the money because I have had to meet all the manufacturing expenditure without receiving any of the returns. And now you demand 5000 more copies, which I have just told Clark to print when he has made the necessary corrections on the plates. And he, too, wants to know what about the collected edition. How can I possibly set to work on that when I have to write ephemeral stuff for the American press to keep the wolf from the door.

You see how it is. I must get my money back and my time paid for sooner if I am to carry on.

By the time you get this, we shall have met at Ayot; but as we shall talk of everything except business I send this to make my necessities clear.

ever

G. Bernard Shaw

The **preface** to *Back to Methuselah* contained an extract from Shaw's 23 March **1906** Fabian Society lecture on Charles Darwin. London bookbinders **Leighton** Son & Hodge (later Leighton-Straker) cased Shaw's books for Constable; their warehouse was fire-bombed in 1941 (see Letter 169).

113 / To Arthur Brentano

10 Adelphi Terrace WC2
20th March 1922

[TLS: Cornell]

My dear Brentano

About that collected edition of my works (not that I seem to have much chance of collecting it just now): –

Your letters on this subject were quite conclusive against the project as far as you and I are concerned; for I cannot undertake the expense of such an edition, and though no doubt you could, it would not be good business for you. I have therefore been casting about for some third party who can cover ground enough to venture on such a speculation.

The other day I had a talk with Mr George Brett, alias The Macmillan Company. He thinks he can operate on a scale which would not be worth your while, as you have the biggest bookshop in the world to look after; and he says he will take on a complete uniform edition of all my works, to be sold in sets or separately. He believes he can arrange with you to supply you with copies bearing your imprint for sale in the area you cover. He is keen on business because he let me slip through his fingers many years ago, and has been wanting to get even with himself for it ever since.

How does this strike you? G.B. was extremely friendly in his tone about you; and of course he urges that this is a publisher's job, and that his 75 travellers can cover the country, and especially the middle west, which he considers a big market for me which has not yet been effectively touched, in a way impossible to a fortunate man like yourself, with whom publishing is only a side line. Naturally I lent a ready ear, as my sanity as an author and my cupidity as a man crushed by war taxation makes me discontented with the small sales I have in the States. At the same time I have no illusions about my being a best seller; and what really impresses me is the fact that your energy and resources must be mopped up by your stores in New York, Washington, Paris etc. to such an extent that publishing can only get the leavings of them. And this question of the collected edition brings matters to a head ...

I may confess that I am continually expecting you to retire and enjoy yourself, leaving me in the hands of a mere abstraction called Brentanos, for which I have no personal affection whatever.

Faithfully,

G. Bernard Shaw

Macmillan president **George** P. **Brett** had let *Man and Superman* **slip through his fingers** in 1903 (see Letters 70 and 71). In a few weeks (on 12 April) Shaw would write a receipt to Brentano's for their Shaw **sales in the States** for the year 1921: the net sum in royalties to Shaw was $17,195.35, after a deduction of $1495.25 income tax at 8% (ALCS: Cornell). Brentano's had asked only 2% in 1918 (see Letters 100 and 101), while in 1941 Shaw was complaining that 'The U.S.A. also takes 15%. Result, ruin' (Letter 169).

114 / To Otto Kyllmann   10 Adelphi Terrace WC2
14th October 1922

[TLS: BL; CL 3]

My dear Kyllmann

You and Co are the mildest mannered sharks that ever forced an author
on the rates ... Since the first of January I have paid out to Clark and
Leighton £1354-1-1; and before the year is out I may have to pay them as
much again. Even if you paid me now, I should have only £32-18-5 surplus on the six months. How am I to live on that? If you like, make up my
account to the 29th of last month, and let me have the money in my bank
on the 31st December; but this is my last word: if you cannot do that, I
must retire from the business, and publicly announce that the publication of my works is no longer commercially practicable.

　You cannot reverse the order of Nature, which is, that great authors
should bankrupt their publishers, not that publishers should bankrupt
great authors ...

Desperately (I was depending on you)
G.B.S.

Kyllmann must have **paid** Shaw immediately, for on the 18th Shaw wrote to him, 'And you
had the money in your pocket all the time!!! Really ——! I shall go out and buy a new car'
(CL 3, 785). Dan Laurence writes: 'Shaw wasn't jesting. On 3rd January 1923 he paid out
£800 ("on account") for an A.C. Coupé' automobile (CL 3, 785). Grant Richards went
bankrupt in April 1905, Brentano's in March 1933.

115 / To The Forum Publishing Co.   10 Adelphi Terrace, London WC2
29th March 1924

[TLS: Yale]

*In June 1904 University of North Carolina mathematics professor Archibald
Henderson (1877–1963) had written to Shaw stating his intention to become his
biographer. The result was three massive tomes:* George Bernard Shaw: His Life
and Works *(1911),* Bernard Shaw: Playboy and Prophet *(1932), and* George
Bernard Shaw: Man of the Century *(1956). The following letter stems from
Shaw's wish to provide Henderson with some needed income by collecting their literary exchanges previously published in the* Fortnightly Review. *Although publication with* Forum *did not materialize, eight months later Shaw sent Harper &*

Brothers a revised set of terms (see Letter 117), and they published the book as
Table-Talk of G.B.S. on 17 April 1925. Royalties were shared equally, but at
Shaw's insistence Henderson received sole editorial credit.

Gentlemen

I am sending you this letter by the hands of Dr Archibald Henderson,
who is the proprietor of the copyright of all that part of the MS entitled
The Table Talk of Bernard Shaw which is not written by myself.

In my opinion this book, if sold for $1.50, will easily bear a 20% royalty.
If it were wholly by me I should have got 25% as a matter of course from
my own publishers. The 20% royalty applies only to selling prices not ex-
ceeding $1.50. On inflated prices I should expect a considerably inflated
royalty.

I will not assign my copyright, nor license the publisher for a longer period than five years. If our relations prove satisfactory there is no reason
why we should not go on after the expiration of this term; but we must
both have power to break at the end of five years at most, or sooner if the
publisher allows the book to go out of print, or retires from business, or
becomes bankrupt, or breaks the other clauses of the agreement.

The book must be published in the course of the current season in an
edition of not less than 5000 copies. It must be copyrighted in the names
of Archibald Henderson and Bernard Shaw. Accounts must be made up
to every 30th June and 31st December, and the royalties due therein paid
on or before the 25th March and 24th September next ensuing. The authors are to be entitled to six copies each of every edition (not being
merely a reprint) issued under the agreement. All rights, including serial
rights, remain the property of the authors; and the authors are to be free
to exploit the serial rights notwithstanding anything to the contrary contained in the agreement.

Subject to the above conditions I undertake to complete by my signature any agreement that Dr Henderson may make with you for the publication of the book; so that you may announce it and proceed with its
manufacture without delay.

Faithfully
G. Bernard Shaw

P.S. The royalties would be payable half to Dr. Henderson and half to
myself; and the agreement would be with us jointly and severally.

116 / To Charles Ricketts   Ayot St Lawrence, Welwyn, Herts.

29th May 1924

[ALS: Colgate]

On 2 October 1924 Constable published a deluxe, limited edition (750 copies) of Saint Joan with sixteen plates (12 in colour) by painter and art critic Charles Ricketts (1866–1931). This was the first illustrated edition of any Shaw work. On 3 March 1946 Shaw complained to Archibald Henderson, 'The pictures were designed as theatre costumes and not as book illustrations. The result was a monster' (quoted in Laurence I, 156). See figure 4.

My dear Ricketts

The enclosed is a draft of the agreement I should suggest. I am sending a duplicate to Kyllmann. It is necessary to have such an instrument, as otherwise there would be complications if any of us dropped dead, as I might now quite reasonably do at any moment.

As there will be no sort of sense in, or raison d'être for this volume apart from your designs, my claim on it is rather against my conscience. Clause 7 is based on the assumption that there is not much more than (if as much as) £100 profit to be made on the enterprise, which would give you £50, Constable £50, and me what I deserve. But if Kyllmann seriously expects anything better (he is a sanguine youth) the figures can be amended accordingly with a view to a similar result.

You will have to discuss processes with Kyllmann: indeed all the details, including the price of the volume, ought to be settled before we execute the agreement. Half-tone blocks on China clay paper cost so much less than photogravure and collotype and so forth that we must be explicit.

ever

G.B.S.

The price of the volume was £5.5.0.

117 / To Harper & Brothers   [10 Adelphi Terrace WC2]

11th November 1924

[SHDU: HRC; CL 3]

For background to the following letter, see Letter 115. Additions in brackets are in CL.

Dear Sirs

I have to apologize for my unconscionable delay in dealing with the agreement concerning this book. If I could have signed the copy sent me [by] Mr Henderson I should have done so and returned it straight off; but I found I had to redraft it and amplify it, and so it got put off. I now enclose you the result of my redrafting.

The changes I have made – at least those that do not explain themselves – are as follows.

The agreement takes the form of a licence to publish. This is necessary because a subsequent clause obliges the authors to defend the copyright in case of infringement. And it saves a tedious reservation of the rights other than those involved.

Your clause about holding you harmless in the event of proceedings for libel could have no effect in law except possibly to subject both the publishers and the authors to a prosecution for having signed it. We can neither make nor unmake the law of the land by our private contracts: we can contract only within the limits of the law. For instance, if you publish a statement by us that the President has six wives and made a couple [of] millions out of the oil scandals you could not escape the legal consequences by producing an agreement to hold you harmless signed by me or by anyone else. The law will hold you responsible for your own actions no matter what agreements you may have in your desk; and you can no more shift the onus of printing and publishing a libel than of committing a murder. All you can ask of me or of Professor Henderson is an assurance that the book contains no libel hidden in such a way that you could not by the exercise of due care in your business detect it. I have accordingly confined the clause to this point.

I have done away with the provision that the contract shall be renewable every five years. There is no sense in this. The first five years is your security that you will have time to exploit the capital you must sink in the manufacture [of] the book. After that you are safe if you can see six months ahead. Consequently I have put it that if we are [still?] together at the end of the five years we then go on subject to six months' notice. This means that we go on indefinitely without having to bother about five year periods until we quarrel; and even then you have the enormous force of inertia on your side, so that unless you treat us quite unbearably we shall not want to change.

I am not disposed to make any concession as to export copies and the like, because I know by experience that every cent I concede will go, not into your pockets, but into those of the colonial bookseller. Besides, the agreement does not cover the colonies, which will presumably be exploited by the publisher of the English edition if there is one. Half-price editions to schools do not touch books like this one; and if it did I should still maintain that the publisher must not make such transactions profitable at the author's expense. Somebody has to be unsqueezable or else the whole business of writing and publishing will become a sweated trade.

The limit of $50 for proof correction may have been reasonable in the XIX century; but today $50 would not pay for deleting three sentences. If you want me to agree to a limit at all you must make it $50,000. There is only one effective way of protecting yourself. Before signing the agreement get the copy from Professor Henderson and ask him whether it is definitive, like the Bible. Make him get my final corrections, if not, and put in his own before you send it to the printer. You will then be as safe as it is possible to be against having much more than the printer's own literals to correct.

I do not think there is anything more in my draft that makes any practical difference to you. I have put in the general clauses at the end to enable us to extricate ourselves if the firm should go to the bad and let us down or get tired of the book. The word 'wilful' in this clause is put in, not uncivilly, but to protect you in the event of your being prevented from carrying out any part of the agreement by circumstances beyond your control: always the possibility in these days of strikes.

If you wish to go ahead at once without waiting for the draft to be fair copied and duly executed by the parties, you may take this letter as an undertaking on my part to execute the fair copy and to be bound by the terms of the draft meanwhile. I have accordingly affixed my signature to each part of it.

faithfully
[G. Bernard Shaw]

Shaw made similar changes when **redrafting** his 1937 Penguin contract for *The Intelligent Woman's Guide* (see Letter 118), replacing the clause about libellous, defamatory, obscene, or improper material with 'any hidden libels,' adding in a footnote: 'A publisher cannot evade his responsibility for every word of the author's. He might as well murder his mother-

143

in-law and produce in defence a contract in which the author agreed to hold him blameless for all murders committed by him' (quoted in Hare, 58). The **English edition** of *Table-Talk* was published on 11 June 1925 by Chapman and Hall; the contract (drafted by Shaw) contained the highly unusual clause that if the book did not sell 2000 copies within two years of publication, the publishers would pay the authors the royalty on that number anyway (see Weintraub, 211). The clause proved unnecessary.

118 / To Otto Kyllmann   Reid's Palace Hotel, Funchal, Madeira
                                     21st January 1925

[ALS: BL; CL 3]

'I am so utterly distracted by impossible arrears of business that I have taken a passage for Madeira on the 26th, because that is cheaper than St Helena,' Shaw had told Kyllmann on 16 December 1924 (APCS: UNC). The Intelligent Woman's Guide to Socialism and Capitalism *(1928) began as* 'A Guide for the Study Circles and Other Bodies desirous of investigating Socialism,' *the result of a request from Charlotte Shaw's sister, Mary Cholmondeley, for some ideas on socialism to present to a Shropshire women's study circle. In a 25 September self-drafted Constable advertisement, Shaw claimed that his book was the first work on economics and political science addressed specifically to women (CL 3, 900). Composition was long and arduous: Shaw wrote to Brentano's on 24 January 1926 that 'the job has been a very heavy one – worse than half a dozen plays' (TPCS: Cornell). The ellipses in the following letter are in CL.*

My dear Kyllmann

I have not settled the name of the book yet, except it will be The Intelligent Woman's Guide to ——. Whether the —— will be Capitalism or Socialism or both I dont know: really the book will be What Everybody Ought to Know and Everybody Pretends to Know & Most People Dont Know. Capitalism has not been explained; and I am, so far, the only person who knows what it really is.

My preface to the Webbs' English Prisons Under Local Government is being reprinted as a separate book in America by the National Council of Protestant Episcopal Churches! via Brentano. We might, when I return, discuss an English edition from the American plates. I dont think it would damage Webb's book now: rather the contrary. It is a nailer of a preface ...

                                     ever
                                     G. Bernard Shaw

The I.W.'s Guide will be at least 50,000 words, I expect: most of them already in black & white, and very dull – a Shavian novelty.

English Prisons Under Local Government (1922) was by leading Fabians Sidney and Beatrice **Webb**. The **separate book** was *Imprisonment*, published by Brentano's ('Issued by the Department of Christian Social Service of the National Council of the Protestant Episcopal Church') on 30 April 1925 and in 1944 by the Philosophical Library as *The Crime of Imprisonment*. When finally published on 1 June 1928 (by Constable at 15s. and Brentano's at $3.00), the **I.W. Guide** exceeded 200,000 **words**. 'It has been a terrible job for me,' Shaw told William Maxwell on 22 July 1927 when sending him the first set of corrections. 'I was appalled to find how badly I had botched my work. Old age, I suppose' (TLS: NLS).

119 / To Otto Kyllmann   Kirkwall [Orkney Islands]
                                                        20th August 1925
[APCS: BL; CL 3]

The Shaws toured Scotland and its islands from 17 July until early October.

My dear Kyllmann

I always use the very largest type (set solid to get it larger) compatible with portability. People who never complain of the Temple Shakespear (because it is leaded, I suppose) complain of my type. Well, set up one of my three-play-three-preface volumes for them in large pica, and see how they like it. I am writing to The London Mercury about it. The Wagnerite is short: if I have to use smaller type for the new book it will be because it is too long for pica.

                                                        G.B.S

For the **Temple Shakespear**e, see Letter 63. Shaw's letter, entitled 'The Typography of G.B.S.,' appeared in the September issue of *The London Mercury* (see Introduction).

120 / To Thomas Nelson & Sons   [4 Whitehall Court SW1]
                                                        24th November 1927
[ACCS: UNC; FP: CL 4; PP: Henderson]

Shaw wrote the following reply at the foot of a 21 November letter from Thomas Nelson & Sons (London) requesting permission to include the third scene from Saint Joan in a book intended for secondary schools. Shaw sent Nelson's letter to Kyllmann with the following imprecation: 'Blast all schools and schoolbooks! They are making literature loathed' (quoted in CL 4, 78).

NO. I lay my eternal curse on whomsoever shall now or at any time hereafter make schoolbooks of my works, and make me hated as Shakespear is hated. My plays were not designed as instruments of torture. All the schools that lust after them get this answer, and will never get any other from

G. Bernard Shaw

While the Shaws vacationed in Italy (24 July–6 October 1927), servants moved their belongings to No. 130, **4 Whitehall Court** on 28–30 July, the Adelphi Terrace having been scheduled for demolition (it was not torn down until 1936). On 9 August 1925 Shaw told Curt Otto that he would consent to a 'special University edition' of his works only if he 'were allowed to preface each volume with a foreword in red ink warning students that I am not responsible for the remarks and explanations of the Liar and Fool who has perverted my play into an **instrument of torture**' (ALS: Colgate).

121 / To G. Bernard Shaw　　　　50 West 47th Street, New York City
4th June 1928

[TLS: HRC]

William Griffith, an editor at William H. Wise & Co. (founded 1920), had contacted Shaw on 27 April for permission to publish some Shaw quotations. Shaw replied on 10 May that the ones Griffith had sent were mere 'scraps of newspaper reports of public speeches, inaccurate and perfunctory. The first one is quite foolish; and its selection as a "best thing" indicates that your selector regards me as an imbecile' (TLS: WU).

Dear Mr Shaw

I wish to thank you for your note of May 10, repudiating the statements attributed to you in the newspapers and I can assure you that we would not think of reprinting them in our forthcoming year-book in two parts, entitled respectively THE EUROPEAN SCRAP BOOK and THE AMERICAN SCRAP BOOK, under the circumstances.

I would like, however, to have you represented in the European section of this compilation of the *best* things that have been published, painted or otherwise found expression during the twelve months ending with June, 1928.

The American newspapers are quoting at considerable length from your new book THE INTELLIGENT WOMAN'S GUIDE TO SOCIALISM AND CAPITALISM which Brentano's issued last week.

I have been in communication with Brentano's with regard to the possibility of reprinting some passages from this book. They ask me to write to you direct. We would, of course, give full credit to yourself and your publisher and would also print an editorial note setting forth the great merits of this latest book of yours, which I note you refer to as your 'last Will and Testament to humanity.'

Awaiting your advice, I beg to be

Most Sincerely,
Wm. Griffith

'Bernard Shaw Exhorts America on Socialism,' the preface to the American edition of *The Intelligent Woman's Guide to Socialism and Capitalism*, appeared in **The European Scrap Book: The Year's Golden Harvest of Thought and Achievement** (1928).

122 / To William Griffith

[no address
undated: ca. June 1928]

[TLS: WU]

On 6 July Wise & Co. agreed to pay the Authors' League one hundred dollars to reprint the 'Foreword to the American Reader' from The Intelligent Woman's Guide *(TEL: Bucknell).*

Dear Sirs

In answer to your letter of June 4th, if you are going to make up a book out of copyright matter, had you not better come to some arrangement with the Authors' League about it? My less fortunate professional colleagues find it hard to live in competition with non-copyright work that is at the disposal of publishers without having to compete with copyright matter given to the publishers for nothing as well. If you do not pay the authors individually you can at least pay the general body of authors the equivalent of a reasonable royalty on the book. I cannot as a matter of professional etiquette let you off scot free.

Faithfully
G. Bernard Shaw

The **Authors League** of America (formed 1912) is the national society of professional authors and dramatists.

123 / To G. Bernard Shaw [no address]

18th June 1929

[PP: Unwin]

George Allen (1837–1907) and Sons (founded 1871) merged with Swan Sonnen-schein in 1911 to form George Allen & Co. Ltd. The firm became George Allen & Unwin Ltd in 1914 (until 1986) when Sir Stanley Unwin (1885–1968), previously employed by his father's stepbrother T. Fisher Unwin, purchased a controlling interest. The following two letters concern a postcard from Shaw to Henry Charles Duffin, author of The Quintessence of Bernard Shaw *(Allen & Unwin, 1920), whose proofs Shaw 'heavily annotated' (Unwin, 175) for the revised 1939 edition. The offending paragraph reads as follows: 'Why, oh Why did you throw all that good money to the sharks? It is all very capital for them and for me; but for you! – well, it can't be helped, d—n it' (quoted ibid., 176). The 'd—n' is most likely Unwin's bowdlerization.*

Dear Mr Shaw

I have just been examining some letters and postcards, written by you to Mr H.C. Duffin, which are now on view at Hodgsons and are to be sold on Thursday.

You are entitled to think I am a 'shark,' and that I 'take every possible advantage of an author.' You are, I imagine, privileged to say as much as you do (and more) in *private* letters to Mr Duffin. But I should be surprised to learn that the law permits you to authorize the sale of your libellous remarks by public auction, with the consequent publicity this gives to my customers, the booksellers – not to mention the public at large.

I think you would find it very difficult to 'justify' your statements about me in a Court of Law, but that is, I hope, an irrelevant question, because I refuse to believe that you had, or at any rate have, any wish or intention to injure me. You have on several occasions shown me a courtesy and consideration (notably in connection with my book, *The Truth About Publishing*) which you would hardly have extended to a 'shark.'

The first step is clearly for Lot 467 to be withdrawn from the sale, and we have telegraphed and written to Mr Duffin to this effect.

I think you will agree that the next move is with you. Obviously the matter is urgent, and I am accordingly sending a copy of this letter to

148

you, by express registered post, to Ayot St Lawrence, in case you happen
to be there.

> Yours sincerely,
> Stanley Unwin

Hodgson's, in Chancery Lane, London, was an auction house for old and rare books. Shaw
had shown **courtesy and consideration** in allowing one of his letters to be published in
Unwin's *The Truth About Publishing* (1926). Unwin published Letters 123 and 124 (among
others) in *The Truth About a Publisher: An Autobiographical Record* (1960).

124 / To Stanley Unwin

[no address]
19th June 1929

[PP: Unwin]

*Unwin replied to the following letter on 20 June: 'Thank you very much for your
most courteous letter. I felt sure that you had forgotten what you wrote, and that
your action was prompted solely by a generous wish to benefit Mr Duffin. I do not
agree with you that a publisher must take every advantage he can obtain, but I do
agree that the author should take care of himself and join the Authors Society ...
Thanking you once again for your charming letter – which I do not propose to
sell!' Although Unwin did not claim 'damages,' 'I did claim possession of the
libellous letters and postcards' (Unwin, 178).*

Dear Mr Stanley Unwin

I am very sorry. I was on the point of wiring Duffin and Hodgson when
my secretary rang up from London to say that Duffin has withdrawn the
letters. The present mania for relics (posthumous) is a terrible nuisance
to me. My letters fetch large sums; and I have no power to prevent their
sale. I can prevent multiplication of copies, as the owners possess only
the material sheet of paper; but I cannot prevent the exhibition of the
sheet in an auction room for inspection by purchasers. It seems to me,
however, that such exhibition must constitute publication as distinct
from infringement of copyright, and that a libeled person therefore has
a remedy against the auctioneer or his principal or both.

At all events your protest has, I am glad to note, proved promptly effective.

I always tell young authors who consult me that publishing is a gamble in which the publisher, who must make one best-seller pay for several duds, must take every advantage he can obtain, and that it is up to the author to take care of himself. That, I think, is sound.

Of course I had forgotten all about my counsel to Mr Duffin when I said he could sell my letters; but I certainly did not mean to absolve him from all discretion in the matter.

Shark is a generic term, used without malice. But it shouldn't be thrown about in public.

I greatly regret the annoyance the incident has caused you, and crave your forgiveness for my share in it.

> Faithfully,
> G. Bernard Shaw

Shaw uses his favourite analogy, **publishing is a gamble**, with Dodd, Mead (Letter 166) and Daniel Macmillan (Letter 170), in 'Sixty Years in Business as an Author' (1945), and in a 22 November 1932 letter to G.H. Thring published in Thring's *The Marketing of Literary Property* (1933): 'It may therefore be assumed that all publishers whose business is concerned with contemporary copyright literature are gambling on the inscrutable caprices of public taste' ('A Letter to the Author from Bernard Shaw' in Laurence and Leary, *Flyleaves*, 135). Shaw uses **shark** as a **generic term** in Letters 92 (authors), 102 (himself), 114 (Otto Kyllmann and Constable), and 170 (Alexander Macmillan, Longman, and Bentley, as denounced by Walter Besant).

125 / To G. Bernard Shaw 10 & 12 Orange Street,
Leicester Square, London WC2
24th July 1929

[TLS: UNC]

The Apple Cart: A Political Extravaganza (completed in December 1928) had premiered on 14 June in Warsaw (in Polish) and was first presented in English at the Festival Theatre, Malvern, on 19 August 1929 (4 performances). It opened in London on 17 September and ran for 258 performances. At the bottom of the following letter from Otto Kyllmann, Shaw has scribbled: 'I won't publish it until I have another play to make a substantial book of it. At least not unless I change my mind. Tell the booksellers to go to the blazes. G.B.S.' The Apple Cart first appeared in German translation with S. Fischer (Berlin) on 19 October. Constable published it (with Saint Joan) only on 22 August 1930, as volume 17 of the Collected Edition (its first publication in English), and separately on 11 December 1930.

My dear Shaw

We are getting almost daily enquiries about THE APPLE CART.

Have you decided whether you will publish it separately and if so, when?

Of course, if you are not going to write a preface, may we not publish it just as it stands, at say 3/6 in paper, and 5/– in cloth?

If you don't want it published while it is being acted in Malvern – though, of course, the ideal date of publication would be the day after the first performance – may we announce it for early in September?

If you have definitely decided against publication this year, can you let me know so that we can tell the booksellers?

Sincerely yours
O. Kyllmann

The Apple Cart inaugurated the **Malvern** Festival (at Malvern, Worcestershire), founded by Sir Barry Jackson (1879–1961) to showcase Shaw's plays.

126 / To William H. Wise & Sons

4 Whitehall Court, London SW1
8th November 1929

[TLU (c): HRC]

William H. Wise & Co. (New York) published the Ayot St Lawrence Edition of Shaw's works in thirty volumes between 1930 and 1932. In answer to the following letter, company president William H. Wise (1879–1945) replied on 27 November that his firm appreciated 'the absolute necessity of persuading the American public to take you "as seriously as they take George Washington" – or more so, if possible. All our endeavors will be bent in that direction, and we shall guard against anything that smacks of the "Smart Aleck"' (TLS: HRC).

Dear Sirs

When executing the necessary agreements for the Collected Edition of my works I promised Mr Lowell Brentano that I would send you a draft of the lines on which the edition should be announced and advertised. Accordingly I enclose a sketch of the form I recommend your prospectus should take. Nothing is omitted from it that would be likely to prove attractive. The rest of your publicity work can be founded on it.

I enclose also three of the most suitable recent photographs of me. I have purchased licenses to reproduce these in the United States from the proprietors of the copyright; so you may go ahead with them without any fear of infringing their rights.

In marketing my works in their entirety the difficulty is that instead of having one public I have in effect several publics living in compartments that do not communicate. My reputation as a playwright may be left to take care of itself, as all the people who care for plays know all about it. But many people who dont care for plays do not know that I have written plays and stories. Then there are the fundamentalists who think I am a notorious atheist and the patriots who think that the war was between America and England on the one side against Germany and Bernard Shaw on the other. Above all, there are the hundreds and thousands of people who have very vague notions about me, but who are out for culture for their families and will, to satisfy their parental consciences buy anything that is attractively encyclopedic. The Britannica circulation is one of the most important in the market; and you must advertise with one eye always on it. If you push me as a writer of plays – which is just where I need no pushing – you will risk repelling many of your most likely customers. Rub this well into your publicity experts.

And will you impress on them by every method of persuasion and intimidation in your power that my correspondence with you is strictly private and confidential. The first impulse of a publicity expert when he sees a scrap of handwriting is to rush off with it to the nearest newspaper and sell it without the slightest regard for its privacy or to its effect on the public. For instance, the publication of this letter would wreck your enterprize; but all your publicity experts, if you let them know of its existence will go down on their knees to you to let them publish it as a splendid Shavian joke. They are quite capable of publishing my suggestions for your prospectus as a special article written by me for the newspaper syndicates. I therefore exhort you to exercise the greatest discretion, as otherwise it will be impossible for me to communicate with you at all. I am speaking from bitter and repeated experience when I say that however smart the American publicity expert may be in the ordinary course of his business, he becomes, the moment my name is mentioned, an ignoramus who takes me for a fool and a freak, and strains every nerve to impress that view on people who, left to themselves, would take me as seriously as they take George Washington. Never forget that without the support of these unsophisticated souls that the success of the collection depends [*sic*]; and keep all your Smart Alecks under lock and key until you are through with it.

I hope soon to begin sending you proofs of the British collected edition to set up from. Meanwhile I should like to see a specimen page of your own format. Unlike most authors I am something of a fancier of fine printing; and I may be of some use in the matter. My last big book is being exhibited here as a triumph of artistic commercial printing; but when Brentano's American printer tried to copy it line for line he completely spoiled it by disregarding the margins, which are just as important as the typesetting.

As to type I have examined dozens of the new designs; but there is nothing better, nor as good as, the old Caslon; and this can now be had on the monotype machines. I prefer machine setting: its results are now superior to those of hand setting.

Faithfully
[G. Bernard Shaw]

Shaw may be alluding to the repercussions of his controversial *Common Sense About the War* (1914), whose stance – that all warring parties were to blame – was considered unpatriotic and provoked outrage. The 14th edition of the *Encyclopedia Britannica* (1929) sold very badly, in part due to the Depression. Wise used the plates from Constable's **collected edition to set up** his 'Ayot St Lawrence' Edition. Shaw's **last big book** was *The Intelligent Woman's Guide to Socialism and Capitalism* (1928). Shaw told T.E. Lawrence that the **American** edition 'was set up page by page and line for line; but by altering the size of the page and tampering with the **margins** they utterly ruined it' (quoted in Laurence 1, 173).

127 / To Stanley Unwin
[no address]
9th December 1929

[PP: *Publishing*]

Unwin explains what prompted Letters 127 and 128: 'Libel is a serious matter. At one time, the Authors' Society and the Publishers Association jointly approved a most unsatisfactory clause which seemed to throw upon the publisher the onus of proving the intention of the author to libel (an almost impossible feat), whereas the onus should surely be upon the author to show that the libel was unintentional (a much more practicable task)' (Publishing, 88).

The difficulty about that clause is that people cannot be persuaded that the law of the land cannot be superseded by private contract. If a publisher commits a murder he cannot put another man into the dock by producing an agreement to that effect which the other man has signed. Similarly, if he publishes a criminal libel he cannot proffer the writer of the libel as a scapegoat on the strength of a private agreement. It is not clear even that the execution of such a document is not an offence. It is a sort of conspiracy, and might even run into maintenance and champerty.

All that is of any use to a publisher is a declaration by the author that the book contains no hidden libel: that is, a libel which the publisher could not discover by ordinary diligence in reading the MS, and an undertaking to indemnify the publisher against the costs of a civil action based on such a libel ...

[G. Bernard Shaw]

Maintenance law deals with a person's financial obligations; **champerty** is the unethical sharing in the proceeds of a lawsuit (usually by an attorney).

128 / To G. Bernard Shaw   [no address]
12th December 1929

[PP: *Publishing*]

It would indeed be unpleasant to be convicted of maintenance and champerty, but as a publisher I run greater risks than that almost daily!

I fully realize the points you make and had you and I been deputed to draft a clause on behalf of our respective trade unions we should, I hope, have achieved something more satisfactory than the one of which you rightly complain. The difficulty of drafting a libel clause that has any *legal* value is doubtless wellnigh insuperable. But to a publisher the legal aspect is seldom paramount, because in practice an agreement between an author and a reputable publisher binds only the publisher. Its chief advantage to the publisher is negative, i.e. it limits what can be demanded of him. Most authors (but by no means all) are incredibly careless – a clause that is legally valueless may be exceedingly useful in practice in making the author think twice, thus saving the publisher from the effects of carelessness.

When I apply your definition 'hidden libel' to a recent case (settled out of court) when my firm had the pleasure of paying about £500 I find a curious situation. The libel was obvious to the author and it was pure carelessness that *he* passed it. It was not obvious to us, but it would be untrue to say that we could not have discovered it. Furthermore, a prompt apology from the author would have averted an action for damages, but he failed either to acknowledge the complaint or to advise us that he had received it. No clause will help over this last difficulty, but anything that gives a careless author some *feeling* of responsibility is by no means without value to the publisher.

All of which is not to deny that theoretically you are perfectly right, and personally I should like to see the Authors' Society libel clause revised.

[Stanley Unwin]

129 / To G. Bernard Shaw

50 West 47th Street, New York City
4th March 1930

[TLS: HRC]

On 25 February Lowell Brentano had written to Shaw to reassure him that his firm, despite 'idle gossip' in the press about its financial difficulties, had secured the assistance of 'some of our best friends among the publishers' to repay a $350,000 loan (taken out five years ago) due on 1 March. 'I am sure that any anxiety you may have had will be relieved by this letter' (TLS: HRC). On 1 March he wrote to announce that despite 'irresponsible statements' and inaccurate press reports, Brentano's 'have obtained a five year extension of credit which amply takes care of our needs,' assuring Shaw that the firm's situation would in no way interfere 'with our desire and ability now and in the future to publish your books' (TLS: HRC). In the following letter William H. Wise expresses his eagerness to take over from Brentano's. Although the Collected Edition would appear under his imprint (as the Ayot St Lawrence Edition) beginning on 22 September (until 21 June 1932), sales were affected by the Depression and 'most of the edition eventually was remaindered at vastly reduced prices [see Letter 153]. The three volumes added to the English [Constable] edition in 1934 and 1938 were never added to the American issue' (Laurence 1, 194). Neither would there be a 'special DeLuxe Edition' in 750 sets at $450 per set that Wise would propose to Shaw on 12 April (TLS: HRC); Kyllmann called it 'quite ludicrous' on 29 April (TLS: UNC). The Ayot St Lawrence Edition sold at $315 per set by subscription ($10.50 per volume).

... The New York papers published a report recently that Brentano's were temporarily embarrassed financially because of a large note issue maturing the first of this month. No doubt you have heard something of this. I have not talked with Mr. Lowell Brentano about their affairs but have no doubt everything will work out satisfactorily. We certainly hope so. A committee of creditors (all of whom are publishers) are said to be directing their financial affairs for the present and it is rumoured that these publishers plan to take Brentano out of the publishing business, and confine their efforts to retail book-selling. I can't understand what possible excuse there would be for this and hope it isn't true. If such a policy is adopted, we believe there would be advantages in having us handle your trade editions as well as the subscription edition and would like to talk with you before you close with anyone. I do not want you to take this as an attempt on our part to enter the field against Brentano. If their publishing department is to be continued I hope you won't find it necessary to make a change. – W.H.W.

130 / To Otto Kyllmann   Ayot St Lawrence, Welwyn, Herts.
                             31st May 1930

[ALS: UNC]

Kyllman had written on 30 May that he saw 'no objection to publishing the plays before volume 6, if some of them are passed for press before this volume. We cannot, of course, wait until we have twenty volumes ready. We must start publishing in July, and I suggest that we make a beginning with the first five, and then follow on at intervals' (TLU (c): UNC).

My dear Kyllmann

Five volumes be blowed! Consider an instant.

For composition &c we must now owe Clark something like £4000.

We ought to get The Apple Cart out at ordinary prices at the end of this year, as well as Immaturity; and we are pledged to give the C.E. several months start.

We *must* give the purchasers something solid for their money – something that will make them feel that they have the whole WORKS and have only the trimmings to collect – above all, something that will bring in £20,000 net; and this means 20 volumes on the nail.

A five volume start would be a wretched fiasco. Our broadside, when it *does* come, must be a thundering one; and I am slaving to that end. Set your teeth, and fix 20 volumes as the absolute minimum. After that we can breathe awhile.

ever

G.B.S.

Thirty **volumes** in the *Collected Edition* were published between 26 **July** 1930 (Shaw's birthday) and 24 February 1932; three others (one on 7 June 1934, two on 1 July 1938) brought the total to thirty-three volumes. **The Apple Cart** was published on 11 December 1930 at 5 shillings. On 31 May 1923, after rereading his first novel in view of the **C.E.**, Shaw had written to Kyllmann that *Immaturity* was 'so horribly ridiculous to me that I am utterly incapable of judging it' (CL 3, 827). It was extensively revised before publication (its first) as volume 1 of the *Collected Edition*.

131 / To Jonathan Cape

[no address]

26th October 1930

[ANS: Princeton]

Publisher Jonathan Cape (1879–1960) had written on the 23rd to ask if Shaw wished to read a manuscript entitled George Bernard Shaw: The Evangelist of the Middle Class: 'The subject matter is interesting, it being G.B.S.' (TLS: Princeton). *Shaw placed an asterisk after 'interesting' and replied at the bottom of the letter:*

Not to me. I have rows of these dreary treatises on my shelves, and have never been able to read one of them. My consolation is that as probably nobody else can read them either they do not damage my sales as much as might be expected. Unless the thing is a work of genius I will return it unopened with my curse if you are heartless enough to inflict it on me. G.B.S. 26/10/30

132 / To Otto Kyllmann

Ayot St Lawrence, Welwyn, Herts.

1st December 1930

[ANS: UNC]

In 1926 the Globe Publishing Company, a subsidiary of Macmillan, had published The Plays of Bernard Shaw: Pocket Edition *in 12 volumes, the first collected edition of Shaw's plays in England, also advertised as the Globe Edition. On 21 November 1930 Roland Heath of Macmillan wrote to Kyllmann that there was 'no doubt that our customers are expecting to be supplied with this new title [The Apple Cart]. May we print an edition of 3,000 copies on similar paper to our other volumes? We should be greatly obliged if you would consider this and let us know the terms on which it could be arranged. For the sets we paid at the rate of £1 for the 12 volumes, that is to say 1/8 per volume. This new book is about half the size of the other volumes so possibly the royalty would be adjusted accordingly. We would of course, undertake to sell this book only with complete sets, or to our existing Shaw customers, and it would be quite satisfactory to us to commence selling our volume set three months after your date of publication' (TLS (c): UNC). Shaw's comments (dated 1 December 1930) are on the recto and verso of the second page of Heath's letter.*

It is evident that unless we allow the Globe sets to include The Apple Cart we must shut down on the sets altogether. And I dont think we should do that unless and until we are prepared to take up the £5–5-0 set business ourselves, with all the special travelling machinery it involves.

It is also evident that the Globe cannot increase the price of the sets. They will have to throw in an additional volume (or play, if they combine it with St Joan) for nothing. Therefore, provided they give us no trouble and put us to no expense, I am quite willing to treat our bargain with them as one for complete sets and authorize Clark to supply them at their own cost without any extra payment to us. Whether they are paying us enough at present is another matter. We should notify them that the present edition of The Apple Cart is the last that will appear in the old format, and that when the Fournier edition has supplanted it the whole question of these sets will come up for revision.

The foregoing does not, however, apply to single copies to complete the old sets, if the old purchasers have to pay for the completing volume. On turning it over every way I think we must turn down that part of the proposal flatly. The purchasers of the old sets have what they paid for: a set complete up to date of purchase. There is not room in their boxes for another volume. If they want The Apple Cart they must buy it from us: that market is part of the consideration for which we licensed the Globe enterprise. Of course if any retailer, Globe or bookseller, were to ask us for copies in a special binding and cut down to a special size, we could quote a special price (not a reduced one) if the order were large enough to be worth while; but this would be part of the ordinary course of business and would not place The Globe in a favored position. Nor need we care how many they order and sell, since if the booksellers complain we can say 'We will do the same for you if you give us the order.' I think this is the correct attitude. It disposes of all the questions about 3 or 6 months start, payment for the new volume &c &c. If they will take a million copies on the day of publication so much the better.

It is clear that their sale of sets without The Apple Cart must now have stopped dead. If they have any stock left they must buy Apple Carts from us under the preceding paragraph to complete them. I think we must keep them in this condition for six months before allowing them to print the A.C. for themselves as contemplated in my second paragraph.

I think this is the sum of my wisdom in the matter.

I come up to town late tomorrow afternoon, arriving at Whitehall Court about five.

G.B.S.

Ayot 1/12/30

The Apple Cart became volume 13 in the last of the Globe edition's six printings (1932), which totaled 13,000 sets. William Maxwell pointed out that Shaw's Caslon plates were worn out, suggesting complete resettings in small-pica **Fournier** for Constable's *Standard Edition* (37 volumes issued 1931–51). Kyllmann proposed the name 'Fournier Edition' on 15 May 1931 (TLU (c): UNC). Although Shaw stipulated that the edition should have no name (Laurence 1, 206–7), it was published as the Standard Edition; he refers to 'my Standard Edition' in Letter 147.

133 / To Otto Kyllmann 4 Whitehall Court, London SW1
4th December 1930

[TLS: UNC]

From 1892 to 1922 Shaw carried on an epistolary romance with celebrated actress Dame Ellen Terry (1847–1928). American lawyer and publisher Elbridge L. Adams (1866–1934), owner and director of the Fountain Press (New York), had bought Shaw's letters from Terry's executors in order to obtain publication rights. Shaw later admonished Adams (12 July 1930) because he had 'recklessly given £3000 for the letters without securing the copyright' and then 'deliberately spent another £3000 on the Terry copyrights, still without acquiring mine and again without letting me know what you were doing. You then began threatening to publish my letters without my license and defying me to stop you. Any less patient man than I would have thrown you out of the window into the Thames' (CL 4, 194).

My dear Kyllmann

... The latest from Adams is that the Century Co. have offered a royalty of 30% on a selling price of $5. I have received this offer so very ungratefully, being accustomed to 25% on $1.50, that nothing will happen for the moment: in fact I want to leave the question of the trade edition open until we are through with the five guinea edition. I am writing at considerable length to Adams today upon all the points mentioned in your letter of the 18th. Meanwhile the only change in the situation is that he has veered from Putnams to The Century. I have cabled him to keep quiet and not waste publicity by premature cacklings about his treasure; but as he seems to have nothing else to do it will be rather hard to hold him in ...

> Faithfully
> G. Bernard Shaw

Ellen Terry and Bernard Shaw: A Correspondence, with a preface by Shaw, was published by Constable and the Fountain Press on 4 September 1931 and by G.P. **Putnam**'s Sons on 2 October. Shaw reiterated his caveat about **premature cacklings** to Adams six months later (in Letter 135).

134 / To Otto Kyllmann   4 Whitehall Court, London SW1
                                4th June 1931
[APCS: UNC]

Constable published the first 'Omnibus Edition' of Shaw's works, The Complete Plays of Bernard Shaw, *on 14 May 1931, in a first impression of 25,000 copies and a second (pre-publication) one of 10,000. On 3 June, Kyllmann informed Shaw that he had 'about 8,400 Omnibus left, and it is not selling very rapidly ... My own advice is not to print any more and let us sell off what we have. I think if we could definitely state that it will not be reprinted we could sell all those we have quite rapidly' (TLU (c): UNC).*

Whew! 8400 left, and going slowly! That seems conclusive. By all means announce at once that the 1931 O. will not be reprinted, and will soon be unobtainable. Do not put it in a form that would bar another Omnibus some years hence.

Also announce flatly that there will be no Omnibus of prefaces uniform with the O. of plays. Here again we must not bar a volume of Select Prefaces. Neither, however, must we suggest it.

I think if we call the O. the 1931 O, and qualify the Prefaces as uniform with it, we shall leave ourselves free enough.

'Mr. Bernard Shaw has set aside all other work to complete a new play entitled Too True To Be Good, which has occupied him since his return from the East. It is not a sequel to The Apple Cart; and it is not a historical play like St Joan. Its main theme is the dissolution of established morals by the shock of the war; but the examples may prove unexpected. The play will be published by Constable & Co.'

This is all I can suggest for a paragraph.

G.B.S.

'Although the publisher had advertised in 1931 that the omnibus edition "will never be **reprinted**," Shaw contracted with Odhams Press Ltd in 1934 to license his plates for an edition to be offered as a sales promotion, at bargain prices, exclusively to readers of the *Daily Herald*' (Laurence 1, 200). The Shaws had recently **returned from the East**; Shaw had begun *Too True to be Good* on 5 March, his first morning at sea of their four-week Mediterranean tour.

135 / To Elbridge L. Adams   4 Whitehall Court, London SW1
                                                            19th June 1931
[TLU (c): UNC]

Dear Elbridge Adams

Kyllmann has just shewn me the dummy copy. It is not so bad for America; but there is one damnable blot on it. The cloth with which the case is covered is buckram of the kind that is used only to bind up pamphlets for office use, as it resists hard wear, and its ugliness and stickiness and fingermarkableness doesn't matter. For an *édition de luxe* it is out of the question. You could never shew your face in decent society again after you condescend to it.

What is needed is either a beautifully dyed linen like the one in which my English Collected Edition is bound, or else a fine green leather. You had better buy a lot of chameleons and let them loose in a tree. They will immediately turn a bright green. Then catch them again and skin them before they have time to turn brown. You may find some difficulty in getting 6000 chameleons in time; but at all events you see the idea.

As to your notion of going around for three months sobbing out all the tender bits in the letters and getting them quoted in the press, it is simple lunacy. Why do Americans take such delight in rushing to open doors with battering rams? Every passage you give away to the press – every description of the book you give to the public – means 500 copies off the sale of the book. Dash it all, Lafayette, is there any sense in refusing big money for serialization because it would spoil the sales and then spoiling the sales by producing all the bad effects of serialization at great cost and labor?

You are not to be trusted ten yards out of my sight.

Distractedly

[G. Bernard Shaw]

A **dummy copy** is a mock-up of a book or magazine; **buckram** is a heavy, durable, coarse cloth fabric stiffened with glue. The *Collected Edition* was bound in 'jade green Irish **linen**,' the *Standard Edition* in 'Venetian red fadeless Sundour Fabric' (Laurence 1, 183, 206). Gilbert du Motier, Marquis de **Lafayette** (1757–1834), served as an unpaid volunteer in the Continental Army 1777–81 during the American Revolutionary War (1775–83).

136 / To Otto Kyllmann　　　　Ayot St Lawrence, Welwyn, Herts.

28th June 1931

[ANS: UNC]

Kyllmann had sent Shaw a cable from Elbridge Adams: 'PUTNAMS REQUEST LIMITED EDITION SHOULD NOT BE NUMBERED FEARING DIFFICULTY OF SELLING HIGHEST NUMBERS WILL YOU CONSENT THIS MODIFICATION ON THE CONTRACT?' (TLS: UNC). Shaw replied at the bottom of Kyllmann's letter:

This seems to me foolish. The man who gets No 3000 will be glad to learn that there are 2999 other fools to keep him in countenance and that he has just received the last one. The collectors will expect a number as a guarantee that no more than 5000 have been printed. This last consideration is surely conclusive. Limited supercharged editions *must* be numbered. At least so it appears to me. G.B.S. 28/6/31

Examples of **numbered limited editions** include Constable's *Collected Edition* (1930–8): 1 to 1000 (and twenty-five lettered A to Y); Wise's Collected Edition (1930–2): 1 to 1790; and Constable's *Buoyant Billions* (1950): 1 to 1000 (and twenty-five lettered A to Y).

137 / To William Maxwell

[Malvern Hotel] Malvern
14th August 1931

[ACCS: HRC; CL 4]

The Shaws attended the Malvern Festival from mid-August to mid-September. For the Standard Edition, *Shaw chose a Baskerville type to set off emphasized words in the text, thus avoiding the use of italics or his usual method, wide letter-spacing.*

I have carefully studied the two alternatives to this Baskerville; and it seems to me by far the best. Plantin is horrible: it changes the color of the letterpress. Fournier italics is all right where italic is needed; but I still feel that if italic is to be used for the stage directions it must not be used for anything else. Baskerville struck me at first sight, as it struck you, as not being sufficiently distinctive. But I then made the curious discovery that it *is* distinctive when it is in the right place. The words *cynical* and *keystone* on the same page do not stand out. Well, they shouldnt. But the word *before* (3rd line from foot) does stand out as it ought to. And it does not blotch the prevailing color of the letterpress or spoil the page in any way.

I therefore plump for Baskerville.

G.B.S.

The printers and engravers who gave their names to typefaces mentioned by Shaw include Christophe **Plantin** (1520–89), William Caslon (1692–1766), John **Baskerville** (1706–75), Pierre Simon **Fournier** (1712–68), and William Miller (1788–1874).

138 / To Otto Kyllmann

Ayot St Lawrence, Welwyn, Herts.
12th October 1931

[ALS: UNC]

Shaw soon regretted his decision to let William Maxwell use a Fournier typeface for the Standard Edition, *writing to Kyllmann on 9 September, 'I curse the day I ever deserted Caslon' (TLS: UNC). The envelope for the following letter is marked 'Personal.'*

My dear Kyllmann

If you are ruined so am I. I had to pay Clark £3000 yesterday for this in-sane Fournier reprint; and Heaven knows how many more such cheques he will demand before I am through with it. I have to find £2000 for the Royal Academy of Dramatic Art to get the builders out. I dare not calcu-late what my taxes will be on the 1st January. And there are other things which mean that unless I can realize on the Collected Edition I shall be in Queer St. So do what you can for me as soon as you can. Dont say 'Oh, old Shaw is rich: he can wait.' He can't, blast him. How much can I count on, and when, without knocking you off the gold standard? The question is not desperately urgent; but it is real. I shall, I think, want some thou-sands pretty badly to get me to the end of the year. You need not lie awake at nights; but you must console me with something more definite than 'from time to time.' You know I shan't resort to the premises if you are at all reasonable ...

> In haste and financial panic (which will abate)
> G. Bernard Shaw

The **Royal Academy of Dramatic Art** was established in 1904; Shaw joined the RADA Coun-cil in 1911. In 1927 he donated £5000 toward the cost of a new building (opened in 1931); the **£2000** appears to be a further contribution. The origin of the expression to 'be **in Queer Street**' is unclear, but it means 'to be in financial straits.' The name appears in Charles Dickens (an early and important influence on Shaw) in chapter 55 of *The Pickwick Papers* (1837) and in *Our Mutual Friend* (1865), whose Book the Third opens with 'Chapter 1: Lodgers in Queer Street.'

139 / To Otto Kyllmann   Ayot St Lawrence, Welwyn, Herts.
12th June 1932

[APCS: UNC]

On 24 December 1931 the Shaws sailed to South Africa, arriving in Cape Town on 11 January 1932. On 10 February, while driving to Cape Elizabeth, Shaw lost control of the car (he was speeding) and crashed. He sustained minor injuries but Charlotte was seriously injured, and it was while she was recuperating at Knysna that he wrote The Adventures of the Black Girl in Her Search for God *in eighteen days. After reading it, William Maxwell suggested that it would make an attrac-tive and saleable illustrated book and recommended draughtsman and wood engraver John Farleigh (1900–65). On 8 May Shaw sent Farleigh a list of twelve*

'Suggested Subjects' and a cheque for five guineas for 'one trial drawing' (CL 4, 296–7). On the 11th Kyllmann wrote to Shaw urging him to let Constable issue the book as 'separate from the Standard Edition, and then later include it in the volume of short stories ... I think 5/– would be quite a suitable price and I know we could sell a good many thousands ...' (TLU (c): UNC).

I have talked it over with Farleigh and found, as I expected, that he had conceived the book in terms of the Standard Edition page and type, which suits his style. For a smaller page I should have chosen another draughtsman. Nothing will make 13,000 words worth five shillings. We must make a feature of the thinness of the book (like The Gregynog Press Davies) and sell it for half a crown. It ought to be sixpence.

Anyhow we must experiment in the breakaway from high prices which is now inevitable. We are back to the two shilling novel already. A pamphlet which ought really to be a broadsheet and be hawked on the pavement is dear at half a crown ...

G.B.S.

In 1928 *Selected Poems of W.H. Davies* (285 copies) appeared with Welsh publishers **Gregynog Press** (founded 1922), who published *Shaw Gives Himself Away* (300 copies) on 6 November 1939. On the topic of a **breakaway from high prices**, Shaw would write to Kyllmann on 8 August 1932 that *The Black Girl* 'may tempt the people I want to get at to indulge in the extravagance (for them) of two and six. I should like to sell 250,000 in the first five minutes after publication. I am utterly sick of the futile handful of plutocrats to whom five shillings is nothing: I want to impose a heroic sacrifice on those to whom **half a crown** is a twelfth of their weekly income' (APCS: UNC). *The Black Girl*, published on 5 December 1932 at 2s.6d., was a best-seller and was reprinted fourteen times between 1932 and 1936.

140 / To Howard C. Lewis   4 Whitehall Court, London SW1
                                 14th December 1932

[ALS: Brown; FP: *Saturday Review of Literature*]

Shaw sent the agreement below to Howard Corwin Lewis (1890–1952), vice-president of Dodd, Mead & Co., with the following note: 'The enclosed, written in great haste, must do to protect you until we can make a regular contract covering the whole field of our operations. In the concluding clause the word "wilfully" is inserted to meet the contingency of delay by circumstances over which you have no control – strikes, for instance' (ALCS: Cornell). As part of 'To G.B.S. On His Eighty-Eighth Birthday, the Saturday Review of Literature *(New York) for 22 July*

1944 reproduced it (p. 14) with the caption: 'Photograph of a provisional con-
tract, written by Shaw for the publication of "The Black Girl" and illustrating his
remarkable precision and clarity in business relations with his publisher.' Shaw
capitalizes 'Fifteen' presumably for emphasis.

I hereby license Messrs. Dodd Mead & Company Incorporated of 443
Fourth Avenue in New York City to print and publish a story written by
me entitled The Adventures of the Black Girl in Her Search for God with
the illustrations by John Farleigh (as published in London on the fifth
day of December in the present year) for a period of five years terminat-
ing on the thirtyfirst day of December one thousand nine hundred and
thirtyseven on the following conditions.

I am to receive a royalty of Fifteen per cent on the retail price of all
copies sold under this license.

Accounts to be furnished to me half yearly to Midsummer and New
Year and the sums due to those dates to be paid to me by a draft on Lon-
don on or before every twentyfifth day of March and twentyninth day of
September first following.

I am not to license any other publisher to publish the story during the
term of this license in the United States of America.

This license does not extend to Canada.

I guarantee that I have acquired from John Farleigh his license to reproduce his illustrations and decorations for a fully paid consideration
covering the duration of this copyright.

The book is to be manufactured in the United States in compliance
with the Copyright Act and published in time to secure my copyright
there.

Should the story be allowed to fall virtually out of print, or the publishers commit an act of bankruptcy, or willfully violate the conditions of this
license, it shall cease and I shall be free to license any other publisher in
the United States notwithstanding anything to the contrary declared or
implied above.

G. Bernard Shaw

Four of Farleigh's woodcut **illustrations** paired with Shaw's sketches are reproduced in
Hugo, *Bernard Shaw's 'The Black Girl.'* Shaw expanded the last sentence in 1933: 'Should the
Publishers at any time during the term of this Agreement find themselves unable or unwill-
ing to operate within its clauses and conditions or should they retire from their publishing

business or materially change its general character or should they commit an act of bank-ruptcy the licenses herein contained with all obligations of the Author to the Publishers under this Agreement shall forthwith cease' (TDU (c): Brown). *The Black Girl* was pub-lished in February 1933, Dodd's first Shaw publication.

141 / To G. Bernard Shaw

[no address]
28th December 1932

[TEL: Brown]

The Shaws had begun their world tour on 16 December, boarding the Canadian Pacific liner Empress of Britain *at Monaco. The following cablegram was ad-dressed to 'Bernard Shaw, passenger Empress Britain transport, Cairo.'*

BRENTANO SITUATION EXTREMELY CRITICAL. BANKRUPTCY WITH-IN THIRTY DAYS APPARENTLY INEVITABLE. HAVE CONSULTED BEN-JAMIN STERN IN YOUR INTEREST AND OURS. HE SUGGESTS YOU CABLE HIM IMMEDIATELY INSTRUCTIONS TO ACT AS NECESSARY IN AFFECTING TRANSFER OF OLDER BOOKS TO US IN ORDER TO FORE-STALL ANY ATTEMPT TO DISPOSE OF YOUR PROPERTY WITH OTHER BRENTANO ASSETS.

DODD

142 / To Lowell Brentano

At Sea, World Cruise
6th January 1933

[TLS: Oregon; CL 4]

Dear Lowell Brentano

Now that I have at last a moment's leisure on board ship I must send you a line to express the wrench to my personal feelings which my change of Publishers cost me. I held on as long as I could with any sort of prudence – in fact longer; but you will probably not appreciate this until you are forty years older. An older hand than you would have known that the re-port you sent me about the action of your Bankers was decisive. I made every possible inquiry in quarters which, if not actively friendly, were at least quite disinterested; but I could get no scrap of reason for hoping that the Bankers would not foreclose in February, and involve me without benefitting you.

If you can transfer your stock of my books to Dodd Mead before your creditors remainder them at waste paper prices, so much the better.

I do not know what is happening or what is going to happen; but I assume that there is some chance of the bookshop's going on under the old name. If you sell the goodwill you will, I suppose, be pushed out on the grounds that the family management has not been successful since the death of your father. You evidently over-capitalised in anticipation of an extension of business that did not take place. Now, they'll blame you and your relatives for the crash; and it might be well for you in making a settlement to do your best to avoid being both squeezed out and prevented from using your name in any future adventures.

Whether Dodd Mead will do any better for me in the way of distribution remains to be seen. They gave up book selling long ago, and therefore do not enjoy the discount which enlarges the fund out of which royalties come; so I am changing my plan and accepting lower royalties on a guaranteed minimum circulation. Our 1931 results were so bad that I foresaw that I must either make some change, or accept the position of an extinct volcano in America.

All this is only to help you to think your affairs over. We, my wife and I – are distressed at the possibility of you – you two – finding yourself in a difficult financial situation which my action will not tend to improve.

But it really couldn't be helped; so feel as charitable as you can about it; and do not forget that there is nothing like three or four bankruptcies for building up a big fortune nowadays.

faithfully

G. Bernard Shaw

For Brentano's **report**, see headnote to Letter 129. A letter authorizing the **transfer** of 'plates, sheets, bound copies and all such copyrights as this concern may have; also its surrender of all publishing rights' to Dodd, Mead & Co. was drawn up on 16 January (TLS: Brown). Shaw most likely refers to the **two** Brentano brothers, Lowell and Simon. Brentano's was declared **bankrupt** in March and bought out by the firm of Coward, McCann. 'Shaw was the only author-creditor who, because of the ironclad terms of his contract, received 100% of the moneys due to him, the others having to be content with about 35¢. in the dollar' (CL 4, 319). Those moneys amounted to $15,914, 'covering everything up to January 1, 1933' (TLS: Brown).

143 / To Lowell Brentano   R.M.S. *Empress of Britain*
approaching Honolulu from Japan
14th March 1933

[ALS: Oregon; CL 4]

Shaw had castigated the United States for its shortcomings in 'A Message to America,' a BBC short-wave broadcast from London (via the CBS network) on 11 October 1931. On 11 April 1933, under the auspices of the non-profit Academy of Political Science, he did so in person, addressing an audience of over 3500 in New York City's Metropolitan Opera House (and millions via NBC radio). His topic: 'The Future of Political Science in America.'

Dear Lowell Brentano

... I am sensible of the friendly way in which you have helped the transfer to Dodd Meads; and if I were forty years younger there is no saying what we might do together; but my sands are nearly run out; and I have no time for moneymaking, nor any desire for the limelight except to get out of it. My brief appearance in New York will be to say some unpopular but necessary things to your people before I die.

I shall have to keep as quiet as possible on the 11th April and sleep on the ship; for to tackle and hold a big audience for an hour at 77 is – though with care I can do it – something that will use up all my forces.

I am rather horrified at the threatened spectacle of a publisher turning playwright. Now if it were the other way – !

Who is to support your wife – and *you*?

ever

G. Bernard Shaw

The 11th of **April** began with a whirlwind four-hour drive through Manhattan with Howard C. Lewis and company president Frank C. Dodd. That evening, during his **hour**-and-forty-minute address, Shaw said numerous **unpopular but necessary things**, criticizing everything from Hollywood immorality, unemployment, and capitalism to the Constitution and the Statue of Liberty. On 17 April Lewis wrote to Otto Kyllmann that Shaw's address had 'created a very favorable impression' and that his audience had been 'enthusiastic and sympathetic' (TLS: UNC). The following day Shaw met with his American copyright attorney Benjamin H. Stern and with publisher William H. Wise. For details of Shaw's brief visit, see Laurence, '"That Awful Country." Dodd, Mead published the address on 28 July, Shaw assigning his royalties to the Academy of Political Science. Lowell Brentano subsequently became a successful novelist and **playwright**.

144 / To Otto Kyllmann   Ayot St Lawrence, Welwyn, Herts.

17th July 1933

[ALS: UNC]

Constable published Shaw's New York lecture as The Political Madhouse in America and Nearer Home *on 29 August; Dodd, Mead had done so on 28 July under the innocuous title* The Future of Political Science in America.

My dear Kyllmann

I enclose an introduction – called an Explanation – for the lecture; but I am doubtful about the sales; and your plan to call in Farleigh and make the book a companion to The Black Girl convinces me that you are quite mad about my works ... By all means let us have an attractive jacket or even a vividly colored case in a cellophane jacket; but it must not be black and white.

And then what are we to call the damned thing? The Future of Political Science is all right for a lecture; but it wont do for anything short of a big treatise in book form. How are we to let the public know exactly what it is buying? The proper title would be Political Science in America: is Ours any Better? A Lecture. But that sounds too dry and is too long. The best subtitle I can think of at present is

The Political Madhouse in America and Nearer Home. A Lecture ...

always

G. Bernard Shaw

The cover (minus 'A Lecture') was not **black and white** but white lettering on a blue background. 'An indeterminate number of advance copies was bound in unlettered brown paper wrappers' (Laurence 1, 215).

145 / To Otto Kyllmann   [Malvern Hotel, Malvern

undated: ca. 26th July 1933]

[ANU: UNC; CL 4]

The Shaws attended the Malvern Festival from 24 July to 15 September. Shaw wrote the following note on a sample title page, which read: 'THE POLITICAL MADHOUSE IN AMERICA AND NEARER HOME *A Lecture With an Explanation by* BERNARD SHAW 1933.'

This won't do, because it suggests an anonymous lecture with an explanation by me. As the whole book is by me there is no need to mention the explanation, as there would be if it applied to a book by somebody else. And there is no publisher's imprint, a pernicious and illegal innovation.

The design is all right; but the designer was not supplied with the proper copy. If he is Farleigh, better send him the accompanying corrected page, and ask him to fill in with a picture of me kicking the statue of Liberty off its pedestal.

John **Farleigh** designed only the lettering for the book's cover. On a proof leaf, Shaw drew his comical **picture** (reproduced in CL 4, 351).

146 / To Otto Kyllmann Malvern Hotel, Malvern
2nd August 1933

[ALS: UNC; CL 4]

The following letter is an example of Shaw's attention to detail, in this instance which colours to use for the cover of The Political Madhouse *and how best to display the book's price.*

When selling a cheap line the first rule is to mark the article with its price in plain figures. A book by me *might* cost anything up to 7s/6d; and people will be afraid to ask for it unless they know that two bob is the limit.

Nothing on earth will make a flat tint of white on green look well. A flat white bit of paper on a tea-rose bush would look like litter. Orange on green would be all right. If the lettering is to be white the ground must be Worcester blue. Black would recall the Black Girl and is therefore ruled out. The green on white, especially that particular shade of green, gives the book an Irish Roman Catholic air, repellant to all good Protestants.

If the figure 2/– looks too haberdashery Farleigh might add another line PRICE ONE FLORIN. 'Two shillings' looks and sounds cheap and nasty, but Florin is Apostolically Imperial and attractively novel.

One should study bookbuyer's psychology.

G.B.S.

The **tea rose** has yellowish or pink flowers. Shaw alludes to the famous **Worcester blue** and white porcelain. A **haberdashery** carries accessories used in clothing, in particular men's wear; for Shaw, **2/–** may have looked too flagrantly commercial (as in Lewis Carroll's Mad Hatter, whose top hat advertises itself with *In this Style 10/6*). When published, *The Political Madhouse* bore the legend 'PRICE ONE FLORIN' (in the same type size as Shaw's name). A British **florin** (1849–1970) was worth **two shillings**.

147 / To Dodd, Mead & Co.   4 Whitehall Court, London SW1
                                                          22nd September 1933

[TLS: Cornell]

Shaw had met president Frank Courtenay Dodd (1875–1968) and vice-president Howard C. Lewis in New York on 11 April and below replies to a letter written by their firm that very day. Shaw writes to the firm's senior members: president (1916–30) and then chairman Edward H. Dodd; his cousin Frank C. Dodd, president (1931–42) and then chairman; Arthur M. Chase; Edward S. Mead (d. 1894); vice-president Lewis (president 1942–52); and Frank Moore Colby. Their letter 'of the 15th, just to hand' to which Shaw replies in a postscript is presumably dated 15 September.

Dear Dodds both, Chase, Mead's Ghost, Lewis,
old Uncle Tom Cobley and All

At last I have snatched a couple of days to attend to that neglected matter of our agreement. I enclose a draft on which you can make your comments. If I have forgotten anything essential let me know and I will draft additional clauses.

Now as to the points mentioned in your letter of 11th April.

I will have nothing to do with schools and colleges at any price: no book of mine shall ever with my consent be that damnable thing, a schoolbook. Let them buy the dollar editions if they want them. By a school edition they mean an edition with notes and prefaces full of material for such questions as 'Give the age of Bernard Shaw's great aunt when he wrote You Never Can Tell and state the reasons for believing that the inscription on her tombstone at Ballyhooly is incorrect.' The experienced students read the notes and prefaces and not the plays, and for ever after loathe my very name.

As to anthologies, it is my custom to blackmail the publisher to the extent of a donation to the Society of Authors (or the Authors' League of ·

America), which thereupon answers for the consents of all the authors involved. How much do you find it practicable to extort by your method?

As to amateur fees they are not worth collecting from a business point of view because it is my practice to allow professional terms (5% on the gross receipts when they do not exceed $250) to all the Little Theatres provided they get drunk with it in the regular professional way. I do so because it is the devoted efforts of these little people that keep the drama alive; and if I leave them to French or any other agent, they are charged fees of $25, which they cannot possibly pay out of receipts that may not reach $5. So I do the job myself, as the fees are so small that they sometimes hardly cover the postage. This is good business for me in the long run; but it would not attract you.

The limit of five years will probably be quite forgotten by us, as the agreement goes on automatically to all eternity if we are satisfied with it. But if Frank goes mad, and Edward takes to drink, and Chase is hanged, and Lewis takes to publishing pornographic literature and is Comstocked for it, how am I to get out unless I can break at six months notice. The five years is only to secure you a run of that length for every book before you sink your capital in it. Besides, you may want to get rid of me in case I become too infamous for any respectable publisher to touch me.

I think that is all that is not dealt with in the agreement. When we get it through I will consider what to do with the money that is in escrow. Your account of sales is ghastly. Some of those old books are as dead as doornails at the ridiculous prices which Brentano insisted on charging. In my Standard Edition here I have combined them into volumes in such a way as to make family reading enough to justify their cost. My forthcoming volumes are a set of three plays with two prefaces: Too True To Be Good, Village Wooing, and On The Rocks, which will be a very tidy $2 worth, and a volume of my short stories including the Black Girl with illustrations by John Farleigh, equally bulky. These will, I think, certainly be ready before the end of the year.

faithfully

G. Bernard Shaw

P.S. In reply to yours of the 15th, just to hand, the Too True volume is actually set up and ready for press as far as the three plays are concerned; but of the two prefaces only half of the first is written. I shall get the rest finished as fast as I can. Simultaneous publication is indispensable for copyright purposes; so I shall not let Constables get the start of you.

As to the Madhouse I had intended to serialize the English preface in America so as to secure its appearance in the American papers on the day of publication; but Kyllmann misunderstood the situation and shot the book out before I had time to arrange anything. By all means include it in the next edition if one is called for. I suggest that you send proofs round to the papers as a news item with the announcement of the new edition. Do as you think fit, anyhow ...

When we have agreed on the draft contract we had better let Benjamin Stern look over it in case the phraseology is not legally correct.

Shaw plays on a line from the popular Devon folksong 'Widecombe Fair' (published 1890), in which '**old Uncle Tom Cobley and all**' ride an old grey mare to the fair. In 1905, when Anthony **Comstock** (1844–1915), founder of the New York Society for the Suppression of Vice (founded 1873), objected to *Mrs Warren's Profession* – calling Shaw an 'Irish smut dealer' – Shaw coined the word 'Comstockery' in an article in the *New York Times* (26 September). For further comments on **schoolbook** editions, see Letters 120, 150, and 179. Despite Shaw's claim that Brentano's charged **ridiculous prices**, their Shaw books were usually priced at $1.50, a fair equivalent to Constable's 6 shillings. Constable charged 7s.6d. for *Too True To Be Good, Village Wooing, and On The Rocks* (1934), while Dodd, Mead sold it for $2.50, not **$2**.

148 / To Otto Kyllmann   4 Whitehall Court, London SW1
25th January 1934

[ALS: UNC]

My dear Kyllmann

As to the Short Stories and the prefaces I agree, though July is a bad date for the prefaces, which demand very long winter evenings when people will read anything.

But as to the Collected Edition it seems to me impossible to rush out a single volume costing a guinea at the moment when an equally desirable one is offered at seven and sixpence. Either we must treat the Collected Edition as up to date at the time and have done with it, or else make the additions to it in batches of three or four at a time. The policy of adding my new books to it, volume by volume, in competition with the Standard Edition is out of the question.

It is very difficult to guess how many of the purchasers of the 30 Collected volumes will go through with it to the end. Some bought on speculation, some will get cold feet, some are dead (young people dont buy Collected Editions), some had realised what idiots they were with the Standard Edition available etc etc etc.

My popularity does not increase. On The Rocks has flopped after an inglorious run of nine weeks to receipts that it would be flattery to call mediocre ...

Faithfully,
G. Bernard Shaw

There were three **additions** to the *Collected Edition* (volumes 31, 32, 33): *Too True to be Good: Village Wooing: On the Rocks* (1934), *The Simpleton of the Unexpected Isles: The Six of Calais: The Millionairess* (1938), and *London Music in 1888–89* (1938). Shaw had instructed Kyllmann on 5 January to 'shoot out the **single** Collected Too True, as the collectors are howling for it; but dont blame me if you dont get the money back' (ALCS: UNC). The book was published on 15 February by Constable (22,000 copies) and Dodd, Mead (5000 copies). Shaw had reason to regret **rushing out** the volume: a schoolboy pointed out 'a hideous mistake in the Too True volume on p. 155 on the cross head. Seventh commandment (adultery) should be sixth commandment (kill) ... Mend the plate instantly, and blush' (CL 4, 375), Shaw wrote to R. & R. Clark on 9 June. *On the Rocks* ran for seventy-three performances at the Winter Garden Theatre (London), 25 November 1933–27 January 1934 (roughly Shaw's **nine weeks**).

149 / To Grant Richards

[no address]
23rd May 1934

[TLS (tr): HRC]

Richards had sent Shaw (whose letters he wished to quote) the proofs of his second volume of memoirs, Author Hunting *(see Letter 45), published later that year.*

Dear G.R.

I enclose the proofs with one or two suggestions and one deletion of a sentence or two of no public importance. The one about the Kelmscott Press – one of the phenomena of the time – is, I think, topically interesting enough to be mentioned; and it explains the letters better.

You should call the book The Tragedy of a Publisher who allowed himself to fall in Love with Literature. The publisher who does that, like the picture dealer who likes pictures or the schoolmistress who gets fond of her pupils, is foredoomed. A certain connoisseurship in the public taste is indispensable; but the slightest uncommercial bias in choosing between, say, Bridges' Testament of Beauty and a telephone directory, is fatal.

The stuff is very readable: you have a pleasant style.

I hereby authorize you to quote in full in your book (except for the one deletion marked) all the letters in galleys 17 to 36, typescript pp 143 to 159, and the two letters about Davidson. Only dont put my name on the title page or Constables will drop down dead.

Is this sufficient? If so, dont bother to reply.

always yrs.

G. Bernard Shaw

For the **Kelmscott Press**, see notes to Letters 32 and 74. Poet laureate (from 1913) Robert **Bridges** (1844–1930) achieved widespread popularity with the 4000-line poem *The Testament of Beauty* (1929). Suffering from depression, Scottish poet and playwright John **Davidson** (1857–1909) drowned himself. Shaw's **two letters** (one to John Lane, one to Richards) explain how he had assisted Davidson with £250 to write what turned out to be a failed melodrama. At Shaw's suggestion, Richards used the second paragraph of this letter as the epigraph of *Author Hunting*.

150 / To Dodd, Mead & Co.   4 Whitehall Court, London SW1
                                        10th September 1934

[TLS: Brown]

American author John B. Opdycke (d. 1956) wrote numerous works on English language usage, including the much-reprinted Harper's English Grammar (1941).

Dear Dodd Mead

... As to the school edition I will not entertain that on any terms. I was horrified when, under date May 30th, Mr John B. Opdycke sent me an announcement made by you that I had consented for the first time to the publication of one of my plays in a school edition. For this you will be called to account on the great Day of Judgment. Three Masters of the English Drama was not sanctioned by me as a school book but as an ordinary piece of literature with the ordinary editorial introductions necessitated by the inclusion in the volume of Shakespear's play and Dryden's.

By a school edition I mean one with a schoolmaster's preface, a glossary, and a set of impertinent notes containing as many dates as possible; so that the examiners may have something to set questions about in their loathsome papers. The experienced student does not read the play: he reads the notes, and acquires a lifelong antipathy to the unfortunate author. The uglier the print and binding the more scholastic the effect.

I have refused offers for these horrors from every country in Europe where literature is a school subject. I shall refuse every such offer from America. I will not have my books prefaced or annotated or meddled with in any way by other hands than my own; and as to having them listed under the abhorrent heading of school or text book I will pursue the scoundrel who does it to the confines of his native hell.

I have no objection to teachers forbidding students to read my books, nor to your preparing editions of single plays exactly as I wrote them to meet the ensuing demand; but I will not have my name detested and my plays avoided by young Americans as the name of Shakespear and his plays are now detested and avoided. So tell your 'excellent text book publisher' that I should just like to catch him at it ...

Faithfully

G. Bernard Shaw

Three Masters of the English Drama: Shaw, Dryden, Shakespeare, edited by Roland Ketchum and Adolph Gillis, was published by Dodd, Mead in 1934.

151 / To William Maxwell

4 Whitehall Court, London SW1
20th October 1936

[ALCS: NLS]

In August Shaw had written to Allen Lane (1902–70), nephew of publisher John Lane and founder (on 1 January 1935) of Penguin Books Ltd, recommending that The Worst Journey in the World, *by his friend Apsley Cherry-Garrard, be added to his list. 'Lane replied that the book he really wanted was* The Intelligent Woman's Guide to Socialism' *(Holroyd, Bernard Shaw, vol. 3, 373). In May 1937 Penguin published an expanded version of the* Guide *(in two volumes) entitled* The Intelligent Woman's Guide to Socialism, Capitalism, Sovietism and Fascism *(with two new chapters) to inaugurate Lane's Pelican Books series. The one-volume cloth edition had sold at fifteen shillings; the paperback volumes were sixpence each.*

... Prepare for a shock. The Penguin Press wants the Intelligent Woman's Guide. A sixpenny edition would be the salvation of mankind. I have replied that it contains 200,000 words, and needs an additional chapter. That is as far as we have got.

I am told that you have an implacable down on the Penguins. Why? Is their printing sweated?

Odhams might be an alternative if they would rise to it. But they couldnt get it down to sixpence or (in 2 vols) a shilling.

Ponder these things at your convenience.

G.B.S.

Odhams Press Ltd (1920–83) had published omnibus editions of Shaw's plays (1931; expanded editions 1934, 1938, 1950) and prefaces (1934; expanded edition 1938).

152 / To G. Bernard Shaw

Office of the President
28th October 1936

[TLS: HRC]

Beneath Dodd's signature in the following letter, Shaw has written 'Cable at full rate Dodd New York Go ahead I agree Bernard Shaw.' However, Shaw must have had second thoughts: on the carbon copy of this letter, at the section requesting that Shaw waive his royalty, we read the manuscript note, 'Not accepted by Shaw – straight 10%' (TLU (c): Brown).

Dear Mr Shaw

Ben Stern sent us a copy of Basil Blackwell's volume on WILLIAM MORRIS, which contains your charming introduction. At your request, Mr Stern took our interim copyright late in August, but in order to complete the copyright of this preface, it will be necessary to publish formally within four months after interim deposit. But, of course, as Stern says, you know more about our copyright than anyone does! It is evident, however, that if protection is to be completed, formal publication must take place sometime in December. This is possible, and I have the following suggestion to make, subject to your approval:

We will be delighted to publish the Preface as a small book, about the size of THE FUTURE OF POLITICAL SCIENCE IN AMERICA, and pay you a roy-

178

alty of ten per cent of the published price. Though the potential demand must necessarily be limited, I feel reasonably confident that we can sell a sufficient number of copies to Shaw collectors, libraries, etc., to liquidate the production expense and perhaps a bit more. With some hesitation, I suggest, however, that unless we sell 500 copies within a year that you waive your royalty. But I am quite willing to abide by your decision as to that.

As time is pressing, won't you kindly cable your acceptance or declination of this proposal at once? Frankly, it is the only method that I can see of protecting the work on this side.

Are you likely to have another volume of plays for 1937? I hesitate to ask this early, but we like to know as far in advance as possible what is coming along.

I do hope you had a pleasant summer and that both you and Mrs Shaw are in good health.

With kindest regards,

Very sincerely yours,
Frank C. Dodd
DODD, MEAD & COMPANY, Inc.

For attorney **Benjamin Stern**, see Letter 100. William Morris's daughter May (1863–1938) edited her father's collected works in twenty-four volumes (1910–15). Shaw's **charming introduction** to *Morris as a Socialist*, volume two of May Morris's *William Morris: Artist, Writer, Socialist*, published by leading Oxford bookseller **Basil Blackwell** (1889–1984) on 1 July 1936, was entitled 'Morris as I Knew Him.' Dodd, Mead published *William Morris as I Knew Him* on 3 December 1936 in an edition of 1000 copies.

153 / To G. Bernard Shaw   50 West 47th Street, New York City
3rd December 1936

[TLS: HRC]

Under the signature of president John J. Crawley, William H. Wise & Co. had distributed a two-page letter addressed to 'Dear Friend': '... While the small remaining quantity lasts, you may have the celebrated de luxe limited edition of THE COLLECTED WORKS OF BERNARD SHAW for less than 20¢ on the dollar – less than ⅕th of their actual value! ... *Only 1,790 numbered sets were made, of which only a few remain. They sold at $10.50 a volume – $315 for the set of 30 volumes.' Wise was now offering each set at 'only $3 monthly until the total price*

of $60 for the 30 volumes is paid – less than ⅕th of the original $315 price!'
(TLS (c): Brown)

Dear Mr Shaw

You will be interested, I hope, in learning that the major portion of the last five hundred sets of the Ayot St Lawrence edition of your works was distributed by our direct-by-mail sales department last month.

These thirty-volume sets cost us on an average of $80.00 a set to manufacture some five years go, and we were finally able to dispose of them at a mark down retail price of $60.00 a set, to be paid for in monthly installments of $3.00 over a period of twenty months.

We still have some forty to fifty sets to distribute, and because of the large investment which we have heretofore had in this property we were unable to undertake the promotion of the low-priced edition contemplated in your letter of January 3, 1935. We now believe that with the more expensive edition out of the way the time is ripe for us to promote a special edition and would like to make the necessary tests during the early part of 1937.

Under the terms of our present license agreement with you, our contract expires on December 31, 1936. We would like very much to have you extend the agreement in its present form for an additional one hundred and twenty days, from December 31, 1936 to April 30, 1937.

We believe that within that time we will be able to make the necessary arrangements to promote your COLLECTED WORKS on a more popular basis.

May we hear from you accordingly.

Yours very truly
WM. H. WISE & CO. INC.
John J. Crawley
President

On 3 January 1935 Shaw had approved a **low-priced edition** of his works: 'I hereby license you to print and publish a twelve-volume set of selected works of mine and to sell them and not otherwise at a retail price of not less than thirty dollars ($30) per set' (TLU (c): HRC). The project did not materialize.

180

154 / To Otto Kyllmann Victoria Hotel, Sidmouth
18th September 1937

[TLS: UNC]

Bernard Shaw, Frank Harris and Oscar Wilde (1937) by Robert Harborough Sher-
ard (1861–1943) was an attack on Frank Harris's (1856–1931) biography Oscar
Wilde, His Life and Confessions *(1916). John Lane would reissue Harris's book*
in 1939, with a preface by Shaw. 'To save his [Harris's] widow from destitution I
have edited it and written a preface in which I have made hay of Sherard's recent
book as goodnaturedly as possible. He called Harris a liar on every page without
convicting him of a single falsehood.' (Shaw to Hesketh Pearson, 4 July 1938, CL
4, 503).

My dear O.K.

... Have you read a book entitled Shaw, Frank Harris, and OSCAR WILDE
by R.H. Sherard? Harris's widow is in Nice, destitute. She says I can do
her only one service besides giving her a few pounds for which she has
never asked. That service is to write a preface to Harris's Life and Confessions of Oscar Wilde, which can easily be edited so as to make it proof
against any possible litigation by Lord Alfred Douglas or anyone else. I
dont think it has ever been published in England for fear of such litigation. In a rash moment I read Sherard's book; and the bait was irresist-
ible: I have wasted half my time here in slicing Robert Harborough
Sherard into many more pieces than there are letters in his long name.
The preface is practically finished; and it remains to find a publisher who
will advance Mrs Harris a few hundred pounds to set her up in a teashop
in Nice on account of royalties.

I am informed by the financially scandalized Miss Patch that you are
down £1412 on my dues up to the 30th June 1936, and that you have giv-
en up even sending in accounts. And my bills for Bassetto will come in
presently. I dont believe you have a notion of how the affairs of the firm
stand; and you certainly know nothing of mine. I shall send in an accoun-
tant to verify Miss P's figures and ascertain your assets; for I can't let you
go on like this: it will continue to get worse and worse until we are both
in Portugal Street. That's the worst of publishing: it obliterates all conscience ...

G.B.S.

The Shaws stayed in **Sidmouth**, on the East Devon coast, from 22 August to 3 October. Wilde's former lover **Lord Alfred Douglas** (1870–1945) had written a preface for Sherard's book; he also assisted Shaw with his 1939 preface by providing 'marginal notes and letters' (CL 4, 489). Frank and Nellie Harris had settled in **Nice** in 1923, marrying only in 1927. Harris died shortly before his *Bernard Shaw: An Unauthorised Biography* (1931) was published (with Shaw's extensive proof revisions following Harris's death). **Miss** Blanche **Patch** (1879–1966) was Shaw's private secretary from 1920 until his death in 1950. Constable published *London Music in 1888–89,* Shaw's reviews under the pseudonym Corno di **Bassetto**, on 23 September. The London Bankruptcy Court was located at 5 **Portugal Street**.

155 / To Otto Kyllmann

Victoria Hotel, Sidmouth
23rd September 1937

[TLS: UNC; CL 4]

My dear O.K.

Let me now explain my sudden attack of business rapacity, and why you must now as fast as you can get out of my debt and keep out of it.

Charlotte and I have been heavily preoccupied with our positively last wills and testaments, which are at last executed and safe in the strong rooms of our respective solicitors.

It is mine which concerns Constable & Co. I am now in my 80second year, which means that my death may occur at any moment: indeed, actuarially, I am dead already.

Suppose I die tomorrow, or this afternoon (motoring on these Devonshire lanes is hazardous), what happens to you? You will find yourself not in the hands of Charlotte or any friendly and squeezable private executor, but in the grip of the Public Trustee, whose mill grinds quickly and grinds exceedingly large. It would be a case of your money or your life: cash down or Portugal St.

It was this new situation which I felt bound to present to you in as violent a manner as possible. Strictly speaking you should insure my life for the debt; but the premium would be colossal.

Meanwhile I cannot pretend that I am suffering any serious personal privation for lack of the money; so you may take a week or two to consider it. I did not mean it to arrive as a welcome home: I had no idea that you were returning from Ireland. Why did you go to that fantastic country? There are worse places, provided you can always get away from it.

We shall probably stay here until the end of the month or thereabouts.

A letter from Odhams just arrived informs me that they never took on the prefaces, but that if I have a large remainder on hand they will get rid of it for me on terms to be arranged. Have we any such remainder?

always yours
G.B.S.

These were not the **positively last wills and testaments**; those were published in Holroyd, *Bernard Shaw*, vol. 4, where Charlotte's (91–100) is dated 2 September 1937 and includes a 27 November 1940 codicil, and Shaw's (101–15) is dated 12 June 1950, five months before his death on 2 November. **Motoring** on **hazardous Devonshire lanes** may have evoked memories of Shaw's 1932 car accident in South Africa (see Letter 139). Shaw seems to be using '**fantastic**' in its slightly pejorative sense of unreal, strange, or bizarre. **Odhams** not only **took on** whatever stock of the *Prefaces* remained in the Leighton-Straker warehouse, but contracted for an enlarged edition of 20,000 copies in 1938.

156 / To Dodd, Mead & Co.

4 Whitehall Court, London SW1
10th December 1937

[TLS: Brown].

The following is an unusual departure from Shaw's habitual and adamant objections to having his work anthologized (see Letters 120, 147, and 150). See also Shaw's 1948 'stereotyped' postcard, which reads (in part): 'Bernard Shaw's books and plays, being on sale in his own editions and subject to various publishing contracts, are not available for anthologies or school editions' (Laurence 2, 831). F.S. Crofts & Co. (founded 1924) of New York merged with the D. Appleton-Century Co. in 1948 to form Appleton-Century-Crofts, Inc.

Dear Sirs

Mr Frederick Crofts representing the firm of F.S. Crofts & Co visited me lately in London. They wish to include my play Arms and the Man in an Anthology of Victorian Literature which they are issuing. They offer a royalty of 1% on the retail price of all copies sold and to advance $100 on account forthwith. I consented to this, subject to your complicity in the transaction. I understand that they have secured this; so will you please take the matter in hand and collect from Crofts & Co., crediting half the payments to my account. The limits to the duration of this arrangement are to be as if it formed part of our general agreement.

Faithfully
G. Bernard Shaw

157 / To Howard C. Lewis   4 Whitehall Court, London SW1
25th November 1938

[ANS: Cornell; CL 4]

On 2 September 1936 Shaw had allowed the American Foundation for the Blind to make 300 copies of a recording of Caesar and Cleopatra *as* Talking Books for the Blind *(TLS: Brown); Dodd, Mead (presumably with Shaw's permission) had contracted for 300 copies of* The Devil's Disciple *on 26 August 1938 (TLU: Brown). The following is a reply to Lewis's 16 November 1938 request for Shaw's approval to do the same for* Candida.

I dont approve at all. I never object to Braille, because the blind can't read the play in the ordinary editions. But they *can* go to ordinary performances. And I strongly object to the existence of records made without any guarantee of the quality of the performance. It is one thing to record a performance by Miss Katharine Cornell and her company. That would be available for the whole English speaking world, blind or seeing. But a record made by a firm of nobodies with a cast of nobodies – no, damn it, no no no no no NO ...

G.B.S.
25/11/38

Celebrated American actress **Katharine Cornell** (1893–1974) starred in *Candida, The Devil's Disciple*, and *Saint Joan*.

158 / To William Maxwell   4 Whitehall Court, London SW1
8th March 1939

[ALCS: NLS]

Shaw's Geneva, *illustrated with sixteen plates and forty-three line drawings by Feliks Topolski (1907–89), was published by Constable on 15 June. Shaw called Topolski 'an astonishing draughtsman: perhaps the greatest of all the Impressionists in black and white' (CL 4, 537). Shaw told Maxwell on 24 July: 'Kyllmann wants me to do a Topolski Charles' (APCS: NLS). Topolski illustrated Constable's* In Good King Charles's Golden Days *(17 November) and the Penguin (screen version) edition of* Pygmalion *(1941).*

Dear Maxwell

Unfortunately this Topolski edition is, like the Political Madhouse, a side line for me. I am not paying for it: Kyllmann does all that; and I go half profits with him. He knows that if it were in my hands it would go to Brandon St; but he says that you wont make a competitive price for him and that his man not only is much cheaper but can reproduce Topolski's work on separate sheets with special skill. This will make it possible to sell at five shillings. (I said either two shillings or two guineas). In the face of this I cannot insist, as the speculation is K's and not mine. It is solely on Topolski's account that I have consented to this abnormal edition ...

G.B.S.

Printers R. & R. Clark were located in **Brandon St**reet, Edinburgh; *Geneva* was printed at the Chiswick Press. It went on sale at 7s.6d.

159 / To G. Bernard Shaw

[no address]
19th June 1939

[TLU (c): Brown]

Shaw's attorney Benjamin Stern was probably approached by Gabriel Pascal (1894–1954), who had recently produced a film version of Pygmalion *(1938). On 24 January 1939 Shaw had sent Pascal an agreement for bringing* The Doctor's Dilemma *to the screen (Dukore,* Bernard Shaw *and Gabriel Pascal, 52), but the project never materialized. The play was filmed only in 1958 under the direction of Anthony Asquith (1902–68), who had directed Pascal's* Pygmalion. *Pascal produced and directed* Major Barbara *(1941) and* Caesar and Cleopatra *(1945), and produced* Androcles and the Lion *(1952), which was directed by Chester Erskine. Shaw had cabled Dodd, Mead about copyright renewal on 14 June.*

Dear Mr Shaw

Your cable concerning the renewal of the copyright on the volume containing THE DOCTOR'S DILEMMA, GETTING MARRIED and THE SHEWING-UP OF BLANCO POSNET was not the first shock we had received concerning this matter. A few days ago Mr Stern advised us that the motion picture producers of THE DOCTOR'S DILEMMA had notified him that the copyright had lapsed; and he pointed out a fact, which had been totally overlooked by us, to the effect that under our contract to you, *we* were responsible for the *renewal* of copyright in your works. (The books we have published ourselves were, of course, copyrighted carefully.)

I can scarcely express to you how deeply chagrined I am to realize that we have apparently been negligent and yet, in justice to ourselves, it is only fair to point out that ever since the contract was made, we have been proceeding on the (erroneous as it appears now) assumption that either you or Mr Stern was attending to *renewals*, as indeed the original copyright certificates were never turned over to us – nor records of the original copyright dates involved, until quite recently. Such records are essential in handling of the hundreds of such matters which go through a publisher's office. The member of our staff who has charge of copyrights is extremely meticulous and our registration cards are carefully filed chronologically, so that automatically they come up for renewal at the proper time and well in advance. That the cards for your books were not so filed explains our lapse, although I am quite aware that it does not exactly exonerate us for not insisting on having the registration certificates at the time we took over the custody of your literary work in America. The long and short of the matter is that copyright has not been renewed on two of the volumes – the one above mentioned and the one containing JOHN BULL'S OTHER ISLAND, HOW HE LIED TO HER HUSBAND and MAJOR BARBARA.

A few days ago I checked up the copyright dates of all your books with Mr Stern, and also searched the copyright records in the New York Public Library. We find that in the case of both THE DOCTOR'S DILEMMA and JOHN BULL volumes, and indeed some of the others, a new copyright was taken out by Brentano in *1913*. Notice of this, however, does not appear on the back of the title page in any of the volumes and we are at a loss to know its meaning. We are now awaiting information from Washington as to just what this copyright involves, with some faint hope that it may sufficiently save the situation ...

So far as piracy is concerned because of lapse of copyright, I cannot believe threat of this is serious, or that any reputable play or motion picture producer would take advantage of it. Indeed, they could scarcely afford to do so. I have known of other instances of this kind in connection with books of prominent authors and to the best of my knowledge, the loss of copyright through a technicality has seldom been used to the disadvantage of the author. Certainly no film producer would pirate the work of an English author because of the lapse of American copyright, knowing that the copyright was still valid in the British Empire and other countries, as he would thus be barred from a valuable field of exploitation.

I am sending you a short cable today, advising you that this letter is on the way, and after we have completed our investigation, I shall write you again. Meantime, I can only express the most abject regret for what seems to me now the most serious error I have made in my long publishing experience, and I hope you will not think too harshly of your loyal and devoted American publishers in their time of trouble and self-abnegation.

Sincerely yours,
DODD, MEAD & COMPANY, Inc.

160 / To Dodd, Mead & Co.

[no address]
1st July 1939

[TLS (c): Brown]

Dodd, Mead replied to the following on 14 July: 'I can only tell you that I was enormously relieved at your postscript ... If all mankind assumed your generous attitude toward the failings of their fellows, the world would be a happier place to live in' (TLU (c): Brown).

Dear Dodds

The dates in Who's Who are no use. They give the year in which the play was written and first performed, but not the date of publication. Thus The Doctor's Dilemma, written and published in 1906; but it was not published until 1911, which made it due for renewal this year. This explains the Brentano dates, which you may take as correct for copyright purposes.

There are other possibilities. A play, being 'a dramatic composition' is exempt from the printing clause and can be copyrighted at Washington by sending a typed copy and a dollar. I have done this in the case of Geneva; and I am not sure that I may not have done so in earlier instances. That apparently only makes the matter worse; but as the text in the published volumes was always a revised one, and was accompanied by new matter in the shape of prefaces etc., their registration would be virtually protected and be renewable as from their date notwithstanding any previous registration.

I presume I can not register film scenarios of the lapsed plays as dramatic compositions and get 28 more years in that way. They will contain new dialogue and new scenes.

I am assuming that the lapse is irremediable – that there is no way out by paying a penalty.

Constables are sending you two copies of the Topolski Geneva. This edition is not in my ordinary routine. It is a speculation of Constables with which I have nothing to do but to take half the profits. I do not know what arrangement they have made with Topolski. 75,000 copies were ordered before publication, they tell me. I will include the play in my standard edition later on, without the illustrations, and with a couple of other plays to make a volume of the usual size. The address of the illustrator is Felix Topolski, 27 Collingham Road, London, S.W.5. The play is registered at Washington as a dramatic composition. I daresay he would be glad if you would undertake an American edition; but I cannot authorize it, as I am not the proprietor of the drawings, as I was in the case of The Black Girl.

G. Bernard Shaw

P.S. Dont worry about the oversight. I make about ten a day myself.

The Doctor's Dilemma was **written and** performed (not **published**) **in 1906**. It was first published in German translation by S. Fischer (Berlin) in 1908 and then in *The Doctor's Dilemma, Getting Married, & The Shewing-up of Blanco Posnet* by Constable and Brentano's in **1911**. Although Shaw had been told that **75,000 copies** of *Geneva* had been **ordered before publication**, 'The actual publication figures for the first impression appear to have been 6500 copies issued in cloth, at 7s.6d., and 3500 in paper boards, at 5s.' (Laurence 1, 233). Shaw would include a revised version of the play in his **standard edition** volume, *Geneva, Cymbeline Refinished, & Good King Charles*, in 1947.

161 / To William Maxwell　　　　　4 Whitehall Court, London SW1
5th November 1939

[TLS: NLS]

Shaw's first 'Penguinized' play was Back to Methuselah *(number 200) in April 1939; the second was the screen version of* Pygmalion *(number 300) in September 1941.*

My dear Maxwell

As I am told that there is no more paper available, there is a job of pure composition for you. Pygmalion has to be pulled all to pieces for the insertion of the additional scenes written for the screen version. You will not need any paper to make these changes and get the plates in order for next printing of Pygmalion.

But this is not the whole story. Allen Lane wants to Penguinize the play. I have consented, and promised to throw in the screen scenes, on condition that you do the printing. I can now tell him that you have the new version to print from. Possibly he may have to raise the price of Penguins to ninepence or nine shillings to get over the paper problem; but that is his affair.

Meanwhile if Kyllmann orders any more Pygmalions do not print them without telling me. The Penguin edition may supersede the Standard to an extent which may make it necessary to keep only a small stock of the latter.

I cannot help thinking that Providence has some mighty design behind this war, and has therefore chosen as its ministers the most complete political dunderheads on record. I have done what I could to stop it; but I might as well lecture to a swarm of wasps on the tensor calculus.

Keep your temper and your health as best you can.

G. Bernard Shaw

The British publishing industry was hard hit by wartime **paper** shortages. For facsimile reproduction of some of **the additional scenes written for the screen version** of *Pygmalion*, see Shand, 'Author and Printer,' 396–7. Shaw's most recent effort to **stop** the Second World War (officially declared on 3 September) was *Geneva*, published on 15 June, with its transparent cast of living **political dunderheads** Bombardone (Benito Mussolini), Battler (Adolf Hitler), and Flanco (Francisco Franco); Shaw would doubtless include Neville Chamberlain, British prime minister since 1937, among the **ministers. Tensors** provide a concise mathematical framework for formulating and solving problems in physics.

162 / To G. Bernard Shaw
Aldine House, 10 Bedford Street,
London WC2
7th February 1940

[TLS: HRC]

Shaw had written to J.M. Dent & Sons on 31 January in response to their request for permission to publish something by him in Modern Humour, *a book in their*

Everyman's Library series. In the following letter, current director Alfred John Hoppé replies to Shaw, using the opportunity to press him for an Everyman volume 'consisting wholly of writings' by Shaw, who ignores the request in his handwritten reply at the top of Hoppé's letter: 'Phone them that they may go ahead, as I accept their offer of 10/– per thousand copies in their letter of the 7th.' Shaw had turned down a similar request by J.M. Dent himself in 1921 (Letter 110).

Dear Mr Bernard Shaw

... We should very much like to see that Shaw passage in the volume, and will even go to the length of keeping a special royalty account for it. To simplify the matter may we make it 10/– per 1000 copies, which is about equivalent to your half-a-farthing a copy (we can't afford more!). I am not sure at present how many copies we shall print for the first edition, but it will not be less than 12,000, and the reprints will be about the same number. The royalty shall be payable, as you suggest, in advance on delivery of the printed sheets of each impression, and not returnable.

Now, dear Mr Bernard Shaw, if this were a volume in *Everyman's Library* consisting wholly of writings by you we could talk business! I have been working at Dents for a good number of years, and I know that from time to time Mr Ernest Rhys has endeavoured to persuade you to grant permission for a volume of two or three of your Plays, or an assortment of a Play or two and some Prose writings to be included in the Library – alas, without success. Recently it has fallen to my lot to take the most active part in arranging new volumes for *Everyman's Library*, and I realise more and more that the chief gap among the Modern Volumes is Bernard Shaw.

Why is it that we cannot have such a volume, please? You will agree, I am sure, that the library has a great reputation, that it does aim at comprehensiveness, and does endeavour to include only worth-while writings, even some works which may not sell well. If the *Penguins* can include Shaw, why not *Everyman's*? We go, at least partly, to a different public, by no means a negligible one. If it is a matter of the business arrangements this can be done through the Society of Authors or direct with you – just as you like – when I can assure you that we shall be as generous as the economics of publishing *Everyman's Library* will allow. We shall in fact be happy to pay you a substantial advance (based on our faith in the potential sales) on account of an equitable royalty; or to come to any other workable publishing arrangement which you may prefer. You must agree that, from all your books, one little *Everyman* volume could be arranged that would not conflict with the sales of any of the existing editions – in fact it might help them! Anyway we start out wishing not to clash with any other volumes.

I hope I have not put this too crudely. We know that Shaw must come into *Everyman* some day. You say in your last letter that *Everyman* goes on forever, but why should *Everyman* have to wait until you are dead thirty years before getting a Shaw volume? Could you spare me a few minutes please? Would you allow me to come along, answer any questions, and get your answer?

Yours sincerely,
A.J. Hoppé, Director
J.M. DENT & SONS LTD.

The **Shaw passage**, the opening scene of act 2 of *John Bull's Other Island* (written 1904, published 1907), appeared under the title *Father Keegan and the Grasshopper* on pages 331–5 in the 369-page **volume** entitled *Modern Humour: A Nosegay of Contemporary Wit* (1940), edited by Guy Noel Pocock and Mildred Mary Bozman. **Ernest** Percival **Rhys** (1859–1946) founded the Everyman's Library (see Letter 19), which he edited until his death. Shaw would **come into** *Everyman* with a volume **consisting wholly of writings by** him not **thirty years** after his death but sixteen, with *The Devil's Disciple, Major Barbara, Saint Joan* (1966).

163 / To Dodd, Mead & Co.

4 Whitehall Court, London SW1
3rd April 1940

[TLS: Brown]

Inspired by Allen Lane's success with Penguin Books, American entrepreneur Robert Fair de Graff (1895–1981) partnered with Simon & Schuster and in January 1939 launched Pocket Books, the first mass-market, pocket-sized paperbacks in the United States. Pocket's 25¢ reprints of standard classics revolutionized the industry. By the end of 1939 Pocket had sold over 1.5 million books.

Dear Dodd, Mead and Co

Mr de Graff's proposal has called my attention to the fact that our five years agreement has expired and that we are not going on at six months notice. And I am much perplexed as to whether I should make any change, and, if yes, what? I am in the queer position of having a publicity so enormous that all advertising of my books seems superfluous; but the fact remains that nobody buys them in the U.S.A. Out of 38 titles in your account for Feb–Aug 1939, only a dozen sell sufficient to be worth finding shelf room for; and of these only 4 sell more than two a day. As the prestige attaching to my name is so grossly delusive from the business point of view, is it worth your while to go on with it?

The truth seems to be that my market is changing from the highly respectable old established section that you represent, dealing in nothing cheaper than $2.50 to the comparatively disreputable adventurers pushing 25 cent editions by reckless advertising, canvassing, mail orders etc etc etc. Even when the whole book is by me it will bear a royalty of no more than $5 per thousand copies. You look on and rake off $2.50 of my $5. This makes the business impossible; my books cannot carry two publishers: most of them, as your accounts shew, cannot carry one.

Take this proposal of de Graff's for instance. His $200. As it means only $100 to me, I turn it down at once: it is not worth the time it would take me to say No to it. The whole $200 would be a little better; though I should probably propose instead a royalty of $5 per thousand copies printed: about half a cent per copy. But not if I had to give you half. And so nothing will come of it for either of us ...

In short, I feel that my market has changed in such a way that I must be free in America as I am in England to dispose of my books as best suits the circumstances without being bound to any particular publisher. Constables (Kyllmann) are my regular publishers in London; but the Penguin Press and the Odham's Press sell, by the hundred thousand, editions of my works at prices which Kyllmann could not touch.

But he has no rake-off on these transactions: why should he?

I am not sure if you will care to remain my regular publishers under these conditions. Like Kyllmann I was considerably surprised when you refused to publish my last two plays (with the Topolski illustrations); and if it had not been possible for me to secure copyright by registering them as 'dramatic compositions' I should have had to find another publisher for them; and this incident leaves me in some doubt as to whether you find it worth while to go on with me at all. I have no wish to change as far as my standard editions are concerned, and, generally, the relatively high priced first editions; for your half yearly $2000 and our friendly relations are very agreeable to me; but I must be free as to all the publishing business that you cannot or will not do for me.

You must forgive me throwing all this at your head in a lump without a word of warning; but I am a very unsatisfactory man of business, because I am so busy writing (always two years in arrear) that I leave my affairs without attention for years at a time, and then have to plunge into them lest I should die leaving them in a hopeless mess.

Let me have your reaction at your convenience.

Faithfully
G. Bernard Shaw

Shaw's **last two plays (with the Topolski illustrations)** were *Geneva* and *In Good King Charles's Golden Days*, published by Constable in 1939. Although Dodd, Mead had **refused to publish** them, they issued them (as did Constable) as *Geneva, Cymbeline Refinished, & Good King Charles* in 1947.

164 / To G. Bernard Shaw

[no address]
26th April 1940

[TLU (c): Brown]

Almost from the beginning, writes Dan Laurence, Dodd, Mead 'had acted more as an agent than a publisher, pocketing half the royalties and fees from previously published Shaw works licensed to other houses, and issuing a variety of reprint editions of the plays from the cheaply acquired plates of William H. Wise's Ayot St Lawrence Edition (1930–32), while resisting investment in new Shavian publications' (CL 4, 560).

Dear Mr Shaw

I confess that your letter of April 3rd was something of a shock, although not altogether a surprise, as I had realized for some time that you have been restless over our reiterated demand for half of the proceeds of any by-product rights in your books which are distributed in this country. Nevertheless I have always felt and still feel that this is the only logical position we can take for a number of reasons, which I will try to enumerate.

Our contract is quite unlike your arrangement with Constable, under which *you* own the plates and stock and they act merely as your selling agents. We purchased for a considerable sum all your physical property (plates and stock) in the hands of Brentanos and in addition paid up the back royalties. At the present time Constable have, I believe, little or no investment in plates or stock, as these are supplied by you. We, on the contrary, have a very considerable involvement, both in the old plates and in new ones made since our agreement went into effect. Is it not natural that we should wish to protect our interest in this investment; and also, is it not logical to assume that were you free, without restriction or guidance by us, to sell your books and rights to reprint publishers, to permit inclusion of various plays in anthologies, in short to do anything you liked, regardless of our interest, that the ultimate effect on our property as a whole would be disastrous, and we would be left with little of value to show for our very considerable investment?

Practically every American publisher's contract, whether made direct with the author or through an agent, provides that in event of leasing subsidiary rights to other publishers, the net proceeds shall be equally divided. Such contracts also provide that the publishers shall be the judges as to just what arrangements of this kind shall be made, in order to protect their interests and those of the author.

The publisher has an investment in the physical property, experience of market possibilities, values and credit risks, etc. He should therefore be responsible for determining the expediency of business arrangements permissible under his contract with the author, and if and when such arrangements are made, to see that they are carefully guarded by contracts with the lessee and credit guarantees established in advance. With the best intentions in the world, how could an author (particularly in a distant country) have an intelligent opinion about these matters, or sufficient experience to separate good proposals from the bad, or the proper machinery to carry out such arrangements and collect the sums due?

For instance, you mention William H. Wise as having a large mail order outlet, similar to Odham's. That is true. Mr Crawley, with whom we have done considerable business, is both able and energetic and has built up in a short time a large business. After receiving your letter, I asked him point blank just what he would be willing to do in the way of distributing your plays in one volume, similar to the Odham's edition, a copy of which we both have. He said he thought he could sell a large number of copies by mail, or $1000.00 in advance. In my opinion, that is an utterly inadequate guarantee and royalty, as it would involve the almost certain demise, for instance, of the most valuable item on our Shaw list – NINE PLAYS – which yields you from eight to nine hundred dollars a year, and we would have to reconsider the proposal made to you in my recent letter about a similar collection of SIX PLAYS. It is possible that a much better bargain could be driven with Wise, though I haven't even gone into that, as a one volume 'mail order' edition, which might well be dropped in a year or two, might very seriously damage your property in this country. However, I will, if you wish, see whether a more advantageous arrangement can be made; but as I pointed out above, we would expect an equal division of the profits.

So far as the de Graff proposal is concerned, and others of this kind which I have forwarded to you from time to time, for inclusion of a play here and there in an anthology, I do not feel that they would have any injurious effect on the sale of your books. Indeed it would probably have been possible, had we been permitted the usual freedom in making sales of this kind, to have secured several thousands of dollars of plus revenue for both of us by judicious leasing of rights. I wish heartily that you would say right now that you are willing to grant us this privilege in future, instead of considering cancellation. You might easily be surprised by the eventual results in increased royalty payments. You could also be entirely sure that we would only take advantage of opportunities of this kind when we were convinced that the *net results* would be beneficial to you and to ourselves *as partners*.

We have never handled the works of an author of which we are quite so proud to be the publishers as those of Bernard Shaw. In addition, I have a very high regard for your business judgment; but nevertheless, you are not a trained publisher who knows his market as we do. It seems only reasonable to assume that you might make grave mistakes in weighing publishing proposals put before you and place too much credence in siren songs of concerns which, for instance, might lack the financial ability to carry out their agreements. Remember, too, that these 'extras' are not necessarily factual but a choice between experimental and assured revenues.

Please pardon me if I have seemed to be standing on a rostrum and lecturing a far wiser man than myself. You asked for my reaction and I've given it to you straight from the shoulder!

Ever sincerely yours,

DODD, MEAD & COMPANY, Inc.

Dodd, Mead **paid up the back royalties** of $15,914 (see Letter 142). John J. **Crawley** was president of William H. Wise & Co. The **Odham's edition** was the one-volume 1934 'Omnibus Edition' of the *Complete Plays*. Dodd had proposed a *Six Plays* volume on 17 April, the *Nine Plays* (1935) having 'become permanently established in many schools and colleges as a supplementary text book' (TLU (c): Brown). Shaw replied (on 16 May) that he had no objection, although 'any author who is made a school subject is loathed and avoided for ever after' (TLS: Brown). *Six Plays* was published in 1941, and *Seven Plays* (from *Nine Plays*, lacking *Fanny's First Play* and *Androcles and the Lion*) in 1951.

165 / To Dodd, Mead & Co.
4 Whitehall Court, London SW1
23rd May 1940

[TLS: Brown]

The following and Letter 166 notwithstanding, Shaw retained Dodd, Mead as his American publishers until his death. Shaw's 'recent letter' has not been located.

Dear Sirs

I hereby give you notice that our Agreement dated the 23rd day of January, 1934 must expire on 31st December next. Clause No. 32 of the Agreement provides for this cessation.

Changes in the book business in the United States and elsewhere have made it necessary for me to cancel all agreements binding me to one publisher. I have explained the situation fully in my recent letter to you, of which, by the way, I have received no acknowledgement.

This step will not, I trust, make any difference in our friendly relation. As far as I can foresee, at present, all that part of my business which is concerned with retail prices between $2.50 per volume and upwards need not be disturbed: we can go on as before until further notice. Now that volumes containing the whole of my plays or all my prefaces are obtaining in England at a cost of one dollar, and copies of Back to Methuselah (five plays), Pygmalion, and The Intelligent Woman's Guide can be bought for 12 cents, whilst American publishers are pressing me for books to be sold at 25 cents in hundreds of thousands (I am offered $25,000 down for a new book to be sold at that price), and since such operations are outside your activities I must set myself free to authorize independently of you; for there is no room in such transactions for two publishers, especially when one is only a sleeping partner.

In short, your present exclusive privilege must go, though you will still benefit by the extension of my reading public, which is still very small compared to my general publicity.

My solicitor, Mr. Benjamin H. Stern, of 1 East 45th Street, will secure the delivery of this notice to you. Excuse this necessary formality.

Faithfully,

G. Bernard Shaw

Although Constable sold the following volumes at 7s.6d., Dodd, Mead did so at **$2.50 per volume and upwards**: *The Simpleton, The Six, and The Millionairess* (1936), $2.50; *Geneva, Cymbeline Refinished, & Good King Charles* (1947), $3.00; and *Sixteen Self Sketches* (1949), $3.50. **Back to Methuselah** (1939), **Pygmalion** (1941), **and** *The Intelligent Woman's Guide* (1937, 2 vols.) had been Penguinized at sixpence per volume, roughly **12 cents**.

166 / To Dodd, Mead & Co. 4 Whitehall Court, London SW1

19th June 1940

[TLS: Brown; CL 4]

Dodd had written on the 17th that he had received Shaw's 23 May letter (via Benjamin Stern), enclosing a copy of his 26 April letter, 'on the chance that it was the victim of a U-boat disaster' (TLU (c): Brown). In Letter 167 Shaw calls the following letter 'a masterpiece of casuistry.'

Dear Dodd, Mead & Co.

The war has knocked the postal service into a cocked hat. Your letter in reply to my ultimatum, though dated the 26th April, did not reach me until June, though some later letters had arrived in good time; and at last I concluded that I had struck you dead, and must act at once to make sure that my notice to quit on the 31st December would reach you soon enough. So I instructed my Counselor at Law, Mr Benjamin H. Stern of 1 East 45th Street, to put the notice through formally.

Now comes your letter. I understand it completely; but it only confirms my decision not to continue on the old terms. What it comes to is that you would like to cease publishing my old books and simply to levy a tax of 50% on my royalties from the operations of other publishers. That, dear Dodd, is not business: you would not dream of allowing me to stop writing books and to levy a tax of 50% on all the other books you publish. Let me put my situation to you.

Most books, bar Bibles and Shakespears, have a lifetime of 18 months. The publisher has to risk the cost of manufacture, and must fix the price at a figure which will bring back his money plus the necessary profit on a sale of between one and two thousand copies. The transaction ends with the sale. There is not much in it for the publisher; but it keeps the shop open even when the profits are negligible. Poor business: why does the publisher do it? Because he is gambling on the chance of, say, one in six or ten of the books proving a best seller. This does actually occur: hence the publisher's automobile and other luxuries, which are permanent whilst the author only acquires expensive habits which ruin him when the book is over and the publisher goes on to the next boom.

Meanwhile the publisher has found out that the author is an imbecile in business and so poor and so desperately anxious to see himself in print that he dare not say No to any condition imposed by the publisher and will sell all his rights, film rights, performing rights, translation rights, and his soul and body into the bargain for $50 cash. It is greatly to the credit of the publishers that they do not kill the goose that lays the golden eggs every time, since there are always more geese to kill. But they get together in their autos and agree to demand 50% of the author's income over and above the winnings of the gamble.

Now all this does not apply to my case. I have a reputation which makes the sale of a few thousand copies of anything I write a certainty. The publisher runs no risk of loss of his capital, nor need he advance any; for the printers and binders, hampered by plants which are eating their heads off when they are not busy, will give credit until the sales bring in the money. There is no need to spend anything worth mentioning on advertisement: my publicity advertises itself. The publisher contributes nothing but a fractional part of his overhead and sales machinery. The author has to write the book, which costs him many months of work, and has only that book to fall back on whereas the publisher has hundreds of books. To the 50–50 business the publisher contributes absolutely nothing at all.

Naturally in England I, having always more money lying at my bank on deposit at next to nothing per cent than enough to manufacture my books at a profit of 300 per cent, and being neither a born imbecile nor ignorant and incapable of business, publish on commission. Constable has no printers' or binders' bills to pay; he has the use of the money from the sales of many months and he finally keeps 15% of it for the fractional part of his overhead that I cost him. He is on velvet; yet he tries his hardest to get me on to a royalty basis. I have allowed him to have some books on a 'half profits' arrangement by which he pays for everything and gives me half of the surplus of sale over cost of manufacture (no overhead). My last two plays were published by him on this system because he found a wonderful illustrator at his own cost and for the first time chose the type and designed the book subject to my approval.

These two books with their illustrations you refused to publish in the U.S.; and I should have forfeited the U.S. copyright had I not registered them as 'dramatic compositions' in Washington in typescript. But if I had found another publisher for them you would have demanded 50% without a blush!

Dodd, Dodd, Dodd: what sort of fool do you take me for?

Any capital you invested in me you invested with your eyes open and our agreement before you. You had to make it good within five years; and the operations of Wise were reserved. I have asked for no advances; and you have had every advantage that you could expect from books that live for two years or less. But my books are not for an age but for all time, provided, that is, that the $2.50 editions are followed by cheaper ones and travelled and canvassed and advertised in all sorts of ways that are beyond your resources. You have refused to take any such risks, very wisely; but for your refusal you demand 50% of my royalties. The proportion bereaves me of breath. I will see you in heaven first.

We must either make reasonable arrangements or else part good friends. There is no reason why you should not continue to do my *de luxe* business and skim the cream off my new books before they go into the cheap market with the rest of my old junk, though if you run your prices up to $5 I shall expect more than 15%. But in the cheap market there is room for one author and one publisher; and in that I must be completely free. If I have to give up either the *de luxe* market or the cheap market I shall give up the *de luxe* market and bid farewell for ever to old established responsible publishers. Think it over.

Forgive the brevity of this letter: I havent time to write at greater length.

fraternally
G. Bernard Shaw

In 'Sixty Years in Business as an Author' (1945), Shaw reiterates his view of **the author** as **an imbecile in business**, calling him 'socially untrained by his irresponsible solitude and spoilt equally by success or failure, an incorrigible individualist anarchist, loathing business and its discipline' (p. 58). For similar comments, see Introduction. The **last two plays** were *Geneva* and *In Good King Charles's Golden Days*. Ben Jonson wrote of Shakespeare (in the 1623 First Folio) that 'He was **not of an age, but for all time**!'

167 / To Frank C. Dodd

4 Whitehall Court, London SW1
11th July 1940

[TLS: Brown]

Frank C. Dodd replied to Shaw's 19 June letter on 9 July: 'Of course we never had any rights in the reprints or permission fees here and the only change involved is your freedom to do as you say in this direction without consulting us. Emphatically we do wish to continue as you suggest we may as the publishers of the regular higher priced volumes. Indeed, we would never voluntarily relinquish our proud position as the accredited publishers of Bernard Shaw in America!' (TLU (c): Brown).

I have just received your letter dated the 17th June, enclosing a copy of yours of the 26th April. This, however, I received after many days, and answered at prodigious length. Possibly this answer has reached you by now: if not, I can send you a copy if my secretary can find my shorthand draft. It was a masterpiece of casuistry; but what it came to was that I must be free to engage in alternate methods of publishing with alternate publishers whilst clinging to you for the respectable $2.50 business and for a decent reputation in the book world ...

My compliments to your partners and to your good self.

Always yours
G. Bernard Shaw

168 / To J.M. Dent

[no address]
16th October 1940

[ALS: Colgate]

In 1937 Dent had published The Birth of Language: Its Place in World Evolution and Its Structure in Relation to Space and Time *by Richard Albert Wilson (1874–1949), professor of English language and literature at the University of Saskatchewan, in Saskatoon, Canada. At the same time as he was writing to*

Dent (below), Shaw contacted Wilson (retired in Vancouver) offering to write a preface for his book. Dent wrote to Shaw on 17 March 1941 thanking him for the 10,000-word preface ('It is almost embarrassing!'), adding in a P.S., 'Your title is right. THE MIRACULOUS BIRTH OF LANGUAGE *it shall be' (TLU (c): Colgate).*

Dear Mr Dent

... I did not expect anything very startling to come from Saskatoon; but you have discovered a book by a Professor Wilson of the University there which is the best essay on Emergent Evolution since Samuel Butler's. Couldnt you issue a sixpenny edition and print 100,000 copies? I should like that; for all the Mechanists and their religious opposites ought to be made to read it, and the world contains millions of them.

Faithfully

G. Bernard Shaw

Works by novelist **Samuel Butler** dealing with **emergent evolution** include *Evolution Old and New* (1879) and *Luck or Cunning?* (1886), reviewed by Shaw in *The Pall Mall Gazette* on 31 May 1887. *The Miraculous Birth of Language* was issued on 26 August 1941. On 3 October A.J. Hoppé informed Wilson that the 50,000 copies printed 'have practically all been sold' (TLU (c): Colgate).

169 / To Otto Kyllmann   Ayot St Lawrence, Welwyn, Herts.

24th February 1941

[TLS: BL; CL 4]

Douglas Leighton, of the Leighton-Straker Bookbinding Company, had informed Shaw on 19 September 1940 that their quire stock warehouse had been destroyed the previous night by 'incendiary bombs,' enclosing a list of 'sheets which have probably been lost' (Guelph). On 24 September Shaw wrote to Otto Kyllmann: 'The Germans have done what Constables have never succeeded in doing. They have disposed of 86,701 sheets of my works in less than 24 hours' (CL 4, 578).

Dear O.K.

I am stoney broke, and have paid my January taxes only with the help of the insurance money I got when my books were burnt at Leighton's. On the 25th March you must send me my accounts and pay me up to the 31st December. Wilson tells me that my books are being bought for the soldiers; so you must have a few pounds in hand for me.

I would not press you but for the appalling misfortune of my having received within one financial year £25,000 from the Pygmalion film. This put me into the millionaire class, in which I am taxed 18/– in the pound not only on the £25,000, but on my wife's income and everything else as well. The U.S.A. also takes 15%. Result, ruin. If I were younger I should abandon authorship and become a publisher.

Are you co-operating with Dent in his plan of pricing books at sixpence and a shilling in paper covers? He tempts me assiduously to let him include me in his Everyman library. I have had to let Pygmalion be penguined. My days of respectable publishing are over, I fear.

For many months past I have been hard at work on jobs that will not bring me a penny. I have earned nothing but a couple of casual hundred pounds from the Hearst Press for articles.

Unless you go into the sixpenny business, for which you are quite unfitted, we shall end together in the workhouse.

Charlotte has been very ill in bed for many many weeks, and is recovering very slowly.

This is a nice cheerful letter. I have put off writing it as long as possible; but as you do the same with your payments (very properly) it serves you right.

always yours
G. Bernard Shaw

J.G. **Wilson** was manager of booksellers John and Edward Bumpus Ltd, from whom Shaw made most of his book purchases. Gabriel Pascal's **film** version of *Pygmalion* was released in 1938. **The U.S.A.** took even more in 1941: 'My plays earned £20,000 in America last year [1941]. Of this America took £13,500 in tax; Kingsley Wood [Chancellor of the Exchequer, 1940–3] took £6,340 on the balance; and I was left to starve on £160' (letter of 9 May 1942 to Nancy Astor, quoted in Wearing, *Bernard Shaw and Nancy Astor*, 106). **Dent** director Hoppé had brought up the **Everyman** issue again 'with all deference' on 17 October 1940 (TLU (c): Colgate); see also Letters 110 and 162. For the **Hearst Press**, see Letter 102. In January **Charlotte** Shaw had been **very ill** with lumbago (she died on 12 September 1943).

170 / To Daniel Macmillan   [4 Whitehall Court SW1]
                                                          11th September 1943

[CL 4; PP: Morgan and Nowell-Smith]

Charles Morgan was writing The House of Macmillan (1843–1943), *published in 1943. Daniel Macmillan (1886–1965), grandson of the co-founder (also Daniel), was Macmillan's chairman and managing director. Shaw the octogenarian looks back upon his early struggles to become a published writer and discusses the uncertain nature of the publishing trade.*

Dear Mr Macmillan

I have read the galley slips you sent me concerning myself in Mr Morgan's history of Macmillans with interest and a very agreeable measure of astonishment.

I had no idea that the reports on novels I submitted were so appreciative. I consider them highly creditable to the firm's readers; for they make it clear what was wrong was not, as I thought, any failure to spot me as a literary discovery, but the strangeness at that time of my valuations. In fact they thought more of my jejune prentice work than I did myself; for I really hated those five novels, having drudged through them like any other industrious apprentice because there was nothing else I could or would do. That in spite of their disagreeableness they somehow induced readers rash enough to begin them to go on to the end and resent that experience seems to me now a proof that I was a born master of the pen. But the novel was not my proper medium. I wrote novels because everybody did so then; and the theatre, my rightful kingdom, was outside literature. The coterie theatres in which I first reached the public as a playwright did not then exist.

But of course I did not understand all this at the time. My recollection, until your letter arrived, was far less encouraging. I began, not very wisely, by calling on all the publishers in person to see what they were like; and they did not like me. I did not like myself enough to blame them. I was young (23), raw, Irish from Dublin, and Bohemian without being in the least convivial or self-indulgent, deeply diffident inside and consequently brazen outside, and so utterly devoid of reverence that a phrenologist whom I asked what my bump of veneration was like replied 'Why, it's a hole!' Altogether a discordant personality in the eyes of the elderly great publishers of those days, a now extinct species. As I had a considerable aesthetic culture, and the English governing classes, of whom I knew only what I had picked up from Thackeray and Trollope, had none, they were barbarians to me; and I was to them a complete outsider. I was in fact outside the political world until I had written the first three of my novels; and when I came in I came in as a Marxist, a phenomenon then inconceivable even to Mill, Morley, Dilke, Auberon Herbert, the Fortnightly Reviewers, the Positivists, the Darwinians, and the rest of the Agnostic Republicans who represented the extreme left of the most advanced pioneers in the eighties of the last century. The Transvaluation of Values in which I was an obscure pioneer can hardly be imagined nowadays by people under 70. I was a Nietzschean and an Ibsenist before I had ever heard of Nietzsche or Ibsen.

In view of all this you will see that Macmillans were very much ahead of the older publishers (I tried them all) in recognizing my talent. They corresponded with me a little; and George Macmillan tried to soften my rejection by Alexander, who didn't like me personally, by sending me a long report by Morley, who turned me down as a victim of undigested Ruskin, of whom I had read little or nothing. Meredith turned me down for Chatto without extenuating circumstances. Blackwood accepted my first novel; but afterwards reneged, to the distress of his oldest reader. Smith Elder were polite and asked to see future efforts. None of the rest would have anything to say to me; and even those who gave some attention to my first attempt found its successors more and more impossible. When William Archer made Stevenson read *Cashel Byron's Profession*, and he and Henley applauded it, Bentley, who had refused it, sent for it urgently, and was furious because it was no longer at his disposal; but that was after I had given up novel writing, having designed a mighty work which I found myself too ignorant to finish; so I let its opening section go as *An Unsocial Socialist*. The novels, printed as padding in Socialist magazines, got pirated in America; and when I, being ashamed of them, tried to suppress them, they broke out in spite of me as persistently as they had suppressed themselves before.

Macmillan's attention and George's kindly civility certainly made a difference to me. There are so many amateurs sending in crude MSS to publishers and managers that no beginner can be sure that he is not one of the hopeless failures until his work is accepted, or he has had at least some response indicating that he is not quite out of the question. If Macmillan had simply declined with thanks like nearly all the rest, I should have had to set my teeth still closer.

I am now one of the few who personally remember the Grand Old Men of the publishing world of that day: Alexander Macmillan, Longman, and

Bentley. They were so powerful that they held the booksellers in abject subjection, and were denounced by Walter Besant and his newly organised Society of Authors as remorseless sharks. When they died and were succeeded by their sons, the hereditary system did not always work as well as it did in Bedford Street; and the booksellers got the upper hand. John Murray's Byronic prestige was so select that I did not dream of trying him until years later, when I was an author of some note and had already helped to bankrupt three publishers. I offered him *Man & Superman*. He refused in a letter which really touched me. He said he was old-fashioned and perhaps a bit behind the times; but he could not see any intention in my book but to wound, irritate, and upset all established constitutional opinion, and therefore could not take the responsibility of publishing it. By that time I could command sufficient capital to finance my books and enter into direct friendly relations with the printers (this began my very pleasant relations with Clarks of Edinburgh). I took matters into my own hands and, like Herbert Spencer and Ruskin, manufactured my books myself, and induced Constables to take me 'on commission.'

Walter Besant never understood that publishing, like Insurance and turf bookmaking, is a gamble, with the important difference that whereas an insurer can employ an actuary who will tell him the odds at which chance becomes mathematical certainty, and a bookmaker who bets against every horse can lose on one only and is being supplanted by the tote, the publisher has to take chances which are incalculable, and must therefore play with all the advantages he can get, leaving the author to take care of himself. Besant assumed that a successful book ought to pay for itself only, not knowing that it has to pay for several others which, though they keep the shop open, barely repay the overhead and the cost of their manufacture and sometimes lose even that. A loss of 100% on the swings makes a large hole in a profit of 300% on the roundabouts. If both authors and publishers understood this there would be much less friction in their dealings. But the publisher often knows everything about publishing practice and nothing about its economic theory, whilst the author as a rule knows nothing about either, and is constitutionally unfit to conduct his own business. I served for ten years on the Society's Committee, and know the ropes pretty well.

faithfully
G. Bernard Shaw

In phrenology, a '**bump**' is a cranial protuberance associated with distinct faculties: a bump of 'amativeness' (libido), 'acquisitiveness' (learning), or **veneration** (respect). Some of the London **coterie theatres** where Shaw's early plays were performed included the Royalty, Coronet, Bijou, Strand, Comedy, Avenue, and (more famously) the Royal Court. The novels of William Makepeace **Thackeray** (1811–63) and Anthony **Trollope** (1815–82) satirized English social mores. Shaw became a follower of Karl **Marx** (1818–83) after reading the first volume of *Das Kapital* (1867) in French translation. John Stuart **Mill** (1806–73) advocated 'utilitarianism,' the doctrine that an action's moral worth is determined by its contribution to overall utility. MP John **Morley** (1838–1923) was editor of the *Fortnightly Review* (1867–82) and the *Pall Mall Gazette* (1880–3); his 'political policies made him one of the prime targets of Shaw's socialistic wrath' (CL 1, 30). Radical statesman Sir Charles W. **Dilke** (1843–1911) supported legislation involving trade unions and a minimum wage. Journalist **Auberon Herbert** (1838–1906) was editor of *Free Life*. The **Nietzschean** concept of 'Umwertung aller Werte' ('transvaluation of all values'), commonly known as **the Transvaluation of Values**, is found in Nietzsche's *On the Genealogy of Morals* (1887). **George A. Macmillan** (1855–1936) was the second son of co-founder **Alexander**. George Meredith turned down Shaw for Chapman & Hall, not **Chatto**. In early 1886 William **Archer** received letters from novelist Robert Louis **Stevenson** (1850–94) and poet William Ernest **Henley** (1849–1903) praising *Cashel Byron* as a work 'full of promise' (RLS) containing 'vigour, humour, originality and wit' (WEH) (quoted in Green, *Shaw's Champions*, 12–14). For Richard **Bentley** & Son, see Letters 2 and 3. For **Longman**, see Letter 46. The **hereditary system** worked in **Bedford Street** for G.P. Putnam's Sons. Byron was one of **John Murray**'s most notable authors and a close friend (see Letter 64). For the firm's rejection of *Man & Superman*, see Letter 65. For Ruskin and Spencer, see Letter 81. 'What you lose **on the swings** you gain **on the roundabouts**' is an old fairground saying equivalent to 'six of one, half a dozen of the other.' Shaw **served for ten years** (1905–15) **on the Society** of Authors' Management **Committee**.

171 / To R. & R. Clark   Ayot St Lawrence, Welwyn, Herts.
                                                  28th October 1944
[APCU: NLS]

... My typescripts are not the original MSS of my books: they are only Miss Patch's transcripts of my shorthand drafts. These I tear up, because I have a mortal dread of some future fool-editor deciphering them and publishing them with all their faults and follies as the real authentic genuine holographs. For some reason the draft of St Joan was preserved by Miss Patch, and is now in the British Museum; but I shall die easier if it gets bombed and burnt ...

                                                  [G.B.S.]

The British Library (the former **British Museum**) holds Shaw's 1923 shorthand **draft** of *Saint Joan* (1924), Add Ms 45923, ff. 1–68.

172 / To Otto Kyllmann   Ayot St Lawrence, Welwyn, Herts.

30th December 1944

[TLS: BL; CL 4]

Constable had made £10,000 largely from sales of Everybody's Political What's What?, *which it had published on commission on 15 September at ten shillings. Shaw had just given his approval to the War Department to publish an edition of 6600 copies of* Selected Plays (Androcles and the Lion, Pygmalion, *and* Saint Joan) *in an 'Edition for the Forces,' published in 1945 along with 4010 copies of* Everybody's Political What's What?

Dear O.K.

Ten thousand pounds! What a magnificent swank!

And you nearly persuaded me that, like Walter Scott and Mark Twain, I should be ruined by the bankruptcy of my publisher.

If you can chuck money about like that I can well believe that your excess profits are so enormous that the few pounds the Exchequer leaves you out of the What's-[What] are less than nothing to you.

But, damn it, you are on velvet compared to me. Out of your ten thousand £8619-16-11 has already gone to the Treasury; and more than the rest will follow next June. Meanwhile I have paid the cost of manufacture, and the best part of four years work. Who would be an author on such terms? Who would not be a publisher?

The Penguin Major Barbara (screen version) is now in print: I am correcting it. Ditto the Oxford U. Press World Classic Methuselah. The *carte blanche* I have given the Government to reprint anything of mine for the soldiers may mean a distribution of samples that will act as the big advertisement that I have never yet ventured on[.] I wish you were in the cheap classic line; but I cannot honestly advise you to go beyond your present highpriced groove, which is a very necessary one.

I shall not wish you another hellish new year; but I am afraid we are in for it. As Europeans we are ruined: how we shall get on as islanders remains to be seen. Bootyless battles do not pay.

I have settled into a routine here in which the months fly like minutes. And as the days are at last lengthening I shall soon perhaps see you again.

G.B.S.

Novelist Sir **Walter Scott** (1771–1832) suffered two major financial crises sparked by the collapse of his publishers John Ballantyne & Co. (1813) – in which Scott was a partner – and Archibald Constable & Co. (1825–6). Aside from other failed moneymaking schemes, novelist **Mark Twain** (1835–1910) had invested heavily in the Charles L. Webster & Co. publishing firm, which went bankrupt in 1894. Publication of Penguin's *Major Barbara: A Screen Version* and of the **Oxford World**'s **Classics** edition of *Back to Methuselah* was delayed until 1946: 'It [*Methuselah*] has been a fearful job,' Shaw wrote to R. & R. Clark on 21 December 1944, 'as much that was topical 25 years ago is now dry rot; and I was too damn discursive' (APCS: NLS). In May 1945 (TEL: Brown), Shaw gave *carte blanche* to American poet and anthologist Louis Untermeyer (1885–1977) for his plays to appear in the Editions for the Armed Services, Inc. (New York).

173 / To Otto Kyllmann   Ayot St Lawrence, Welwyn, Herts.
                                             14th August 1945

[APCS: BL; CL 4]

The United States had recently dropped atomic bombs on Japan at Hiroshima (6 August) and Nagasaki (9 August).

Sorry I missed you when I was in town; but what could I have said anyhow? Even if the Whatswhat is finished, there is the Geneva volume to be printed, and the preface to it has been knocked to pieces by the atomic bomb and must be rewritten. Also I have begun a new play. And though Maxwell says there is paper enough available, there is not labor enough: he could not get the jubilee Methuselah out on my birthday.

The Penguin Major Barbara (screen version) is passed for press and is sticking there apparently. I must Penguinize and Odhamize and perhaps Everyman-Dentize (he is always at me for a volume) because our prices are too high for people with less than £1000 a year; but I always hold back until our lemon is squeezed dry and the book not worth your shelf room, whilst the demand for a decent edition is actually revived by a vogue of the cheap one. The gallery success helps the stalls.

G.B.S.

Geneva, Cymbeline Refinished, & Good King Charles was published only in 1947, with Shaw's revisions to *Geneva* in both play and **preface** (the latter dated '1945'), including references to the **atomic bomb**. Shaw had begun his **new play** at sea on 17 February 1936 as *The World Betterer* and returned to it only on 2 August 1945, completing it on 20 November 1946 as *Buoyant Billions*. Shaw's **birthday** was on 26 July.

174 / To R. & R. Clark   Ayot St Lawrence, Welwyn, Herts.

21st November 1945

[APCS: NLS]

To mark Shaw's ninetieth birthday, Penguin's Allen Lane embarked on his riski-
est speculation yet: the publication of the 'Shaw Million': ten volumes issued in an
edition of 100,000 copies each. 'The million sold out in just over six weeks, and
the overwhelming success of the whole enterprise was not seriously impaired by the
fact that the Eire authorities prevented the sale of The Black Girl *on the grounds of*
its "blasphemy"' (Evans, 'Shaw among the Penguins,' 8), the Irish censors having
objected to Farleigh's depictions of the nude black girl. Shaw's 'earnings from the
Million added eventually to £3750' (Morpurgo, Allen Lane, *221)*.

A bombshell!

Penguin is offering to order a million copies of 12 plays in 10 volumes
for my 90th birthday (26/7/1946). They include, of course, all Kyllman's
[sic] list. They and the Oxford U.P's Methuselah must have priority.

This defers the replenishment of the Standard for a year or thereabouts, does it not?

I must now announce the catastrophe to K.

The German Standard can go ahead unaffected.

G. Bernard Shaw

The Penguin series and the Oxford *Methuselah* delayed the reissue of the **Standard** *Edition.*
On the day he wrote to Clark, Shaw **announced the catastrophe** to Otto Kyllmann: 'This is
an atomic bomb; but it will advertise and pay the Standard in the long run' (CL 4, 758).

175 / To G. Bernard Shaw   [no address]

28th November 1945

[TEL: Cornell]

At the top of the first page of this four-page cablegram from Lowell Brentano, Shaw
has written '95 ¢ = 4s/– = $1.' Shortly after receiving the cable, Shaw sent it to
Dodd, Mead (see Letter 176).

HAVE SECURED REPRINT DEAL IN ACCORDANCE WITH RECENT CON-
VERSATION BENNETT CERF WANTS FIVE YEAR LICENSE TO PUBLISH
CANDIDA PYGMALION STJOAN IN ONE VOLUME HIS MODERN LI-

BRARY SELLING AT NINETYFIVE CENTS STOP HE OFFERS TEN CENTS PER COPY ROYALTY WITH FIFTEEN THOUSAND DOLLARS ADVANCE STOP WORLD BOOKS ALSO WANT OPTION ALL TITLES PLAN TO PUBLISH FOUR BOOKS ANNUALLY FOR FIVE YEARS ASK FIVE YEAR LICENSE EACH BOOK WITH RENEWAL RIGHTS ON TERMS TO BE ARRANGED STOP WILL PAY FOUR CENTS PER COPY ROYALTY ON FIRST SEVENHUNDRED FIFTYTHOUSAND BOOKS SOLD FIVE CENTS THEREAFTER AND TWENTYFIVE THOUSAND DOLLARS GUARANTEE AGAINST ROYALTIES TENTHOUSAND NOW FIVETHOUSAND A YEAR NEXT THREE YEARS STOP WILL SELL BOOKS AT FIFTY CENTS BUT WOULD PREFER TO SELL THEM AT ONE DOLLAR PAYING TEN CENTS ROYALTY STOP BOTH FIRMS KNOW OF EACH OTHERS OFFER AND WILL COOPERATE JOINT DEAL WILL ASSURE YOU TOTAL OF FORTY THOUSAND DOLLARS LESS MY TEN PERCENT COMMISSION DEAL FAR EXCEEDS OUR RECENT EXPECTATIONS FOR POPULAR PRICE NATION WIDE DISTRIBUTION PLEASE CABLE ACCEPTANCE THIRTYFIVE FIFTH AVENUE NEWYORK AND AUTHORIZE ME TO FORWARD CONTRACTS FOR YOUR SIGNATURE REGARDS LOWELL BRENTANO.

Bennett Cerf (1898–1971) had co-founded Random House in 1927 as a subsidiary of the **Modern Library** (purchased 1925). In 1933 Cerf won the landmark obscenity court case against James Joyce's *Ulysses* and published the novel in 1934.

176 / To Dodd, Mead & Co.   4 Whitehall Court, London SW1
[undated: ca. 3rd December 1945]

[TLS: Cornell]

Dear Dodds

I have to thank you for the accounts and their settlement. Why do you keep on publishing my old books? They do not pay for the room they take up on your shelves.

I enclose a cable I have just received from Lowell Brentano. I have refused its offers and accepted instead one from Penguin books for a cheaper edition which must run into much greater numbers if it is to pay its way.

The reason I have given to L.B. is that dollar books are your preserve.

But this is more of an excuse than a fact; for you confine your highly respectable old business to books at $2.50, which greatly restricts the circulation at which I aim. For instance The Intelligent Woman's Guide, by the circulation of which I set great store, is out of print in the U.S., because it cannot be bought for a dollar.

The fact that for a new book I have a fan circulation which makes loss on it impossible at any price has the effect that my books are never advertized, as the publisher naturally spends all his advertising money on books that do not sell unless they are pushed. What I need, however, is not press notices, but simply distribution, which means the free distribution of a million copies or so on the principle that if a reader can be induced to read me once he (or she) will come again and pay. During the war I gave the British and U.S. governments *carte blanche* to use my copyrights for loans of books to the troops without any payment to me. And I am now Penguinizing for a royalty of a farthing (half a cent) a copy. This will react favorably on editions at higher prices, but on editions at one dollar much better than two and a half.

Now it is evident that Bennett Cerf and World Books, who have bought up many apparently well established publishing firms, have decided that the day of the $2.50 dollar book has reached sunset and that the $1.00 book is dawning. If they are right I cannot leave myself with no prices between 50 cents or so and 250.

Have you thought about all this at all? Is there any chance of a change in your policy? Here in England, where I manufacture my own books, and Constable sells them on commission, I have Penguinized and let the Oxford University Press add my Methuselah cycle to its World Classic series to sell at 72 cents a copy. One must march with the times, especially when, as in my case, what is aimed at is maximum circulation rather than maximum profit.

Do not reply until you have time and inclination to consider the matter. Your experienced comments will be very welcome.

Faithfully
G. Bernard Shaw

The **cheaper edition** was **Penguin**'s 'Shaw Million' (see Letter 174). Brentano's had priced its cloth-bound edition of *The Intelligent Woman's Guide* at $3.00. The **World Classics** edition of *Back to Methuselah* was published in 1947 and sold for $1.50, not **72 cents**.

177 / To Allen Lane   [no address]
                                                          6th January 1946

[PP: Hare]

*The following is one of many Shaw postcards that 'were removed from the general
[Penguin Books] files and kept separately with Lane's private papers' (Hare, 63).*

The experience of fifty years contradicts you violently. In every return of
sales during that half century the Unpleasants have been markedly below
the Pleasants. The crisis in which my stuff ranked as unpleasant is long
past and forgotten: the adjective is now a senseless cry of stinking fish, utterly unintelligible to the Penguin public. However, the venture is yours:
do as you please. But you will lose sales on any book you label Unpleasant. As a matter of fact they are *not* unpleasant to the present generation.
Old fashioned and sentimental yes; but prudishly pleasant after *Lady
Chatterley.*

Shaw wrote to Lane on 10 January that '*Three Plays for Prudes* would be nearer the mark'
(quoted in Hare, 63). Penguin made British publishing history with D.H. Lawrence's
(1885–1930) ***Lady Chatterley's Lover.*** Limited editions of the (for its day) sexually explicit
novel had been issued in Florence (1928), Paris (1929), and New York (1959, the Grove
Press unexpurgated version). On 2 November 1960 a verdict of 'not guilty' was rendered
following a sensational six-day trial (under the Obscene Publications Act of 1959), and Penguin published the novel on the 10th, selling out its 200,000 copies that day (and a total of
2 million in six weeks).

178 / To G. Bernard Shaw   [no address]
                                                          31st January 1946

[TLU (c): Cornell]

Dodd, Mead replies to Shaw's letter of ca. 3 December (Letter 176).

Dear Mr Shaw

I hope you will forgive the delay in replying to your letter of a number of
weeks ago concerning reprint editions of your books.

    We appreciate highly your evident attempt to protect our interests and
persuade us to go into the $1.00 field of publishing, and it is certainly
generous on your part to decline the tempting offer made you through
Lowell Brentano.

You ask why we keep on publishing your old books. We do so for two reasons: (1) We are *very proud indeed* of being Bernard Shaw's American publishers. (2) The books are profitable because of the sale of the Collected Plays – NINE PLAYS and SIX PLAYS – and a few of the old titles, such as SAINT JOAN; also we did well (for America) with EVERYBODY'S POLITICAL WHAT'S WHAT – at least *we* thought it was very well.

As for bringing out your books for $1.00, of course we could have made arrangements, similar to those offered by Brentano, with specialists in the cheap field, such as The World Book Company, but it never occurred to us to make such an attempt, as you had rescinded all the control we might have had under our original agreement in connection with leases of reprint editions to other publishers. We ourselves are not equipped – and indeed few general publishers are – to sell $1.00 books. It is a completely different market and requires special organisation. We do an enormous business in renting plates and rights to Reprint Publishers, but we have no plans for going into that field ourselves directly.

We are very interested to learn that you are making arrangements with Penguin for the release of 25¢ editions in England and here. We do not believe that these 25¢ editions will affect, seriously, the sale of the higher price editions here, as the potential market is so completely different. Dollar books *would* compete more directly with us.

I have tried to answer your queries with complete candor and at the same time I can assure you that no matter what you may arrange in the cheap edition field over here, we shall try to carry on as your publishers of the original editions, so long as we are able to do so, even against serious opposition.

Incidentally, we have plans for bringing out another volume of COLLECTED PLAYS – uniform with NINE PLAYS and SIX PLAYS – this volume of course to comprise plays which are not in those two volumes. Eventually, this might lead to publication in this form of your complete works; and while the price per volume is high, the price per play is reasonable.

Howard Lewis joins me in sending you our cordial and affectionate greetings.

Very sincerely yours,
[no signature]

Dodd, Mead had acquired Brentano's plates in 1933 and reprinted *Saint Joan* numerous times. Constable published *Everybody's Political What's What?* (1944) at 50,000 copies; Dodd, Mead at 5000 copies. *Seven Plays*, **uniform with *Nine Plays* and *Six Plays***, was published only in 1951. **Howard** C. **Lewis** was company vice-president.

179 / To Dodd, Mead & Co. Ayot St Lawrence, Welwyn, Herts.
26th November 1946

[APCS: Cornell]

Frank C. Dodd had written on 22 October proposing 'a big SHAW READER of some six hundred pages that will appeal to the widest possible public' (TLS: HRC), to which Shaw replied by cable on the 30th: 'SORRY IMPOSSIBLE MY CONTRACTS WITH PENGUIN AND OXFORD UNIVERSITY PRESS FORBID' (TEL: Cornell). Dodd replied on 8 November that Penguin and Oxford 'haven't the slightest objection' to the volume (TLS: HRC). Shaw cabled on the 16th: 'READER SUGGESTS SCHOOLBOOK WHY NOT TWO OMNIBUS VOLUMES OF ALL THE PLAYS AND ALL THE PREFACES INSTEAD OF PICKING OUT THE PLUMS' (TEL: Cornell). Dodd replied on the 20th that they already had two omnibus volumes (Nine Plays and Six Plays) and that what was needed was 'an omnibus of selections covering the whole field of your work in one not too long volume.' Dodd included a royalty report for sales from 1 February to 1 August 1946: 'It is very pleasing to us, and even more so to you, that our two countries have finally agreed to reciprocal waiving of taxes on royalties. Thus, we are able to refund $665.67 which we should have been obliged to pay under the old law' (TLU (c): Cornell). Shaw put the 'reader' issue to rest with the following postcard.

'An omnibus selection' is a contradiction in terms. By an omnibus I mean, not a selection, but *all* the plays or prefaces in a single volume like a family Bible. Experience has convinced me that anthologies are a mistake, though of course in your case it does matter, you being my publishers. But I have to play fair with the Oxford University Press and Penguin. Nothing else new can be done until their exclusive rights period expires.

I will not tolerate the term Reader on any account. A reader is a schoolbook. I hate schoolbooks; and so does everyone else. They only sell because their purchase is compulsory; and their authors are loathed for life.

Thanks for the accounts. Less than $5000! I am still unread in the U.S.A. No matter: it will all go in taxation.

G.B.S.

180 / To Dodd, Mead & Co.　　　　　　　　　　[no address]

12th July 1948

[TLT: Cornell; CL 4]

Dodd, Mead would publish Sixteen Self Sketches *on 3 March 1949 at 10,500 copies, Constable at 50,000.*

Dear Dodds

Drown your designer. There us nothing so ugly in print as a combination of type with ordinary handwriting. If I were a great artist-calligrapher like Michael Angelo, whose handwriting was more beautiful than any fount of type, then a lithograph of my holograph would make any book an art treasure. As it is, it would make any book a disgusting curiosity, like binding it in the skin of some famous murderer.

Your designer ought to know this as well as I do. If he has an incurable fancy for my initials, here they are as I scrawl. They make a sort of butterfly pattern. Let him redraw them artistically and repeat them all over the page as he would in a wallpaper; and the result will perhaps be a presentable end paper for the inside of the cover.

I have changed the title to SIXTEEN SELF-SKETCHES partly because there must be no suggestion of a full dress Autobiography, and also because a title must be easy to speak, easy to spell, and unmistakeable to pronounce.

Autobiography is a hard word. Many people are uncertain about both the spelling and the pronunciation.

The illustrations will follow when Maxwell gets them done.

I shall be 92 on the 26th. Please do not congratulate me. Wish me no returns.

G.B.S.

Although more stylized, the handwriting of artist **Michelangelo** Buonarroti (1475–1564) is, like Shaw's, precise and easy to read. Shaw signed 'GBS' in the left margin near '**scrawl**.' The book contains numerous **illustrations** (photographs).

181 / To Dodd, Mead & Co.　　　　Ayot St Lawrence, Welwyn, Herts.

13th August 1948

[TLT: Cornell]

On 5 August Shaw had written to 'Dodds' that under no circumstances should he 'announce the book as a full dress autobiography,' as it was merely 'a little collection of sketches, mostly reprints ... The book market is bursting with Autobiographies. So SELF-SKETCHES IT MUST BE! ... (TLT: Cornell). Dodds took this to mean that 'SELF-SKETCHES' would be the full title, which he preferred.

Dear Dodds

Somehow SELF SKETCHES *tout court*, is unattractive: it needs another word to give it a swing. What about STRAY S-S? The advantage of SIXTEEN is that it suggests full measure. I am a great believer in sheer quantity. A book should last a family a fortnight. That is why I give at least two or three plays and a couple of prefaces in my standard editions instead of a bare one play. The purchaser may not like either the plays or the prefaces; but he (or she) feels that the book is good value for its price and gives me a good mark for it.

182 / To G. Bernard Shaw   [no address]
                                                1st March 1949

[TLU (c): Cornell]

Shaw replied to the proposal below on 1 April (Letter 183).

Dear Mr Shaw

Manufacturing conditions have made it very difficult to keep the old NINE PLAYS volume going at the low retail price of $5, and in casting about for some way to continue the group volumes without raising the price, we have worked out a scheme which seems to have a number of advantages over the old NINE PLAYS and SIX PLAYS volumes. Our plan is to issue a three-volume set of selected plays – twenty of them in all – and later on if they prove successful, to add another or several more, as conditions permit. I am enclosing the proposed lineup for your information, and I feel certain that you will agree that this gives a much wider representation of your plays at a better price for the public and more royalties for yourself. Each volume would be $5 retail. They will be uniform in size. The plates will be the same as they were in the NINE PLAYS and SIX PLAYS, and the new plays that are added will be uniform typographically. We are planning to have those available by August.

I am anxious to hear from you about our proposal for the publication of your letters.

> With best wishes,
> Sincerely yours,
> DODD, MEAD & COMPANY, Inc.

183 / To Dodd, Mead & Co.   Ayot St Lawrence, Welwyn, Herts.
1st April 1949

[TLS: Cornell]

When Dodd, Mead proposed to Shaw biographer Hesketh Pearson (1887–1964) that he edit a volume of Shaw's selected correspondence, Shaw strongly advised Pearson on 18 January 1943 'to fight shy of the job'; 'I could not possibly co-operate even if I were alive: it would take all my time; and I shall never again have any to spare for picking up my old droppings' (CL 4, 659). Frank C. Dodd's reply to the following is Letter 184.

Dear Dodds

There are two questions on which you are pressing me: both difficult.

First, as to publishing my letters. There are billions of them; and I am adding to them every day. Not until my death can any collection of them be described complete; and their collection, classification and selection would be the work of years by some fanatical Shavian, and quite out of the question as a commercial job. It has been proposed over and over again; but nothing has ever come of it. Put it out of your head.

Second, your proposal to publish my plays in 20 three-volume sets to supersede your 9-6 sets. But this is our Standard practice. You already have my plays in sets of three, priced as library editions.

What is really at issue between us is that I need breaking into a new class of readers who can afford no more than 20 cents for a book, and with this riffraff you, as the oldest and most respected publishing house in the U.S.A. will have nothing to do, even if mass production technique were in your line. In England what I call Omnibus editions of my entire 50 plays, and another of all my prefaces, have been printed and sold out for less than $1 a copy by newspaper syndicates to people producing enough coupons to prove that they take in the newspaper regularly. Also there is the Penguin firm which has sold more than a million of my plays separately for 12 cents apiece. During the war thousands of volumes of my plays were printed for the soldiers, who paid nothing for them.

The effect of all this on my library editions has been to increase their sales to such an extent that I now print 50,000 of a new book of which I should formerly have printed 10,000.

You cannot do this for me; and your sales are so trifling that after the first $2.50 issue the books are not worth their shelfroom and your Shaw business survives only as prestige publishing.

Now prestige publishing is dying fast. It is stone dead in your case and mine because you have as much prestige as you can exploit; and so have I: in fact you are being forced more and more into getting rid of your highbrow reputation and gaining a lowbrow one. You may even have to amalgamate with firms that have not a tithe of your reputation, to avoid being swamped by gangs of mushroom publishers who read nothing but police and sporting news.

This being the situation I can hardly advise you to go on with me at all, and must keep my market open for Omnibuses and Penguins, and bar any further experiments in the 9-6 line; also, at the opposite end of the scale for *éditions de luxe*. I have now in the Press a limited collectors' edition of Buoyant Billions, 1000 copies at $25, selling as fast as Self-Sketches. But these high prices are investments: the people who used to buy a book to read, and pay $2.50 for it, can hardly afford half a dollar. Read the printed card I enclose.

Think over this; and let me know the result of your meditations.

G. Bernard Shaw

According to Dan H. Laurence, Shaw is writing to chairman Edward H. **Dodd** (see *Exhibit*, item 87). In July 1937, when Stanley Unwin suggested publishing Shaw's letters, Shaw replied: 'There are some **billions** of letters of mine in existence' (Unwin, 181); Shaw reiterates his objections in Letter 187. Dan Laurence writes that 'Shaw, by conservative estimate, must in his lifetime have written at least a quarter of a million letters and postcards' (CL 1, xi). The expensive (£6.6.0), **limited** (1025 copies) **collectors' edition of** *Buoyant Billions: A Comedy of No Manners In Prose by Bernard Shaw and in Pictures by Clare Winsten*, published on 15 May 1950, was a commercial failure. In his personal copy, William Maxwell bemoaned 'the horrible title page,' 'silly inept caricatures,' and 'the ruination of my design' (quoted in Laurence 1, 254).

184 / To G. Bernard Shaw [no address]
6th May 1949

[TLS (c): Brown]

Dodd, Mead had written to Shaw on 19 April asking him to consider 'a one- or two-volume selection of letters, a publication which would comprise not more than a tenth or twentieth perhaps of the whole bulk of your correspondence. Such a selection would be a commercial undertaking and thus gain a much wider public circulation than a many-volumed, complete collection, which, as you point out, would probably be a very long-term undertaking' (TLU (c): Brown). Most likely Shaw replied to that letter on the 26th.

Dear Mr Shaw

I have just returned to the office from a Florida vacation and find my associates greatly disturbed over your letters of April 1st and 26th concerning the proposed three volume omnibus of your plays. Possibly you do not fully understand our plan. At any rate, at the risk of annoying you with further details, I want to be quite certain that there is no possible misunderstanding.

In 1935 we issued the omnibus volume of NINE PLAYS which was immediately successful and as you know was used as a premium 'distribution' by the Book of the Month Club to the extent of 63,000 copies. In addition, we have sold about 40,000 copies to the trade.

In 1941 we issued another collection of SIX PLAYS which has sold about 12,000.

It is not our plan to retire these two volumes and substitute three volumes containing twenty in all of your plays, or five more than the present two volumes. The enclosed circular describes the contents. We have consulted many of the important booksellers and they are all enthusiastically in favor of this plan and we anticipate a very considerable success for it. Each volume, of course, will be independent and sold separately, though many people will want to collect the three volumes for their libraries. It seems to us to be an intelligent move toward widening your American public and supplying a demand in an attractive library edition for even more of your plays than are now available, unless bought separately at a much higher price in the standard edition.

I quite agree with you that the sale of the standard editions has been dwindling and it would appear that the NINE PLAYS and SIX PLAYS (or better still, their successors, the three volume proposed set) more completely satisfies the public who want good library editions of your works and cannot afford to buy them by the volume or even three at a time in one volume.

So I beg you *please* to re-consider your decision!

As for the Penguins and other inexpensive editions, any of these which you may arrange here will certainly have our blessing. Indeed, we are completely sympathetic with this amazingly successful effort to widen the distribution of good books. On the other hand, there will always be a demand for these books in more permanent library editions, and I cannot foresee the time when the two will compete to the exclusion of either.

I wish heartily that I might see you once again in London, as Mrs Dodd and I remember so very pleasantly our visits with you and Mrs Shaw in the old days. But unfortunately my wife's health has been poor in the last year or two and there is no prospect of my going abroad again in the near future. I would like particularly to discuss with you publishing conditions in this country, and I think I could convince you that our proposal in regard to the three volume set is sound and intelligent.

With kindest personal regards, I am as always,

> Sincerely yours,
> Frank C. Dodd

185 / To Howard C. Lewis   [no address]
                                           10th May 1949

[ALS: Cornell]

Lewis replied to the following on the 17th, thanking Shaw for his letter 'which, I take it, gives consent to the manufacture and distribution of the three volumes of plays which have been the subject of our recent correspondence' (TLU (c): Brown).

My dear Lewis

As you are still infatuated about $5 Selections, there is no reason why I should not indulge you, as I suppose you can afford to lose a few thousands to gratify your fancy. But why not include Buoyant Billions and Far-fetched Fables &c &c to make up 5 volumes totaling $25?

But I warn you that if I can bring off a complete set in one volume at $1, either of the plays or prefaces, I will do it and ruin you.

Also I must inform you (though you wont listen) that William Randolph Hearst tells me that the war taxation has put such sums as $5 far beyond his means, and that he has to think twice before he spends 5 cents on a luxury.

Here people simply cannot afford the old prices except for art treasures that are investments.

Now your fate is in your own hands.

G.B.S.

Shaw's comments about the financial woes of billionaire **William Randolph Hearst**, who hosted the Shaws in March 1933 at his opulent estate at San Simeon (on the California coast), appear to be facetious.

186 / To Max Reinhardt

Ayot St Lawrence, Welwyn, Herts.
8th June 1949

[TLS: Georgetown]

In late 1947 Shaw and Max Reinhardt (1915–2002), of Reinhardt & Evans Ltd (founded 1947), had discussed a reissue of Ellen Terry and Bernard Shaw: A Correspondence (1931). On 8 January 1948 Shaw wrote that he was 'quite ready to complete our transaction' (TLS: Georgetown). They signed a 'Memorandum of Agreement' on 1 May and the book was published in 1949 – despite Constable's claim to copyright. 'I do not think they [Constable] have a leg to stand on,' Shaw assured Reinhardt on 26 August. 'I do not see how they can prove damages if they should sue for them instead of asserting a right. I never assign my copyright' (TLS: Georgetown). 'Rheinhardt' is Shaw's misspelling.

Dear Max Rheinhardt

I have just seen the advertisement of the Terry book, and learnt with dismay that you have priced it at 18 shillings. You are behind the times: the day of the 18/– book is past: the people who paid it now buy Penguins and have what they save by it confiscated by Cripps. As to a series of reprinted old favorites, which was what you proposed to me, 18/– was out of the question for them: they ranged from 5/– to 12/6d at the very extreme outside. I have never given in to this inflation. Nobody that buys a book of mine shall feel that he has not had full value for the money, which means that the book shall occupy the whole family for a fortnight. My standard volumes contain two full length new plays with my prefaces, and one short one. The price is 7/6d, and the first printing 50,000. That is what my fans expect. You are offering them a reprint of an old book for 18/–. If you sell more than a few thousand at that rate you will be lucky. And your intention of beginning a series of reprints falls through.

Dont trouble to reply. I must put myself in order for 'I told you so' in case –

G. Bernard Shaw

Beatrice Webb's nephew Sir Stafford **Cripps** (1889–1952), Chancellor of the Exchequer 1947–50, increased taxes (in order to stabilize the post-war pound sterling); 'Shaw's tax rate was nineteen shillings and sixpence in the pound (97.5%)' (Conolly, *Bernard Shaw and Barry Jackson*, 175). In 1957 Reinhardt took over The Bodley Head and published Shaw's *Collected Letters 1874–1897* (1965), *Collected Letters 1898–1910* (1972), *Collected Plays with their Prefaces* (1970–4, 7 vols.), and *Shaw's Music* (1981, 3 vols.). Random House took over The Bodley Head, Chatto & Windus, and Jonathan Cape in 1987.

187 / To Dodd, Mead & Co. [Ayot St Lawrence, Welwyn, Herts.]
ca. 1950

[PP: *Exhibit*]

This undated, unsigned draft (in Blanche Patch's hand) is a reply to Dodd, Mead's continued requests to publish Shaw's letters following his refusal of 1 April 1949. Shaw addressed the members of the firm in a similar fashion in Letter 147.

Dear Dodds, Mead, Uncle Tom Cobbley and all

Since all I can say fails to convince you that a selected collection of my letters will be the work of a lifetime and is now commercially impossible, let me now say finally, flatly, positively, pigheadedly, irrevocably, and inexorably that I will not let you attempt it, and that letters from you containing any mention of it will be hurled in the basket with the most profane oaths I can command.

If you come in the fall to continue the discussion I will set all the dogs of Ayot Saint Lawrence on you. You will be welcome only when the subject is barred.

Table of Correspondents

Unless otherwise noted the letters were written by Bernard Shaw.

1 To Macmillan & Co. 1 February 1880   3

2 To Remington & Co. 26 November 1881   4

3 To Richard Bentley & Son 18 February 1882   6

4 To Richard Bentley & Son 31 May 1883   7

5 To Macmillan & Co. 14 January 1885   8

6 To Macmillan & Co. 22 January 1885   9

7 To Swan Sonnenschein & Co. 25 February 1885   10

8 To Swan Sonnenschein & Co. 1 March 1885   11

9 To Swan Sonnenschein & Co. 16 March 1885   12

10 To Swan Sonnenschein & Co. 30 March 1885   13

11 To William Swan Sonnenschein 2 May 1887   14

12 To William Swan Sonnenschein 28 November 1887   15

13 To William Swan Sonnenschein 31 December 1887   16

14 To William Swan Sonnenschein 4 January 1888   17

15 To T. Fisher Unwin 4 September 1888   18

16 To T. Fisher Unwin 19 November 1888   19

17 To G. Bernard Shaw from the Walter Scott Publishing Co.
21 February 1889   20

18 To G. Bernard Shaw from the Walter Scott Publishing Co.
25 February 1889   21

19 To Will H. Dircks 3 September 1890   21

20 To T. Fisher Unwin 4 March 1891   23

21 To T. Fisher Unwin 22 April 1891   25

22 To John Lane 22 November 1892   26
23 To Grant Richards 13 November 1893   27
24 To Frederick H. Evans 14 August 1895   28
25 To T. Fisher Unwin 9 September 1895   29
26 To T. Fisher Unwin 6 December 1895   30
27 To T. Fisher Unwin 11 February 1896   31
28 To T. Fisher Unwin 24 February 1896   33
29 To John Lane 3 June 1896   33
30 To John Lane 29 June 1896   34
31 To Grant Richards 8 November 1896   36
32 To Grant Richards 27 March 1897   37
33 To John Lane 10 April 1897   38
34 To Grant Richards 19 May 1897   39
35 To G. Bernard Shaw from Grant Richards 20 May 1897   40
36 To Grant Richards 21 May 1897   41
37 To Grant Richards 26 August 1897   42
38 To Grant Richards 28 August 1897   43
39 To Grant Richards 25 September 1897   44
40 To Grant Richards 8 October 1897   45
41 To Grant Richards 3 January 1898   46
42 To Grant Richards 20 August 1898   47
43 To Grant Richards 9 September 1898   48
44 To Grant Richards 2 December 1898   50
45 To Grant Richards 5 December 1898   50
46 To G. Bernard Shaw from Grant Richards 24 May 1899   51
47 To Grant Richards 29 May 1899   53
48 To Herbert S. Stone & Co. 4 October 1899   54
49 To Grant Richards 8 May 1900   56
50 To Grant Richards 31 May 1900   57
51 To Grant Richards 13 September 1900   57
52 To Grant Richards 30 November 1900   58
53 To Grant Richards 30 December 1900   60
54 To Grant Richards 23 January 1901   60
55 To J.E. Lyons ca. 4 May 1901   62
56 To Grant Richards 21 May 1901   62
57 To Grant Richards 22 October 1902   64
58 To Grant Richards 7 November 1902   65

59 To Grant Richards 3 January 1903   66
60 To James Brand Pinker ca. February 1903   67
61 To Methuen & Co. ca. 17 February 1903   69
62 To Grant Richards 30 March 1903   71
63 To Grant Richards 4 April 1903   72
64 To John Murray 2 June 1903   74
65 To G. Bernard Shaw from John Murray 9 June 1903   76
66 To John Murray 10 June 1903   77
67 To Macmillan & Co. 19 June 1903   78
68 To Grant Richards 21 June 1903   80
69 To Harper & Brothers 10 July 1903   81
70 To George P. Brett 10 July 1903   82
71 To George P. Brett 13 July 1903   83
72 To Constable & Co. 15 July 1903   83
73 To T. Fisher Unwin 23 July 1903   85
74 To William Dana Orcutt 28 August 1903   86
75 To Otto Kyllmann 9 September 1903   90
76 To Grant Richards 30 March 1904   91
77 To Brentano's 15 June 1904   92
78 To Brentano's 12 August 1904   95
79 To Grant Richards 18 December 1904   96
80 To Grant Richards 31 December 1904   97
81 To Grant Richards 6 January 1905   98
82 To Grant Richards 15 January 1905   99
83 To G. Bernard Shaw from Grant Richards ca. 16 January 1905   102
84 To Grant Richards 17 January 1905   103
85 To R. & R. Clark 11 March 1905   104
86 To Brentano's 1 August 1905   105
87 To Otto Kyllmann ca. 24 March 1907   106
88 To Constable & Co. 26 March 1907   107
89 To John Lane 2 June 1908   110
90 To Curt Otto 24 October 1908   111
91 To Curt Otto 12 November 1908   113
92 To Constable & Co. 7 June 1909   114
93 To Simon Brentano 6 November 1912   115
94 To Simon Brentano 19 April 1913   117
95 To Curt Otto 14 January 1914   119

 96 To Curt Otto 23 May 1914   120
 97 To Brentano's 15 January 1916   121
 98 To Brentano's 22 August 1916   121
 99 To Constable & Co. 11 May 1917   122
100 To Brentano's 25 April 1918   123
101 To Brentano's 7 June 1918   124
102 To Brentano's 22 January 1919   124
103 To Curt Otto 4 October 1919   126
104 To Otto Kyllmann 29 January 1920   128
105 To Curt Otto ca. 20 March 1920   129
106 To Otto Kyllmann 31 December 1920   131
107 To Arthur Brentano 17 January 1921   131
108 To Bernard Shaw from J.E. Spingarn 24 March 1921   132
109 To J.E. Spingarn 7 April 1921   133
110 To J.M. Dent 22 June 1921   134
111 To Curt Otto 28 July 1921   135
112 To Otto Kyllmann 17 December 1921   135
113 To Arthur Brentano 20 March 1922   136
114 To Otto Kyllmann 14 October 1922   138
115 To The Forum Publishing Co. 29 March 1924   138
116 To Charles Ricketts 29 May 1924   140
117 To Harper & Brothers 11 November 1924   141
118 To Otto Kyllmann 21 January 1925   143
119 To Otto Kyllmann 20 August 1925   144
120 To Thomas Nelson & Sons 24 November 1927   144
121 To G. Bernard Shaw from William Griffith 4 June 1928   145
122 To William Griffith ca. June 1928   146
123 To G. Bernard Shaw from Stanley Unwin 18 June 1929   147
124 To Stanley Unwin 19 June 1929   148
125 To G. Bernard Shaw from Otto Kyllmann 24 July 1929   149
126 To William H. Wise & Sons 8 November 1929   150
127 To Stanley Unwin 9 December 1929   152
128 To Bernard Shaw from Stanley Unwin 12 December 1929   153
129 To G. Bernard Shaw from William H. Wise 4 March 1930   154
130 To Otto Kyllmann 31 May 1930   155
131 To Jonathan Cape 26 October 1930   156
132 To Otto Kyllmann 1 December 1930   156

133 To Otto Kyllmann 4 December 1930   158
134 To Otto Kyllmann 4 June 1931   159
135 To Elbridge L. Adams 19 June 1931   160
136 To Otto Kyllmann 28 June 1931   161
137 To William Maxwell 14 August 1931   162
138 To Otto Kyllmann 12 October 1931   162
139 To Otto Kyllmann 12 June 1932   163
140 To Howard C. Lewis 14 December 1932   164
141 To G. Bernard Shaw from Dodd, Mead & Co. 28 December 1932   166
142 To Lowell Brentano 6 January 1933   166
143 To Lowell Brentano 14 March 1933   168
144 To Otto Kyllmann 17 July 1933   169
145 To Otto Kyllmann ca. 26 July 1933   169
146 To Otto Kyllmann 2 August 1933   170
147 To Dodd, Mead & Co. 22 September 1933   171
148 To Otto Kyllmann 25 January 1934   173
149 To Grant Richards 23 May 1934   174
150 To Dodd, Mead & Co. 10 September 1934   175
151 To William Maxwell 20 October 1936   176
152 To G. Bernard Shaw from Frank C. Dodd 28 October 1936   177
153 To G. Bernard Shaw from John J. Crawley 3 December 1936   178
154 To Otto Kyllmann 18 September 1937   180
155 To Otto Kyllmann 23 September 1937   181
156 To Dodd, Mead & Co. 10 December 1937   182
157 To Howard C. Lewis 25 November 1938   183
158 To William Maxwell 8 March 1939   183
159 To G. Bernard Shaw from Dodd, Mead & Co. 19 June 1939   184
160 To Dodd, Mead & Co. 1 July 1939   186
161 To William Maxwell 5 November 1939   187
162 To G. Bernard Shaw from A.J. Hoppé 7 February 1940   188
163 To Dodd, Mead & Co. 3 April 1940   190
164 To G. Bernard Shaw from Dodd, Mead & Co. 26 April 1940   192
165 To Dodd, Mead & Co. 23 May 1940   195
166 To Dodd, Mead & Co. 19 June 1940   196
167 To Frank C. Dodd 11 July 1940   199
168 To J.M. Dent 16 October 1940   199
169 To Otto Kyllmann 24 February 1941   200

170 To Daniel Macmillan 11 September 1943   201
171 To R. & R. Clark 28 October 1944   205
172 To Otto Kyllmann 30 December 1944   206
173 To Otto Kyllmann 14 August 1945   207
174 To R. & R. Clark 21 November 1945   208
175 To G. Bernard Shaw from Lowell Brentano 28 November 1945   208
176 To Dodd, Mead & Co. ca. 3 December 1945   209
177 To Allen Lane 6 January 1946   211
178 To G. Bernard Shaw from Dodd, Mead & Co. 31 January 1946   211
179 To Dodd, Mead & Co. 26 November 1946   213
180 To Dodd, Mead & Co. 12 July 1948   214
181 To Dodd, Mead & Co. 13 August 1948   214
182 To G. Bernard Shaw from Dodd, Mead & Co. 1 March 1949   215
183 To Dodd, Mead & Co. 1 April 1949   216
184 To G. Bernard Shaw from Frank C. Dodd 6 May 1949   218
185 To Howard C. Lewis 10 May 1949   219
186 To Max Reinhardt 8 June 1949   220
187 To Dodd, Mead & Co. ca. 1950   221

References

Bonham-Carter, Victor. *Authors by Profession*. Volume 2: *From the Copyright Act 1911 until the End of 1981*. Los Altos, CA: William Kaufmann, 1984.

Bowes and Bowes. *Catalogue 523*. Cambridge, UK: 1950.

Collini, Stefan. 'Boomster and the Quack.' *London Review of Books*, 2 November 2006: 11–14.

Conolly, L.W., ed. *Selected Correspondence of Bernard Shaw. Bernard Shaw and Barry Jackson*. Toronto: University of Toronto Press, 2002.

Dukore, Bernard F., ed. *Selected Correspondence of Bernard Shaw. Bernard Shaw and Gabriel Pascal*. Toronto: University of Toronto Press, 1996.

Dunlap, Joseph R. 'The Typographical Shaw: GBS and the Revival of Printing.' *Bulletin of the New York Public Library* 64 (1960): 534–47. Reprinted in *The Shavian* 2.3 (February 1961): 4–15.

Ervine, St John. *Bernard Shaw: His Life, Work and Friends*. London: Constable, 1956.

Evans, T.F. 'Shaw among the Penguins.' *The Shavian* 6.4 (Spring 1986): 6–9.

Ford, Ronald, ed. *The Letters of Bernard Shaw to* The Times. Dublin, Ireland, and Portland, OR: Irish Academic Press, 2007.

Gibbs, A.M. *A Bernard Shaw Chronology*. Basingstoke, UK: Palgrave, 2001.

Green, Benny. *Shaw's Champions: G.B.S. and Prizefighting from Cashel Byron to Gene Tunney*. London: Elm Tree Books, 1978.

Hare, Steve, ed. *Penguin Portrait: Allen Lane and the Penguin Editors 1935–1970*. Harmondsworth, UK: Penguin, 1995.

Henderson, Archibald. *Bernard Shaw, Playboy and Prophet*. New York: D. Appleton, 1932.

Holroyd, Michael. *Bernard Shaw*. Volume 2: *1898–1918, The Pursuit of Power*. London: Chatto & Windus, 1989.

– *Bernard Shaw.* Volume 3: *1918–1950, The Lure of Fantasy.* London: Chatto & Windus, 1991.

– *Bernard Shaw.* Volume 4: *1950–1991, The Last Laugh.* New York: Random House, 1992.

Hugo, Leon. *Bernard Shaw's 'The Black Girl in Search of God': The Story behind the Story.* Gainesville: University Press of Florida, 2003.

Jackson, Holbrook. 'Robert Bridges, George Moore, Bernard Shaw and Printing.' *The Fleuron: A Journal of Typography* 4 (1925): 43–53.

Kelly, Katherine E. 'Imprinting the Stage: Shaw and the Publishing Trade, 1883–1903.' In Christopher Innes, ed., *The Cambridge Companion to George Bernard Shaw*, 25–54. Cambridge: Cambridge University Press, 1998.

King, Raphael. *Catalogue 5.* London, UK: 1929.

Laurence, Dan H. *Bernard Shaw: A Bibliography.* 2 volumes. Oxford: Clarendon Press, 1983.

– *Shaw: An Exhibit.* Austin: The University of Texas at Austin, 1977 [catalogue of an exhibit at the University of Texas, 11 September 1977 to 28 February 1978].

– '"That Awful Country": Shaw in America.' In *SHAW: The Annual of Bernard Shaw Studies*, volume 5: 279–97. University Park: Penn State University Press, 1985.

Laurence, Dan H., ed. *Bernard Shaw: Collected Letters 1874–1897.* New York: Dodd, Mead, 1965.

– *Bernard Shaw: Collected Letters 1898–1910.* New York: Dodd, Mead, 1972.

– *Bernard Shaw: Collected Letters 1911–1925.* New York: Viking, 1985.

– *Bernard Shaw: Collected Letters 1926–1950.* New York: Viking, 1988.

– *Bernard Shaw: Collected Plays with Their Prefaces.* 7 volumes. New York: Dodd, Mead & Company, 1975.

Laurence, Dan H., and Daniel J. Leary, eds. *Flyleaves.* Austin: W. Thomas Taylor, 1977.

Mander, Raymond, and Joe Mitchenson. *Theatrical Companion to Shaw: A Pictorial Record of the First Performances of the Plays of George Bernard Shaw.* New York: Pitman Publishing Corporation, 1955.

Maxwell, William. 'Newdigate *v.* Shaw.' *London Mercury* 13 (November 1925): 72–3.

– 'Printing for Bernard Shaw.' *The Listener*, 10 September 1949: 797.

– 'To the Editor of *The London Mercury*.' *London Mercury* 13 (November 1925): 72–3.

Meynell, Gerard T. 'Newdigate *v.* Shaw.' *London Mercury* 13 (November 1925): 72.

Middleton, George. 'Shaw's Royal Royalties: Dramatist Knew Values of Literary Property Rights – and Protected Them to the Hilt.' *Variety*, 9 January 1957: 31.

Morgan, Charles. *The House of Macmillan (1843–1943).* London: The Macmillan Co., 1943; New York: The Macmillan Co., 1944.

Morpurgo, J.E. *Allen Lane, King Penguin: A Biography.* London: Hutchinson & Co., 1979.

Mumby, F.A. [Frank Arthur], and Frances H.S. [Helena Swan] Stallybrass. *From Swan Sonnenschein to George Allen & Unwin Ltd.* London: George Allen & Unwin, 1955.

Newdigate, B.H. 'Book-Production Notes.' *London Mercury* 12 (October 1925): 645–6.

– '"G.B.S." and the Typography of His Books.' *London Mercury* 12 (August 1925): 420.

– 'Meynell *versus* Shaw and Others.' *London Mercury* 13 (December 1925): 189.

Nowell-Smith, Simon, ed. *Letters to Macmillan.* London: Macmillan; New York: St Martin's Press, 1967.

Orcutt, William Dana. *Celebrities Off Parade: Pen-and-Ink Portrait Sketches.* Chicago: Willett, Clark & Co., 1935.

Patch, Blanche. *Thirty Years with G.B.S.* London: Victor Gollancz, 1951.

Pharand, Michel W. 'Getting Published: Grant Richards and the Shaw Book.' *SHAW: The Annual of Bernard Shaw Studies* 27 (2007): 69–80.

– 'A Selected Bibliography of Writings by Bernard Shaw on Publishing, Printing, and Related Topics.' *SHAW: The Annual of Bernard Shaw Studies* 27 (2007): 80–4.

Richards, Grant. *Author Hunting, by an old literary sports man; memories of years spent mainly in publishing, 1897–1925.* London: Hamish Hamilton; New York: Coward-McCann, 1934.

– *Memories of a Misspent Youth, 1872–1896.* London: William Heinemann, 1932.

Rose, Jonathan, and Patricia J. Anderson, eds. *Dictionary of Literary Biography: British Literary Publishing Houses, 1881–1965.* Volume 112. Detroit: Gale Research Company, 1991.

Rhys, Ernest. *Letters from Limbo.* London: J.M. Dent & Sons Ltd, 1936.

Saroléa, Charles. 'G. Bernard Shaw as the Champion of Capitalism: An Open Letter on the New Copyright Bill.' *Everyman*, 7 February 1913: 521–2.

Shand, James. 'Author and Printer: G.B.S. and R. & R. C[lark].: 1898–1948.'

1948. In *Books and Printing: A Treasury for Typophiles*. Revised edition, ed. Paul
    A. Bennett, 381–401. Cleveland: The World Publishing Co., 1951

Shaw, Bernard. 'The Author's View: A Criticism of Modern Book Printing.' *The
    Caxton Magazine* 2 (January 1902): 119–21. Reprinted as *Bernard Shaw on Mod-
    ern Typography* (Cleveland: Horace Carr, 1915) and *On Modern Composition*
    (London: H.J.B. Craven, 1921).

– 'A Letter to the Author from Bernard Shaw.' In G. Herbert Thring, *The Mar-
    keting of Literary Property: Books and Serial Rights*, xi–xxiii. London: Constable,
    1933. Reprinted in *Bernard Shaw: The Complete Prefaces*, Volume 3: *1930–1950*,
    ed. Dan H. Laurence and Daniel J. Leary, 131–40. London: Allen Lane, Pen-
    guin, 1997.

– 'Mr. Bernard Shaw on "imbeciles" who are "afraid to say no."' *The Author* 41
    (Spring 1931): 88.

– 'Notes on the Clarendon Press Rules for Compositors and Readers.' *The
    Author* 12 (1 April 1902): 171–2.

– 'Sixty Years in Business as an Author.' *The Author* 55 (Summer 1945): 56–58.

– 'The Typography of G.B.S.' *London Mercury* 23 (November 1925): 524.

Sotheby, Parke-Bernet. *George Bernard Shaw: A Distinguished Collection of Letters,
    Manuscripts and First Editions*. New York: Sotheby, Parke-Bernet, 1972.

Todd, William B., and Ann Bowden. *Tauchnitz International Editions in English
    1841–1955: A Bibliographical History*. New York: Bibliographical Society of
    America, 1988.

Unwin, Sir Stanley. *The Truth About a Publisher: An Autobiographical Record*. New
    York: The Macmillan Co.; London: George Allen & Unwin, 1960.

– *The Truth About Publishing*. 1926. Revised edition. New York: The Macmillan
    Co., 1960.

Wearing, J.P., ed. *Selected Correspondence of Bernard Shaw. Bernard Shaw and Nancy
    Astor*. Toronto: University of Toronto Press, 2005.

Weintraub, Stanley, ed. *Bernard Shaw: The Diaries 1885–1897*. 2 volumes. Univer-
    sity Park and London: The Pennsylvania State University Press, 1986.

– *Bernard Shaw's Nondramatic Literary Criticism*. Lincoln: University of Nebraska
    Press, 1972.

Whyte, Frederic. *William Heinemann: A Memoir*. London: Jonathan Cape, 1928.

Index

Academy of Political Science, 168
Adams, Elbridge L., 158–61
Allen, George, 29, 147
Allen, Grant, 73; *The Woman Who Did*,
 40–1
American Foundation for the Blind,
 183
American Scrap Book, The, 145
Archer, William, 8–9, 25–6, 203, 205
Asquith, Anthony, 184
Astor, Nancy, 201
Atalanta, 35–6
Authors League of America, 146, 171
Ayot St Lawrence, xxv, 119, 130, 136,
 148, 221

Bacon, Francis: *Essays*, 91
Bain, Francis William: *A Digit of the
 Moon*, 60
Balfour Declaration (1917), 134
Balzac, Honoré de, 44, 70
Barker, Harley Granville, 102
Baskerville, John, 162
Bayreuth Festival, 35, 80
Belloc, Hilaire: *The Jews*, 133
Besant, Sir Walter, 85, 149, 204
Bible, 86–90, 142, 197, 213

Blackwell, Basil, 177–8
bookshops, booksellers, bookselling:
 29, 37, 86, 97–8, 106–8, 110, 116, 118,
 129, 131–2, 137, 142, 149–50, 155–8,
 167, 201
*Book of a Thousand Nights and a Night,
 The*, 60
Brentano, Arthur, 93, 131–2, 136–7
Brentano, Lowell, xvii, 93, 150, 154–5,
 166–8, 208–9, 211
Brentano, Simon, xvi–xvii, 93, 115–19,
 131, 167
Brett, George Platt, 82–3, 137
Bridges, Robert: *The Testament of
 Beauty*, 175
British Museum, 4, 8, 60, 205
Bulwer-Lytton, Edward: *The Last Days
 of Pompeii*, 111
Bumpus, John and Edward, Ltd
 (booksellers), 201
Buonarroti, Michelangelo, 214
Burne-Jones, Sir Edward, 90
Burnett, Frances Hodgson: *Little Lord
 Fauntleroy*, 32
Burrelle's (press cutting bureau), 115–
 17
Burton, Sir Richard Francis, 60

Butler, Samuel: *Erewhon Revisited*, 53; *Evolution Old and New*, 200; *Luck or Cunning?* 200; *The Way of All Flesh*, 53

Byron, George Gordon, Lord, 75, 204–5

Caslon, William, 162
Camelot Series (Scott Library), 22–3
Campbell, Mrs Patrick, 30; *My Life and Some Letters*, xxii
Carlyle, Thomas, 44, 70
Carroll, Lewis, 171
Cassell, John, 19
Caxton, William, 46–7
Cerf, Bennett, 208–10
Chamberlain, Neville, 188
Champion, Henry Hyde, 14–15
Chase, Arthur M., 171–2
Cherry-Garrard, Apsley: *The Worst Journey in the World*, 176
Chesterton, Gilbert Keith, 91; *The New Jerusalem*, 133
Cholmondeley, Mary, 143
Clark, Edward, 44, 128
Clark, Robert, 44
Clemens, Cyril, xxiii–xxiv
Cobden-Sanderson, Thomas J., 89–90
Colby, Frank Moore, 171, 221
Combes, Émile: *Une campagne laïque*, 111
Comstock, Anthony, 173
Copyright Act (1911), xiii, xxiii–xxiv, xxx, 63, 165
Copyright Treaty (Berne Convention, 1886), 13, 55–6
Cornell, Katharine, 183
'Corno di Bassetto,' 24–5, 180–1
Crane, Walter, 22–3
Crawley, John J., 178–9, 193, 195
Cripps, Sir Stafford, 220–1

Crofts, Frederick, 182
Crossland, John R., xxii

Darwin, Charles, 136
Davidson, John, 175
Davies, W.H., xxiii; *Selected Poems of W.H. Davies*, 164
Dent, Joseph Malaby. *See under* publishing houses
Dickens, Charles: *Our Mutual Friend*, 163; *The Pickwick Papers*, 163
Dilke, Sir Charles W., 203, 205
Dircks, Will H., 20–3
Dodd, Edward H., 171, 216–17
Dodd, Frank Courtenay, xvii–xviii, 168, 171–2, 177–8, 199, 213, 216, 218–19
Dodd, Moses Woodruff, 106
Douglas, Lord Alfred, 180–1
Doyle, Sir Arthur Conan, 112
Drummond, Charles J., 24
Dryden, John, 110–11, 175; *Fables, Ancient and Modern*, 111
Duffin, Henry Charles, 147–9; *The Quintessence of Bernard Shaw*, 147
Dunlap, Joseph R., xxv–xxvi; 'The Typographical Shaw: GBS and the Revival of Printing,' xxv

Echegaray, José: *Mariana*, 30; *The Son of Don Juan*, 30
Editions for the Armed Services, 207
Egan, Pierce, 7–8; *Boxiana*, 7
Encyclopedia Britannica, 151–2
Erskine, Chester, 184
European Scrap Book, The, 145–6
Evans, Frederick H., xii, 28–30, 41–2, 74
Everyman's Library Series (J.M. Dent), 134, 188–90, 201, 207

Fabian Society, xi, 17, 21, 24, 57–8, 103, 136

Farleigh, John, 163–5, 169–70, 172, 208

Farr, Florence (Mrs Edward Emery), 24, 26–7

Field & Roscoe (solicitors), 100, 102

Ford, Henry, 133

Fournier, Pierre Simon, 162

France, Anatole, 110–11

Franco, Francisco, 188

Galignani (Paris bookstore), 112

Gordon, David, 20–1

Gosse, Sir Edmund, 26, 110–11

Graff, Robert Fair de, 190–1, 194

Griffith, William, 145–6

Gurly, Walter John, 7

Harris, Frank, 180–1; *Bernard Shaw: An Unauthorised Biography*, 181; *Oscar Wilde, His Life and Confessions*, 180

Harris, Nellie, 180–1

Hearst, William Randolph, 124–6, 201, 220

Heath, Roland, 156

Heinemann, William. *See under* publishing houses

Henderson, Archibald: *Bernard Shaw: Playboy and Prophet*, 138; *George Bernard Shaw: His Life and Works*, 138; *George Bernard Shaw: Man of the Century*, 138; *Table-Talk of G.B.S.*, 139–43

Henley, William Ernest, 203, 205

Herbert, Auberon, 203, 205

Hitler, Adolf, 188

Hodgson's (auction house), 147–8

Hogg, Wentworth, 58–9

Holloway Prison, 67, 69

Hoppé, Alfred John, 188–90, 200–1

Hubbard, Elbert, xxv, 55–6, 89–90

Ibsen, Henrik, xiii, 24–6, 32, 42, 44–5, 203; *Hedda Gabler*, 26; *The Lady from the Sea*, 25–6; *Rosmersholm*, 24

Independent Theatre Society, 27, 36

International Socialist Congress (London), 35–6

Irving, Sir Henry, 37

Jackson, Sir Barry, 150

Jackson, Holbrook, xx

Jewish Territorialist Organization, 134

Jonson, Ben, 199

journals, periodicals, newspapers: *The Academy*, 22–3, 84–5; *The Author*, 86; *British Weekly*, 91; *Church Reformer*, 22–3; *The Conservator*, 95; *Cosmopolis*, 35–6; *Daily Herald*, 160; *Daily News*, 22–3, 91; *Dearborn Independent*, 133; *The Economist*, 99; *The Fleuron: A Journal of Typography*, xx; *The Free Lance*, 84–5; *Free Life*, 205; *Fortnightly Review*, 138, 203, 205; *Illustrated London News*, 28; *Lady's Pictorial*, 84–5; *Liberty*, 56, 95, 134; *London Mercury*, xx, 144; *Methodist Times*, 22–3; *New Review*, 32; *New Statesman*, 121; *New York American*, 124, 126; *New York Times*, 117, 121, 173; *News Chronicle*, xxiii; *Our Corner*, 13, 19–20, 24; *The Outlook*, 84–5; *The Pall Mall Gazette*, xi, 22–3, 27, 33, 200, 205; *The Queen*, 84–5; *Review of Reviews*, 27–8; *Saturday Review*, 30, 84–5; *Saturday Review of Literature*, 164; *The Savoy*, 35–6; *Scots Observer*, 22–3; *Scottish Leader*, 22–3; *The Speaker*, 84–5; *The Star*, xi, 24–6, 33; *Time*, 10; *The Times*, xvi, 26, 106–9; *To-Day*, 7–8, 13; *Wilshire's*

Magazine, 95; *The World*, xi, 8, 24, 26, 28, 33–4

Joyce, James, *Ulysses*, 209

Karsh, Yousuf, xxv
Kelly, Katherine E., xiii
Kennington, Eric, xviii
Ketchum, Roland (and Adolph Gillis): *Three Masters of the English Drama: Shaw, Dryden, Shakespeare* (containing *Caesar and Cleopatra, All for Love, Julius Caesar*), 175–6
Kimball, Hannibal Ingalls, 43
Kipling, Rudyard, 112
Kyllmann, Otto, xvi–xvii, xxvi, 83, 90–1, 106–7, 114, 123, 125, 128, 131, 135–8, 140, 143–4, 149–50, 154–64, 168–70, 173–4, 180–4, 188, 191, 200–1, 206–8

Lafayette, Gilbert du Motier, Marquis de, 161
Lamb's Tales from Shakespere, 24
Lane, Sir Allen, xviii, 176, 188, 190, 208, 211
Lane, Edward William, 60
Lane, John. *See under* publishing houses
Langford, Joseph M., 3–4
La Rochefoucauld, François, duc de, *Réflexions ou Sentences et Maximes morales*, 75
Lawrence, D.H.: *Lady Chatterley's Lover*, 211
Lawrence, T.E., 152; *Revolt in the Desert*, xxiii
Leighton, Douglas, 200
Leighton Son & Hodge (bookbinders; later Leighton-Straker), 136, 138, 182, 200

Lewis, Howard Corwin, xvii, 164–5, 168, 171–2, 183, 212–13, 219–20
Lowrey, Francis, 18
Lucas, E.V., 129; *Edwin Austin Abbey: The Record of His Life and Work*, 128–9
Lyons, J.E., 62, 65

Macmillan, Alexander, 4, 149, 203, 205
Macmillan, Daniel (1813–57), 4, 201
Macmillan, Daniel (1886–1965), xxii, 149, 201–4
Macmillan, George A., 203, 205
Mahomet, 91
Malvern Festival, 150, 162, 169
Mansfield, Richard, 30
Marx, Karl, 8; *Das Kapital*, 205
Matthews, Elkin, 26
Maude, Aylmer, 102–3
Maxwell, William, xiv, xxi, xxv–xxvi, 128, 144, 158, 162–3, 176–7, 183–4, 187–8, 207, 214, 217
Mead, Edward S., 106, 171–2, 221
Meredith, George, 203, 205
Meredith, William Maxse, 114, 123
Methuen, Sir Algernon, 68
Metropolitan Opera House, 168
Meynell, Gerald T., xxi
Mill, John Stuart, 203, 205
Miller, William, 162
Modern Humour: A Nosegay of Contemporary Wit, 188–90
Moore, George, 36; *Confessions of a Young Man*, 18
Morgan, Charles: *The House of Macmillan*, 201–2
Morley, John, 203, 205
Morris, May: *Morris as a Socialist*, 178; *William Morris: Artist, Writer, Socialist*, 178
Morris, William, xiv, xix–xxi, xxvi, 38,

86–9, 178; *The Roots of the Mountains,*
xx, 58
Murray, John (1745–93), 75, 204–5
Murray, Sir John (1851–1928). *See
under* publishing houses
Mussolini, Benito, 188

Nathan, George Emanuel, 123
Net Book Agreement (1899), xvi, 110
Newdigate, Bernard H., xx–xxi
Newman, John Henry Cardinal: *Apolo-
gia pro Vita Sua,* 78
New York Society for the Suppression
of Vice, 173
New York Theatre Guild, 129
Nietzsche, Friedrich, 77–8, 203, 205
Nordau, Max Simon, 133–4; *Entartung,*
134

Opdycke, John B.: *Harper's English
Grammar,* 175
Orcutt, William Dana, xix, 86–9
Osgood, James R., 15
Otto, Curt, 111–13, 119–20, 126–30,
135, 145

Paris Peace Conference, 124
Pascal, Gabriel, 184, 201
Patch, Blanche, xxiv, 180–1, 199, 205,
221
Paul, Saint, 77–8
Payne, John, 60
Pearson, Hesketh, 216
Pease, Edward R., 21–3
Pennell, Joseph, 24
Pinero, Sir Arthur Wing, 36, 58; *The
Notorious Mrs Ebbsmith,* 30; *The Second
Mrs Tanqueray,* 30, 32
Pinker, James Brand, xvii, 64–71, 93
Plantin, Christophe, 162

printing firms: Chiswick Press, 57–8,
184; R. & R. Clark, xii, xiv–xvi, xxi,
xxv, 39–41, 44–6, 48–9, 51, 56–7, 61–
2, 71–2, 84, 86, 88, 90, 94, 100, 102,
104–5, 128, 131, 136, 138, 155, 157,
163, 174, 184, 204–8; Hazell Watson
& Viney Ltd, 71; Unwin Brothers,
24, 31
publication, simultaneous British and
American, 36–7, 71, 79, 86, 173
Publishers' Association, 106, 109, 152
publishing:
– advertising, advertisements, xv, 5, 16,
22, 61–6, 72, 79–81, 84, 86, 91, 106,
114–16, 143, 150, 191, 197–8, 210,
220; Grant Richards, 50–3, 64, 92
– agreements, contracts, legal documents, xii, xxii–xxiii, 25, 39–40, 43,
50, 52, 54, 56, 67–8, 79, 95, 108, 110,
113, 121, 131–2, 150, 153, 171–3, 182,
184, 190, 193, 220; Brentano's, 93–4,
116; Constable, xv; Dodd, Mead,
xvii, 164–5, 171–2, 195–6, 198;
Harper & Brothers, 139–42; Henry
& Co., 27; Methuen & Co., 69; Grant
Richards, 39–42, 66, 72, 96, 100;
Swan Sonnenschein, 14; Tauchnitz,
119–20, 126–30
– commission publishing, xv, xvii, 5–
6, 13, 23, 45–6, 54, 56–7, 65, 67, 72–
3, 79, 91–2, 99, 116–17, 197, 204, 206,
210
– copyright, xxiii–xvii, xxi–xxiii, 5–6,
10–14, 19, 23, 31–3, 39, 47, 55–8, 62–
3, 71, 75, 79, 81–6, 90–1, 105, 113,
118, 122–3, 139, 141, 146, 148–51,
158, 165, 173, 177, 184–7, 191, 198,
220
– cost of Shaw's books: xviii, 5, 10, 16,
23, 25, 37–8, 43–6, 60, 66, 86, 110,

120, 139–40, 144, 154, 157, 164, 169, 172–3, 178–9, 184, 188–9, 191, 195–9, 206, 209, 210, 215–17, 219–21
- earnings, income (American), xvii, xxviii, 81, 115, 123, 125, 137, 167, 195, 213
- earnings, income (British), xvi, 91–2, 114, 122, 124, 135, 201, 206, 208
- *éditions de luxe*, 27, 44, 46, 58, 154, 160, 198, 217
- electroplates, 12, 90–1, 93
- fair wages, xiv, 23–4, 41, 70–1
- illustrations and illustrated editions, 23, 27, 42, 140, 163–5, 183, 187, 191–2, 198–9, 208, 214, 217
- photographs, 27–8, 41–2, 51, 66, 151, 214
- printing requirements (apostrophes, bindings, design, ink, margins, paper, spacing, spelling, title pages, typefaces, typesetting, type sizes, typography), xiv, xix–xx, 20–1, 23, 43–4, 46–51, 58, 61–2, 87–91, 94, 128, 131, 144, 152, 170, 214
- proofs, xix, 13, 43, 49, 51, 53, 57–8, 61, 74, 78, 87, 147, 152
- royalties, xv, xxiii, 5, 10–13, 19, 22, 34–5, 39–44, 43, 59, 68, 70, 79, 81, 83, 91–3, 96–100, 105, 117, 125–9, 146, 157, 159, 165, 167–8, 178, 180, 182, 189, 193, 198, 209–10, 215; Brentano's, xvii, xxviii, 115, 123, 137; Constable, 92; Dodd, Mead, xviii, 177, 191–2, 195, 213; Harper & Brothers, 139; John Lane, 34; Grant Richards, 40–1, 46, 64–5, 91, 96, 100; Swan Sonnenschein, 10, 13
- school editions, anthologies, readers, xxii, 142, 144–5, 171, 173, 175–6, 182, 193–5, 213 .

- stagerights and stagerighting, xiii, 30–2, 71
- stereoplates, xx, 11–12, 14–15
- taxes (American), xvii, 93, 123–5, 137, 196, 201, 213, 220
- taxes (British), xvi, xvii, 114, 125, 127, 163, 200–1, 206, 213, 221
- typefaces, xx, xxv–xxvi; Baskerville, xxvi, 162; Caslon, xix–xxi, xxv–xxvi, 48, 88, 94, 128, 131, 152, 158, 162; Fournier, xxvi, 158, 162–3; Imprint, xxi; Miller, 131; Old Style, xxvi; Plantin, 162; Scotch Roman, xxvi, 131
publishing houses: George Allen & Co. Ltd, 10, 147; George Allen & Unwin Ltd, 29, 147–8, 152–4; Appleton-Century-Crofts, Inc., 182; Arden Press, 128; W.H. Baker & Co., 26; John Ballantyne & Co., 207; Richard Bentley & Son, 3–4, 6–8, 149, 203–5; W. Blackwood & Sons, 4, 203; The Bodley Head, 26, 221; Boni and Liveright, 122; Brentano's, xii, xvi–xvii, xxvi, 13, 37, 55–6, 79–80, 85–6, 91–6, 105–6, 108, 110, 115–19, 121–6, 131–2, 136–7, 143–6, 152–5, 167, 172–3, 185–7, 192–3, 210, 212; —, bankruptcy of, xvii, 92–3, 105, 117, 138, 166–8; Jonathan Cape, xxiii, 156, 221; Cassell & Co., 18–19; The Century Co., 159; Chapman and Hall, 143, 205; Chatto & Windus, 8, 203, 205, 221; William Collins Sons & Co., xxii; Archibald Constable & Co., 207; Constable & Co., xii, xv–xvii, xxv–xxvi, 13, 23, 41, 74, 80, 83–6, 91–2, 106–10, 114–15, 119–20, 122–3, 126, 128–32, 134–6, 140, 143–4, 149, 155–64, 169, 173–5, 180–4,

187, 191–2, 196–7, 200, 204, 206–7, 210, 213–14, 220; Coward, McCann, 167; F.S. Crofts & Co., 182; J.M. Dent & Sons Ltd, 73–4, 81, 134, 188–90, 199–201, 207; Digby, Long & Co., 73–4; Dodd, Mead & Co., xii, xvii–xviii, xxvi, xxxi, 105–6, 149, 164–78, 182–7, 190–9, 208–21; The Doves Press, 42, 89–90; Duckworth & Co., xxiii; S. Fischer, 149, 187; The Forum Publishing Co., 138–9; Fountain Press, 158–9; Fox, Duffield & Co., xvi–xvii; Samuel French, 58–9, 171; The Globe Publishing Co., 156–8; Gregynog Press, 164; Harcourt, Brace & Co., 132–3; Harper & Brothers, 15, 37, 55–6, 78–9, 81–2, 126, 138, 140–2; Hearst Press, 124, 201; William Heinemann, 30, 32, 36, 44, 52, 58; Henry & Co., xii, 27, 36, 39, 42; Hurst & Blackett, 3; Hutchinson & Co. Ltd, 73–4; Kegan Paul & Co., 3; Kegan Paul, Trench & Co., 8; Kelmscott Press, xiv, xix, 38, 42, 89–90, 174; John Lane, 26–7, 29, 33–6, 38, 40, 52, 110–1, 175–6, 180, 190; Longman, 51, 53, 68, 72–4, 149, 203, 205; Macmillan & Co., xi, xxii, 3–5, 7–9, 78–80, 82–4, 137, 156, 202–4; Methuen & Co., 23, 40, 66–7, 69–71; Modern Library, 208–9; The Modern Press, 14; George Munro, 37; John Murray, xv, 62, 73, 74–8; Thomas Nelson & Sons, 144–5; New Age Press, 122; Newman & Co., 5; Odhams Press Ltd, 160, 177, 182, 191, 193, 195; Oxford University Press, 206–8, 210, 213; James Parker & Co., 60; Penguin Books Ltd, xii, xviii–xix, xxiii, 142, 176–7, 183, 187–91, 208–13, 217, 219–20; G.P. Putnam's Sons, 31, 39–41, 159, 161, 205; Random House, 209, 221; Reinhardt & Evans Ltd, 220; Remington & Co., 4–6; Grant Richards, xiii–xvi, xxi, 27–8, 36–54, 56–66, 69–74, 80–1, 91–2, 96–105; —, *Author Hunting*, 50, 174–5; —, bankruptcy of, xv, 80, 92, 96–104, 138; George Routledge and Sons Ltd, 73–4, 108; The Roycroft Printing Shop, xxv, 55–6, 87, 89, 94; Walter Scott Publishing Co., 20, 24–6, 36–8, 42, 45, 53, 94; Simon & Schuster, 190; Simpkin, Marshall, Hamilton, Kent & Co., 22–3, 29, 64; Smith, Elder & Co., 5, 73–4, 203; —, *Dictionary of National Biography*, 85–6; The Stein Co., 37; Herbert S. Stone & Co., xv–xvii, xxvi, 23, 37, 43, 47, 53–5, 79; Swan Sonnenschein & Co., xi, 10–18, 50, 147; Bernhard Tauchnitz, 111–13, 119–20, 126–30, 135; T. Fisher Unwin, xi, xii–xiii, 18–19, 23–6, 29–31, 32–3, 39, 85–6, 107, 147; University Press of Cambridge, 84–9, 94, 104; Charles L. Webster & Co., 207; William H. Wise & Co., xviii, 145–6, 150–2, 154–5, 168, 178–9, 192–4, 198; World Book Company, 210, 212

Putnam, George Haven, 31, 41

Reinhardt, Max, 220–2
Revenue Act of 1917, War, 124
Revenue Act of 1918, 124
Reynolds, Paul R., 31
Rhys, Ernest Percival, 23, 189–90
Richards, Grant. *See under* publishing houses
Ricketts, Charles, 140

Robertson, John Mackinnon, 8
Rodin, Auguste, 90
Routledge, George, 74
Royal Academy of Dramatic Art, 163
Ruskin, John, 99, 203–5; *Fors Clavigera*, 29
Ryley, Madeleine R.: *Jedbury Junior*, 58–9

Scott, Sir Walter (1771–1832), novelist, 206–7
Scott, Sir Walter (1826–1910), publisher, 20
Shakespeare, William, 55, 73–4, 144–5, 175–6, 197, 199; *All's Well That Ends Well*, 85
Shaw, Bernard:
– plays (separate issue): *The Admirable Bashville*, 60, 63, 119; *Androcles and the Lion: A Fable Play*, 130–1, 133, 184, 195, 206; *Androcles and the Lion, Overruled, Pygmalion*, 121; *Annajanska, the Bolshevik Empress*, 129–30; *The Apple Cart: A Political Extravaganza*, 149–50, 155–8, 160; *Arms and the Man*, xii, 26, 29, 32–3, 36, 182; *Augustus Does His Bit*, 129–30; *Back to Methuselah*, xviii, 131–2, 135–6, 187, 195–6, 206–8, 210; *Buoyant Billions*, 162, 207, 217, 219; *Caesar and Cleopatra*, 183–4; *Candida*, 36, 183, 208; *The Dark Lady of the Sonnets*, xxii; *The Devil's Disciple*, 30, 39–40, 60–3, 183; *The Devil's Disciple, Major Barbara, Saint Joan* (Everyman), 190; *The Doctor's Dilemma*, xxi, 184, 186; *The Doctor's Dilemma, Getting Married & The Shewing-up of Blanco Posnet*, 184–7; *Fanny's First Play*, 120, 130, 195; *Geneva*, 183–8, 192, 198–9, 207;

Geneva, Cymbeline Refinished, & Good King Charles, 187, 192, 196, 207; *Great Catherine*, 129–30; *Heartbreak House*, 128–32; *Heartbreak House: Great Catherine: Playlets of the War*, 129–30; *The Inca of Perusalem*, 129–30; *In Good King Charles's Golden Days*, 183, 192, 198–9; *John Bull's Other Island*, 110, 118–19, 190; *John Bull's Other Island and Major Barbara*, xvi, 117; *John Bull's Other Island, How He Lied to Her Husband, and Major Barbara*, 106, 185; *Major Barbara*, 78, 130, 184; *Major Barbara: A Screen Version*, 206–7; *Man and Superman*, xv, 6, 9, 26, 56, 63, 65–7, 71–8, 80–2, 84–93, 95, 104, 112–13, 115, 118–19, 137, 204–5; *The Man of Destiny*, 36–7, 39–40, 42; *Misalliance*, 120, 130–1; *Misalliance, The Dark Lady of the Sonnets, and Fanny's First Play*, 130; *Mrs Warren's Profession*, xv, 36–7, 43–4, 66, 73, 173; *O'Flaherty, V.C.*, 129–30; *On The Rocks*, 172, 174; *The Philanderer*, xx–xxi, 36–7, 41; *Pygmalion*: play (1914), 30, 120, 130, 196, 201, 206, 208; —, film (1938), 184, 188, 201; —, Penguin screen version (1941), xviii, 183, 187–8; *Saint Joan*, xxii, 140, 144, 149, 157, 160, 183, 205–6, 208, 212; *The Simpleton of the Unexpected Isles, The Six of Calais, The Millionairess*, 174, 196; *Too True to be Good*, 160, 172, 174; *Too True to be Good, Village Wooing, and On The Rocks*, 173–4; *Village Wooing*, 172; *Widowers' Houses*, xii–xiii, 9, 26–7, 36, 39–40, 42; *You Never Can Tell*, 36, 38–9, 171
– plays (collected editions): *Ayot St Lawrence Edition* (William H. Wise &

Co.), xviii, 150, 152, 154, 162, 178–9, 192; *Collected Edition* (Brentano's), 117, 136–7; *Collected Plays with their Prefaces*, 221; *The Complete Plays of Bernard Shaw* (Constable's 1931 'Omnibus Edition'), 159–60; *The Complete Plays* (Odham's 1934 'Omnibus Edition'), 195; *Nine Plays*, xviii, 194–5, 212–13, 215, 218–19; *The Plays of Bernard Shaw: Pocket Edition* ('Globe Edition'), 156–8; *Plays: Pleasant & Unpleasant*, xiv, xv–xvi, xix, xxv, 36–40, 43, 47–8, 56, 66, 73, 100, 119, 211; 'The Shaw Million' (Penguin), xviii, 208, 210; *Selected Plays* ('Edition for the Forces'), 206–7; *Seven Plays*, xviii, 195, 213; *Six Plays*, xviii, 194–5, 212–13, 215, 218–19; *Three Plays for Puritans*, xv–xvi, 40, 43, 56, 66, 72–3, 91–2, 100, 102, 115; *The Works of Bernard Shaw: Collected Edition* (Constable), xxv–xxvi, 33, 46, 121, 128, 130–1, 149, 150, 152–6, 158, 160–3, 173–4; *The Works of Bernard Shaw: Standard Edition* (Constable), xxv–xxvi, 46, 158, 161–4, 172–4, 188, 208

– on publishers and publishing, xii, xvii, xxii–xxiii, 28–30, 34, 64, 67–9, 73–4, 83, 85, 90, 132, 138, 148–9, 197, 202–4; 'The Author's View: A Criticism of Modern Book Printing,' xxv; 'Bernard Shaw on Modern Typography,' xxv; 'Book Distribution: Not More Lights, but More Shops,' 86; 'Books and the Public' (letter to *The Times*), 107; 'A Letter to the Author from Bernard Shaw,' 149; 'Notes on the Clarendon Press Rules for Compositors and Readers,' xix; 'Publishers and the Public' (letter to *The Times*), 107; 'Sixty Years in Business as an Author,' xxii, 149, 199; 'The Society of Authors' (letter to *The Times*), 107; 'The Typography of G.B.S.,' xx, 144

– novels: *Cashel Byron's Profession*, xi, xv–xvi, 6–8, 13–16, 18–24, 26, 37–8, 43, 55–6, 60–1, 63–4, 73, 80, 94–5, 119, 203; *Immaturity*, xi, 3–6, 29–30, 155–6; *The Irrational Knot*, xi, 4, 7, 13, 16, 74; *Love Among the Artists*, xi, xvi, 6–7, 19–20, 23–6, 43, 56; *An Unsocial Socialist*, xi, 8–17, 20, 80, 94–5, 203

– other works: *The Adventures of the Black Girl in Her Search for God*, xvii, 163–6, 169–70, 172, 187, 208; 'Bernard Shaw Exhorts America on Socialism,' 146; *Collected Letters 1874–1897*, 221; *Collected Letters 1898–1910*, 221; *Common Sense About the War*, 85, 121, 152; *The Crime of Imprisonment*, 144; 'A Degenerate's View of Nordau,' 134; *Dramatic Opinions and Essays*, 85, 107, 110, 117, 119; 'A Dramatic Realist to His Critics,' 32; *Ellen Terry and Bernard Shaw: A Correspondence*, 159, 220; *Everybody's Political What's What?* xvi, xxv, 128, 206, 212–13; *Fabian Essays in Socialism*, 19–24, 26; *Fabianism and the Empire*, 57–8; *Farfetched Fables*, 219; *The Future of Political Science in America*, xxvi, 168–9, 177; *Imprisonment*, 144; *The Intelligent Woman's Guide to Socialism and Capitalism*, xviii, xxiii, 142–6, 152, 176–7; *The Intelligent Woman's Guide to Socialism, Capitalism, Sovietism and Fascism*, xviii, xxiii, 176, 195–6, 210; *London*

Music in 1888–89, 174, 180–1; 'A
Message to America' (BBC broad-
cast), 168; *Music in London 1890–94*,
33; 'On Going to Church,' xxv, 36,
55, 90; *Peace Conference Hints*, 126;
The Perfect Wagnerite, xv–xvi, 43, 47–
8, 50–3, 80–1, 119, 121–2, 144; *The
Political Madhouse in America and
Nearer Home*, xxvi, 169–71, 173, 184;
The Quintessence of Ibsenism, 20, 24–5,
39, 41–2, 45–6, 55–6, 94–5, 121–2;
The Sanity of Art, 121–2, 134; *Shaw
Gives Himself Away*, 164; *Shaw's
Music*, 221; *Sixteen Self Sketches*, 196,
214–15, 217; 'Socialism at the Inter-
national Congress,' 36; *Table-Talk of
G.B.S.*, 139–43; *What I Really Wrote
About The War*, 121; 'What's in a
Name? (How an Anarchist might
put it),' 56; *William Morris as I Knew
Him*, 177–8
Shaw, Charlotte (née Payne-Towns-
hend), 41, 48, 56, 80, 117, 143, 163,
167, 181–2, 201, 219
Shaw, Lucinda Elizabeth Gurly, 4, 8, 15
Shaw, Lucinda Frances, 4, 8, 15
Sherard, Robert Harborough, 180–1;
*Bernard Shaw, Frank Harris and Oscar
Wilde*, 180
Smith, George, 86
Society of Authors, xxii, 46, 79–80, 83,
85, 98, 106, 113, 123, 127, 148, 152,
154, 171, 189, 204–5
Sonnenschein, William Swan. *See*
Swan, Sonnenschein & Co. *under*
publishing houses
Spencer, Herbert, 99, 204–5
Spingarn, Joel Elias, 132–4
Stage Society, 37, 39, 66
Stead, William T., 27

Stevenson, Robert Louis, 203, 205
Stone, Herbert Stuart, 43
Stern, Benjamin H. (attorney at Stern
& Reubens), 123–4, 168, 173, 177–8,
184–5, 196

Tauchnitz, Baron Bernhard, 113
Tauchnitz, Baron Karl, 113
Taylor, John S., 106
Terry, Dame Ellen, xix, 38, 158
Thackeray, William Makepeace, 202,
205
theatres: Avenue, 29, 205; Bijou, 205;
Comedy, 205; Coronet, 205; Festival
(Malvern), 149; Garrick (New
York), 30, 129; Haymarket, 32, 38;
Independent, 36; Lyceum, 36–7;
Royal Court, 100, 102, 205; Royalty,
xiii, 27, 205; Strand, 37, 205; Terry's,
59; Winter Garden, 174
Thring, George Herbert, 79–80, 83,
98–103; *The Marketing of Literary
Property*, xxii, 149
Times Book Club, The, xvi, 106–10
Tolstoy, Count Leo, 63, 103
Topolski, Feliks, 183–4, 187, 191–2
Traubel, Horace, 95
Trollope, Anthony, 202, 205
Tucker, Benjamin R., 55–6, 94–5, 122,
134
Twain, Mark, xxiii, 125–6, 206–7

Untermeyer, Louis, 207
Unwin, Edward, 24
Unwin, Sir Stanley, xi, xxii, 147–9, 152–
4, 217; *The Truth About a Publisher: An
Autobiographical Record*, 147; *The
Truth About Publishing*, 147–8;
Unwin, Thomas Fisher. *See under* pub-
lishing houses

Vedrenne, John Eugene, 102
Victoria, Queen, 75
The Victoria History of the Counties of England, 115

Wagner, Richard, 35, 51, 47; *Der Ring des Nibelungen*, 47–8, 50, 80–1; other operas, 50
Walker, Adam, 101–2
Walker, Sir Emery, 42, 89–90, 128–9
Walkley, Arthur Bingham, 25–6, 75, 77, 110–11; *Playhouse Impressions*, 26
Ward, Mrs Humphry, 112
Washington, George, 150, 152
Webb, Beatrice, 41–2, 221
Webb, Beatrice and Sidney, xiv, 28, 41, 66; *English Prisons Under Local Government*, 143–4

Wells, H.G., 133–4; *The Shape of Things to Come*, 134
Whitehall Court, xxv, 145
Whitman, Walt, 95
Wilde, Oscar, 36, 69; *Lady Windemere's Fan*, 29
Wilhelm II, Kaiser, 130
Wilson, J.G., 201
Wilson, Richard Albert, 199–200; *The Miraculous Birth of Language*, 200
Wise, William H. *See under* publishing houses
Wood, Kingsley, 201
World Zionist Organization, 134

Zangwill, Israel, 133–4

Selected Correspondence of Bernard Shaw

Bernard Shaw Theatrics, edited by Dan H. Laurence

Bernard Shaw and H.G. Wells, edited by J. Percy Smith

Bernard Shaw and Gabriel Pascal, edited by Bernard F. Dukore

Bernard Shaw and Barry Jackson, edited by L.W. Conolly

Bernard Shaw and the Webbs, edited by Alex C. Michalos and Deborah C. Poff

Bernard Shaw and Nancy Astor, edited by J.P. Wearing

Bernard Shaw and His Publishers, edited by Michel W. Pharand